D1809529

GEORGIA DOUGLAS JOHNSON

THE SELECTED WORKS OF
GEORGIA DOUGLAS JOHNSON

AFRICAN-AMERICAN WOMEN WRITERS, 1910–1940

HENRY LOUIS GATES, JR. *GENERAL EDITOR*

Jennifer Burton *Associate Editor*

GEORGIA DOUGLAS JOHNSON

THE SELECTED WORKS OF GEORGIA DOUGLAS JOHNSON

Introduction by
CLAUDIA TATE

G.K. HALL & CO.
An Imprint of Simon & Schuster Macmillan
New York

Prentice Hall International
London   Mexico City   New Delhi   Singapore   Sydney   Toronto

G. K. Hall & Co.
An Imprint of Simon & Schuster Macmillan
1633 Broadway
New York, NY 10019

Library of Congress Catalog Card Number: 96-23997

Printed in the United States of America

Printing Number
1 2 3 4 5 6 7 8 9 10

Library of Congress Cataloging-in-Publication Data

Johnson, Georgia Douglas Camp, 1877-1966.
  [Selections]
  The selected works of Georgia Douglas Johnson / Georgia Douglas Johnson ; introduction by Claudia Tate.
    p. cm. — (African-American women writers, 1910-1940)
  Includes bibliographical references (p.   ).
  ISBN 0-7838-0038-X (alk. paper)
  1. Afro-American women—Literary collections. 2. Afro-Americans—Literary collections. I. Tate, Claudia. II. Title III. Series.
  PS3519.0253A6 1997
  810.8'09287'08996073—dc20   96023997
                                          CIP

This paper meets the requirements of ANSI/NISO Z39.48.1992 (Permanence of Paper).

CONTENTS

CONTENTS

CONTENTS

Selections from Unpublished Works

GENERAL EDITORS' PREFACE

The past decade of our literary history might be thought of as the era of African-American women writers. Culminating in the awarding of the Pulitzer Prize to Toni Morrison and Rita Dove and the Nobel Prize for Literature to Toni Morrison in 1993 and characterized by the presence of several writers—Toni Morrison, Alice Walker, Maya Angelou, and the Delaney Sisters, among others—on the *New York Times* Best Seller List, the shape of the most recent period in our literary history has been determined in large part by the writings of black women.

This, of course, has not always been the case. African-American women authors have been publishing their thoughts and feelings at least since 1773, when Phillis Wheatley published her book of poems in London, thereby bringing poetry directly to bear upon the philosophical discourse over the African's "place in nature" and his or her place in the great chain of being. The scores of words published by black women in America in the nineteenth century—most of which were published in extremely limited editions and never reprinted—have been republished in new critical editions in the forty-volume *Schomburg Library of Nineteenth-Century Black Women Writers*. The critical response to that series has led to requests from scholars and students alike for a similar series, one geared to the work by black women published between 1910 and the beginning of World War Two.

African-American Women Writers, 1910–1940 is designed to bring back into print many writers who otherwise would be unknown to contemporary readers, and to increase the availability of lesser-known texts by established writers who originally published during this critical period in African-American letters. This series implicitly acts as a chronological sequel to the Schomburg series, which focused on the origins of the black female literary tradition in America.

In less than a decade, the study of African-American women's writings has grown from its promising beginnings into a firmly established field in departments of English, American Studies, and African-American Studies. A comparison of the form and function of the original series and this sequel illustrates this dramatic shift. The *Schomburg Library* was published at the cusp of focused academic investigation into the interplay between race and gender. It covered the extensive period from the publication of Phillis Wheatley's *Poems on Various Subjects, Religious and Moral* in 1773 through the "Black Women's Era" of 1890–1910, and was designed to be an inclusive series of the major early texts by black women writers. The Schomburg Library provided a historical backdrop for black women's writings of the 1970s and 1980s, including the works of writers such as Toni Morrison, Alice Walker, Maya Angelou, and Rita Dove.

African-American Women Writers, 1910–1940 continues our effort to provide a new generation of readers access to texts—historical, sociological, and literary—that have been largely "unread" for most of this century. The series bypasses works that are important both to the period and the tradition, but that are readily available, such as Zora Neale Hurston's *Their Eyes Were Watching God*, Jessie Fauset's *Plum Bun* and *There Is Confusion*, and Nella Larsen's *Quicksand* and *Passing*. Our goal is to provide access to a wide variety of rare texts. The series includes Fauset's two other novels, *The Chinaberry Tree: A Novel of American Life* and *Comedy: American Style*, and Hurston's short play *Color Struck*, since these are not yet widely available. It also features works by virtually unknown writers, such as *A Tiny Spark*, Christina Moody's slim volume of poetry self-published in 1910, and *Reminiscences of School Life, and Hints on Teaching*, written by Fanny Jackson Coppin in the last year of her life (1913), a multi-genre work combining an autobiographical sketch and reflections on trips to England and South Africa, complete with pedagogical advice.

Cultural studies' investment in diverse resources allows the historic scope of the *African-American Women Writers* series to be more focused than the *Schomburg Library* series, which covered works written over a 137-year period. With few exceptions, the authors included in the *African-American Women Writers* series wrote their major works between 1910 and 1940. The texts reprinted include all the works by each particular author that are not otherwise readily obtainable. As a result, two volumes contain works originally published after 1940. The Charlotte Hawkins Brown volume includes her book of etiquette published in 1941, *The Correct Thing To Do—To Say—To Wear*. One of the poetry volumes contains Maggie Pogue Johnson's *Fallen Blossoms*, published in 1951, a compilation of all her previously published and unpublished poems.

Excavational work by scholars during the past decade has been crucial to the development of *African-American Women Writers, 1910–1940*. Germinal bibliographical sources such as Ann Allen Shockley's *Afro-American Women Writers 1746–1933* and Maryemma Graham's *Database of African-American Women Writers* made the initial identification of texts possible. Other works were brought to our attention by scholars who wrote letters sharing their research. Additional texts by selected authors were then added, so that many volumes contain the complete oeuvres of particular writers. Pieces by authors without enough published work to fill an entire volume were grouped with other pieces by genre.

The two types of collections, those organized by author and those organized by genre, bring out different characteristics of black women's writings of the period. The collected works of the literary writers illustrate that many of them were experimenting with a variety of forms. Mercedes Gilbert's volume, for example, contains her 1931 collection *Selected Gems of Poetry, Comedy, and Drama, Etc.*, as well as her 1938 novel *Aunt Sarah's Wooden God*. Georgia Douglas Johnson's volume contains her plays and short stories in addition to her poetry. Sarah Lee Brown Fleming's volume combines her 1918 novel *Hope's Highway* with her 1920 collection of poetry, *Clouds and Sunshine*.

The generic volumes both bring out the formal and thematic similarities among many of the writings and highlight the striking individuality of particular writers. Most of the plays in the volume of one-acts are social dramas whose tragic endings can be clearly attributed to miscegenation and racism. Within the context of these other plays, Marita Bonner's expressionistic theatrical vision becomes all the more striking.

The volumes of *African-American Women Writers, 1910–1940* contain reproductions of more than one hundred previously published texts, including twenty-nine plays, seventeen poetry collections, twelve novels, six autobiographies, five collections of short biographical sketches, three biographies, three histories of organizations, three black histories, two anthologies, two sociological studies, a diary, and a book of etiquette. Each volume features an introduction by a contemporary scholar that provides crucial biographical data on each author and the historical and critical context of her work. In some cases, little information on the authors was available outside of the fragments of biographical data contained in the original introduction or in the text itself. In these instances, editors have documented the libraries and research centers where they tried to find information, in the hope that subsequent scholars will continue the necessary search to find the "lost" clues to the women's stories in the rich stores of papers, letters, photographs, and other primary materials scattered throughout the country that have yet to be fully catalogued.

Many of the thrilling moments that occurred during the development of this series were the result of previously fragmented pieces of these women's histories suddenly coming together, such as Adele Alexander's uncovering of an old family photograph picturing her own aunt with Addie Hunton, the author Alexander was researching. Claudia Tate's examination of Georgia Douglas Johnson's papers in the Moorland-Spingarn Research Center of Howard University resulted in the discovery of a wealth of previously unpublished work.

The slippery quality of race itself emerged during the construction of the series. One of the short novels originally intended for inclusion in the series had to be cut when the family of the author protested that the writer was not of African descent. Another case involved Louise Kennedy's sociological study *The Negro Peasant Turns Inward*. The fact that none of the available biographical material on Kennedy specifically mentioned race, combined with some coded criticism in a review in the *Crisis*, convinced editor Sheila Smith McKoy that Kennedy was probably white.

These women, taken together, began to chart the true vitality, and complexity, of the literary tradition that African-American women have generated, using a wide variety of forms. They testify to the fact that the monumental works of Hurston, Larsen, and Fauset, for example, emerged out of a larger cultural context; they were not exceptions or aberrations. Indeed, their contributions to American literature and culture, as this series makes clear, were fundamental not only to the shaping of the African-American tradition but to the American tradition as well.

Henry Louis Gates, Jr.
Jennifer Burton

PUBLISHER'S NOTE

In the *African-American Women Writers, 1910–1940* series, G. K. Hall not only is making available previously neglected works that in many cases have been long out of print, we are also, whenever possible, publishing these works in facsimiles reprinted from their original editions including, when available, reproductions of original title pages, copyright pages, and photographs.

When it was not possible for us to reproduce a complete facsimile edition of a particular work (for example, if the original exists only as a handwritten draft or is too fragile to be reproduced), we have attempted to preserve the essence of the original by resetting the work exactly as it originally appeared. Therefore, any typographical errors, strikeouts, or other anomalies reflect our efforts to give the reader a true sense of the original work.

We trust that these facsimile and reprint editions, together with the new introductory essays, will be both useful and historically enlightening to scholars and students alike.

INTRODUCTION

BY CLAUDIA TATE

Greater sophistication would spoil the message.Fortunately, to the gift of a lyric style, delicate in touch,rhapsodic in tone, authentic in timbre, there has beenadded a temperamental endowment of ardent sincerity ofemotion, ingenuous candor of expression, and happiest of allfor the particular task, a naive and unsophisticated spirit.

—Alain Locke, Foreword to *An Autumn Love Cycle* by Georgia Douglas Johnson (1928)[1]

The erotic is the nurturer or nursemaid of all our deepest knowledge. . . . Our erotic knowledge empowers us, becomes a lens through which we scrutinize all aspects of our existence, forcing us to evaluate those aspects honestly in terms of their relative meaning within our lives. . . . [W]hen released from its intense and constrained pellet, [the erotic] flows through and colors my life with a kind of energy that heightens and sensitizes and strengthens all my experiences.

—Audre Lorde, "The Uses of the Erotic" (1984)[2]

[R]emember that others judge us by past performances. . . but we judge ourselves by that which we dream and hope to do—our possibilities.

—Georgia Douglas Johnson[3]

xvii

REREADING A (WOMAN) POET OF THE NEW NEGRO RENAISSANCE

Georgia Douglas Johnson was the most anthologized woman poet of the New Negro Renaissance. While she also wrote one-act plays, short stories, and songs, her reputation rests on three collections of lyrical verse—*The Heart of a Woman* (1918), *Bronze: A Book of Verse* (1922), and *An Autumn Love Cycle* (1928).[4] Primarily written in the ballad stanza, the poems in these collections focus on recalled love, lost youth, and inevitable death. Although she racialized *Bronze*, a work that anticipated Gwendolyn Brooks's *A Street in Bronzeville* (1945), Johnson has generally been understood by her critics as a traditionalist and an advocate of genteel culture, who adhered to the Romantic[5] conventions of the nineteenth-century Anglo-literary establishment.

Johnson's somewhat anachronistic verse did not constitute a retreat from the harsh social reality of African Americans during the first decades of the twentieth century. Rather, Johnson's poetic style was part of her strategy of "compensatory conservatism,"[6] which veiled her criticism of racial and gender oppressions behind the demeanor of "the lady poet." This perspective offered her the means to describe freedom, beauty, and especially her renegade sensuality without the censure of her peers. One persistent element of this veiled strategy is irony. What she praised, she also undercut with interrogating whimsy and thereby inscribed a furtive critique of the gender conventions of her day. Thus, beneath the veneer of Johnson's traditionalist verse and genteel public persona, labored a "bold modernist imagination"[7] that used erotic desire to idealize disappointment and irony to cushion the pain.

By recovering Johnson's erotic imagination from clichés about Victorian femininity, I want to suggest that we late-twentieth-century readers can appreciate Johnson's recurring depictions of sensual and often highly sexual perceptions, feelings, actions, and longings in especially her verse but also in her short stories and plays as the calculated attempts of a middle-aged black woman to define and preserve her subjectivity. Johnson used writing to define her life, shape her ambitions, determine her relationships, and accept her disappointments. Her love lyrics in particular are not sentimental abstractions but complex instruments for her intense self-reflection and retrospection. As letters from Johnson's admirers and her unpublished works suggest, writing love poetry was also the means by which she celebrated *and* camouflaged actual romantic conquests and idealized emotional injury.[8]

Johnson was a fascinating woman, who for various reasons—some obvious, others not—failed to fulfill her ambition to be a major poet. Because Johnson's formative years coincided with the period of U.S. modernization, when literature became one staple of a highly politicized mass culture, her life and work form a provocative perspective from which to reread the intersections of race, gender, class, and sexuality. Her career as a woman poet during the New Negro Renaissance also provides an excellent context for reviewing the literary fates of her black female contemporaries such as Zora Neale Hurston, Nella Larsen, Jessie Fauset, Angelina Grimké, and Alice Dunbar-Nelson. Thus Johnson's importance as a literary figure is a product of the volume of her writings and her transitional position in two cultural maps of U.S. literary history.

Neither a subscriber to Victorian ideology nor a fully modern woman, Johnson stood between those of the generation who understood sex as the husband's conjugal right, race as fixed, and poetry as sedate, speculative wonder on the one extreme, and those of the next generation who assumed sexual liberty, fluid racial identities, and a poetic sensibility of social activism on the other. Her contemporaries describe her verse as possessing "exquisite artistry," "poignant pathos," "ardent sincerity," and "ingenuous candor of expression."[9] Despite the fact that Johnson is everywhere concerned with eroticism, this term is effaced in commentaries about her work—probably because her contemporaries feared that any mention of sexuality would invite the racist stereotype of the essential licentiousness of black people. Alain Locke, the veritable dean of the New Negro Renaissance, comes the closest to recognizing Johnson's persistent lyrical ardor in his foreword to *An Autumn Love Cycle*, her third collection of verse, and therefore provides an incisive illustration of how Johnson's black contemporaries read female sexuality.

In the foreword to Johnson's *An Autumn Love Cycle* (hereafter referred to as *Autumn*) Locke promises a gender-sensitive reading of this work by addressing Johnson's somewhat unreserved display of emotions, indeed, her intense sensuality. By commenting on how "the emotions of woman . . . have yet to be carried beyond the platitudes and sentimentalizations of man made tradition" (xv), Locke intimates that Johnson explores what is fundamentally a woman-centered tradition of eroticism—"the Sapphic cult of love"—to describe "the ecstasy of life" (xviii). Adding that Johnson "probes under the experiences of love to the underlying forces of natural instinct which so fatalistically control our lives," Locke implicitly draws on Freudian psychology to explain as instinctive the curious yoking of passion and melancholy in Johnson's poetry.

Locke seems to have detected a libidinal impulse in her verse beyond maternal devotion, indeed, one of transgressive ardor. However, the conventions of his age and race evidently prevented him from publicly addressing his discovery. As a result, Locke retreats from examining the censored content and substitutes an analysis of "the tragic poignancy of Motherhood" (xviii). However, no sooner has he has placed Johnson's transgressive passion in the context of maternal virtue than he concedes that motherhood cannot subsume womanhood. The "real dilemma of womanhood," he explains, encompasses "the antagonisms of the dual role of Mother and Lover" (xviii–xix). But rather than examine this conflict, Locke abandons the project by allowing the powerful cultural valence of motherhood to bind female desire.

For Locke and his contemporaries, female desire was to be bound to motherhood, and motherhood was understood, accordingly, as "the consummation of love" and "the expiation of [female] passion" (*Autumn*, xviii). Although Locke was well aware that Johnson did not address motherhood in this rather candid collection of love poetry, I suspect that he mentions the maternal institution, which is a prominent theme in *Bronze*, published six years earlier, to harness Johnson's renegade passion to respectability. By binding Johnson's depictions of female desire to motherhood, Locke subjugates the power of female sexuality to maternity by insisting that she "has gone straight to the mine of the heart" to explore "her own subjective experience" undoubtedly as a widowed mother (xix), for he believed her work to be "abstractly confessional of a woman's way and view of love."[10] By framing *Autumn* in this way, Locke forecloses the possibility of a "philosophical yield" in her work (xix). For despite his comment on the novelty, indeed, the power of Johnson's eroticism, Locke ultimately follows the gender prescriptions of his age and circumscribes her poetry within a patriarchal economy in which the feminine signifies the body and feelings of the mother and not the mind and ardor of the poet.

Locke not only fashions Johnson to fit early twentieth-century cultural prescriptions of woman as mother, he also portrays her as fitting the description of "the average Negro writer," despite his implicit use of this category to designate male writers. According to Locke the "average" black writer of the early twentieth century was "characteristically conservative and conformist on general social, political and economic issues, [and] something of a traditionalist with regard to art, style and philosophy, with a little salient of racial radicalism jutting out in front—the spear-point of his position."[11] Although these characteristics ostensibly fit Johnson, the label—"average Negro writer"—obscures the fact that she was an ambitious, mature woman, writing when female desire was closely regulated by, to invoke Locke, the "man made tradition," and when the old and new generations were competing to define the aesthetic of New Negro literature.

From the perspective of present-day readers, Johnson is not usually regarded as a "New Negro" but rather as a member of what Robert Bone has labeled "the rear guard."[12] For Bone and us as well, the New Negro or Harlem Renaissance is generally characterized by the works of the younger generation of black writers, "the young Turks," who were mostly male—principally Langston Hughes, Claude McKay, and Wallace Thurman. This is not surprising inasmuch as they were the most productive members of this younger generation who would overshadow the writers of Johnson's generation. The young Turks were also destined to become the dominant canonical figures, because their black nationalistic values were resurgent during the 1960s and early 1970s, when scholars of African-American culture rewrote the literary history of the New Negro Renaissance. These two periods are analogues. As literary historian Nathan Huggins has perceptively observed, the militant self-assertion of those who saw them-selves as New Negroes determined "their search for ethnic identity and heritage in folk and African culture, and their promotion of the arts as the agent which was to define and to fuse racial integrity resonate [in] what we hear about us now, fifty years later."[13] As a result, the black aesthetic of the late 1960s and 1970s rede-fined the New Negro Renaissance as a prototype of the Black Arts Movement. This redefinition distinguished the young Turks as innovative and progressive, as Huggins, Bone, and Darwin Turner (and others) have argued, while classifying the writers of Johnson's generation—W. E. B. Du Bois, Jessie Fauset, William Stanley Braithwaite, for example—as reactionary integrationists, indeed, as "old" Negroes. This viewpoint has helped to obscure Johnson's prominence as the lady poet of the Renaissance.

Recent interpretative strategies of feminism, deconstruction, and cultural studies, however, suggest that we should question such literary topographies at the same time that we begin to reassess the significance of Johnson's work. For we now know that powerful racialist and gendered assumptions (as illustrated) predetermined the literary representations of eros. Because Johnson was a woman, indeed, a lady, her constituency automati-cally relegated her to the status of a very minor poet and a muse for masculine ambition during a period when African-American art became intensely politicized. I contend that Johnson's femi-nized voice was not a retreat from but a radical engagement with the politicized aesthetic of the Renaissance. She used that voice to create a space to enact her own literary ambitions and to formalize an erotic agency that on the one hand, white culture had denied to women and black people in general and on the other hand, black culture had denied to women of the race. Because the Renaissance (and modernism as well) called into question prior social and liter-ary meanings, it offered Johnson an opportunity to mask her appropriation of the masculine prerogative to critique her culture and express sexual agency.

The Renaissance also provided the occasion for a contest between elite and folk culture among black artists. In the words of Locke, the former held that "assimilation was the prevailing idea in Negro endeavor," and the latter "pointed in the direction of distinctive achievement[,] a capitalization of the race's endowments and particular inheritances of temperament and experience."[14] However, as Locke further insisted, the movement from the assimilationist position "was not separatist" in motivation, but "a minority promotion move—an attempt to capitalize" on one's own culture, to move "from propaganda to art, from cultural parade to self-expression" ("A Decade of Negro Expression," 7). As a result, the writers of the younger generation defined themselves in opposition to the then reigning standards of assimilationist literature. To accomplish this task they fastened the "older" generation of writers, which would include Johnson, to a rigidly defined bourgeois conservatism so as to highlight their own originality, liberalism, and self-assertiveness. Even though the older writers—Locke, Du Bois, Fauset, Braithwaite (Johnson's mentor), and Johnson herself—held more varied artistic and social attitudes than the young Turks would ascribe to them, the elders still tended to regard art as a vehicle for racial uplift, as evidence of social advancement.

The elders did not agree that art must address racial topics to accomplish this task. Du Bois's writings are always tinged with racial propaganda, while Braithwaite's poetry suggests no aura of race. Nevertheless, Du Bois and Braithwaite, like their black contemporaries, were conditioned by a post–Reconstruction ethos that made social equality within an integrated political context the goal. They still believed that African Americans could use their "production of literature and art" to demonstrate their "intellectual parity" with white Americans.[15] But unlike Braithwaite, Du Bois was prepared to move beyond demonstration and deploy black literature as a weapon for social justice. Johnson held both positions. She wrote love poems about erotic self-awareness that endorsed Anglo-literary conventions and thereby earned the approval of Braithwaite. But she also wrote racial protest verse and plays with a passionate indignation that pleased Du Bois. Hence Johnson evidently did not strive to make her writings reflect a consistent position but allowed them to delineate an ideological dissidence that embraced the objectives of *both* bourgeois assimilation and folk nationalism.

By contrast, the younger generation of artists, Hughes in particular, attempted to unify their positions under the mantle of political manifestos. Not interested in proving themselves worthy to a white audience, these writers repudiated the "uplift" mission for art. They used art to define black cultural identity. To illustrate the bifurcation of the generational positions, I refer to their 1926 launching of the ill-fated *Fire!!* Principally established by Hughes, Thurman, Hurston, and Gwendolyn Bennett, the quarterly was "Devoted to the Younger Negro Artists." According to Hughes, *Fire!!* "would burn up a lot of old, dead, conventional Negro-white ideas of the past, *épater le bourgeoise* into a realization of the existence of the younger Negro writers and artists."[16] In *Fire!!* they defined their collective artistic agenda by shocking some of the black bourgeois intelligentsia, according to Locke, with their "strong sex radicalism" and, hence, their outspoken repudiation of "any special moral burden of proof."[17] Although Du Bois was among those who disapproved of the young Turks' radical sexuality, he nevertheless celebrated the flowering of Negro literature in the decade of the twenties. For Du Bois that development was fostered by propaganda. In "Criteria of Negro Art," for example, published in the Du Bois edited *Crisis*, he encouraged young black artists "to fight their way to freedom" of expression by refusing to cater to either the white public's demand for black primitivism or the black middle-class's demand for bourgeois propriety.[18] And still, as Du Bois's 1926 *Crisis* survey on black representation reveals, he felt that writers and publishers who overemphasized "the sordid, foolish and criminal among Negroes" would "convinc[e] the world that this and this alone is really and essentially Negroid." Such representation would prevent "white artists from knowing any other types and black artists from daring to paint them."[19]

Georgia Douglas Johnson shared Du Bois's position. In response to the *Crisis* survey questions, she appealed to black artists to let "the world see those who have proven stronger than the iron grip of [racial] circumstance. Let the artist cease to capitalize on the frailties of the struggling or apathetic mass. . . . Depict the best, with or without approbation, and renown."[20] What Johnson meant here by "the best" had little to do with technique and everything to do with class. Like many of her black contemporaries, she felt that black writers had concentrated on portraying "the Negro farthest down" and that "the time is about ripe" for stories that tell "the history of our great middle class"—its "hopes, dreams, yearnings, heartbreaks and yes, even the joys and fulfillments of today."[21]

Nevertheless, Johnson's emphatic endorsement of middle-class values and her very close friendships with Thurman and Hughes in particular undoubtedly complicated her response to *Fire!!*. Johnson's reaction can be deduced from Thurman's undated letters to her. In the fragment of one letter, presumably written before *Fire!!*'s appearance, he requests her assistance in finding subscribers. In another, on *Fire!!* letterhead, addressed to Johnson as "Dear God-mother," he seeks her sympathy and possibly her aid by describing his poor health and financial woes, while accepting her apparent chastisement by mentioning without complaint his receipt of the copy of *Fire!!* that she returned.[22] In this way she expressed her disapproval of *Fire!!*.

The debate over aesthetic values was more than a dispute over black representation. It was a controversy among factions of black writers who disagreed on whether art could or should define a unique black identity. One faction held that the New Negro Renaissance was "unmitigated bunk,"[23] and the other used a racialized aesthetic to mount a heroic effort to assault the racist American landscape. For example, in "Negro-Art Hokum," published in *The Nation* in 1926, black journalist George S. Schuyler attacked the New Negro Renaissance by insisting that Negro art in America was "non-existent": "Negro art there has been, is, and will be among the numerous black nations of Africa; but to suggest the possibility of any such development among the ten million colored people in this republic is self-evident foolishness" (662). Schuyler went on to exclaim that "it is sheer nonsense to talk about 'racial differences' as between the American black man and the American white man" (663). The "Aframerican," Schuyler insisted, "is merely a lampblack Anglo-Saxon" (662).

In response to Schuyler, Hughes published his most famous essay—"The Negro Artist and the Racial Mountain"—in the next issue of *The Nation*. Here Hughes emphatically affirms "the duty of the younger Negro artist . . . to change through the force of his art that old whispering, 'I want to be white,' hidden in the aspirations of his people, to 'Why should I want to be white? I am a Negro—and beautiful!'"[24] This essay became a veritable manifesto for black writers of the new generation:

> We younger Negro artists who create now intend to express our individual dark-skinned selves without fear of shame. If white people are pleased we are glad. If they are not, it doesn't matter. We know we are beautiful. And ugly too. The tom-tom cries and the tom-tom laughs. If colored people are pleased we are glad. If they are not, their displeasure doesn't matter either. (694)

The New Negro writer then is not one who simply demands the opportunity to address topics beyond Victorian respectability. According to Locke, a sympathetic elder, who looked back at the Renaissance from the vantage point of the mid-thirties, the New Negro writer was one who gradually converted "race consciousness from a negative sense of social wrong and injustice to a positive note of race loyalty and pride in racial tradition" ("Propaganda or Poetry," 70). Hence, art became the mode of redress during the decade of the twenties, as in the black literature of the post–Reconstruction era, because African Americans of both periods had no hope of ameliorating the vicious social oppression with civil appeals to due process of the law. As we shall see, for Johnson art was also a means to recuperate shattered hopes. Johnson's volume of poetry *Bronze* and her folk plays were her defenses against the reentrenchment of institutionalized racism whereby black Americans alone would define the terms of their emotional interdependencies.

The interracial hostility of post–World War I matched that of the post–Reconstruction. Segregation, discrimination, and disenfranchisement, mob violence, lynching, and full-scale race riots were the rule rather than the exception. However, the war had conditioned black people to respond aggressively to social injustice. Black soldiers had fought to make the world safe for democracy. They abandoned the accommodationist position of Booker T. Washington and declared their readiness, in the words of Du Bois, "to fight a sterner, longer, more unbending battle against the forces of hell in our own land."[25] The swelling ranks of the

National Association for the Advancement of Colored People (NAACP), which was founded in 1910, reflected black America's growing discontent and its willingness to use militant agitation to demand racial justice. *The Crisis* magazine, the official publication of the NAACP, proclaimed the battle cry. In its pages black Americans not only declared war on racism but on white cultural dependency as well. The New Negro literature was a part of their declaration of independence.

The decided emphasis on the black cultural aesthetics of the Renaissance supported a different objective than that defined by the artistic formulas of the post–Reconstruction period. During that era African-American writers sought to demonstrate their intellectual parity by appropriating Western, genteel, artistic models as the means for promoting social assimilation. Black poets, for example, published works that either avoided or idealized black identity. Black poets like Paul Laurence Dunbar (best known for nostalgic dialect verse) and Braithwaite, as well as such lesser-known poets as Mary Weston Fordham, Priscilla Jane Thompson, Josephine D. Heard, and H. Cordelia Ray, as scholar Joan R. Sherman explains, "emulate[d] the white literary establishment's inspirational, romantic, and sentimental poetry on orthodox subjects."[26] This poetic model shaped Johnson's formative experience as a poet. Such a model, as Sterling Brown would later explain, required the repression of a historicized black identity:

> References to race were avoided or else couched in abstract, idealistic diction. Valuably insisting that Negro poets should not be confined to problems of race or pictures of Negro life, these poets too often committed a costlier error out of timidity at being Negroes: they refused to look into their own hearts and write. (45)

These poets seem not to have questioned their use of Western literary forms or expectations and their subsequent artistic colonization. Their poetry was a passive political strategy for cultural if not social assimilation.

During the New Negro Renaissance, though, race was the quintessential topic of the new aesthetic. The historical fact of segregation was recast from the black rather than the white perspective as separatism for enhancing race pride. "To be black," in the words of literary scholar Benjamin Brawley, "ceased to be matter for explanation or apology; instead it became something to be advertised and exploited: thus the changed point of view made for increased racial self-respect."[27] Assimilation was no longer the prevailing ideal in the distinctive achievements of black artists; rather they now capitalized, as Locke argued, on "the race's endowments and particular inheritances of temperament and experience."[28] Despite their nationalistic redefinition of the politics of racial separation, black people still held the desire to participate in United States polity as full citizens. Into the culturally complex, turbulent, and paradoxical domain of the New Negro ventured Georgia Douglas Johnson with a life-long determination to be recognized as a serious poet.

AN AMBITIOUS, DYNAMIC, AND SPIRITED WOMAN

Georgia Blanche Douglas Camp was born on September 10, 1877, in Atlanta, Georgia, to Laura (neé Douglas) and George Camp, who were respectively half black and Native American, and half black and white.[29] In an autobiographical sketch Johnson recalls that her first school days were in Rome, Georgia, and while still a young child, she moved to Atlanta with her mother (Davis and Freeman, 2). Johnson seems to have been somewhat estranged from her mother, for she mentions in the sketch that her mother was "rather resentful of her daughters" (Johnson and her half sisters) and that her childhood was very lonely. Johnson does not refer to her father beyond mentioning his racial background. Presumably her parents separated sometime around the move to Atlanta. At this time her mother resumed her maiden name, Douglas, an action suggesting that her union with George Camp might have been a common-law marriage. Within a year or two she remarried and became Laura Spaulding.[30] Despite Johnson's apparent ambivalence toward the mother, Johnson displaced her patrimonial name at the time of her marriage and unconventionally proclaimed herself to be Georgia *Douglas* Johnson and not

Georgia Camp Johnson. This act of self-naming transformed the daughter's conflicted devotion into fidelity to her mother.

In 1893 she finished Atlanta University's Normal School and began teaching in Marietta, Georgia. In 1902, after working as a schoolteacher for nearly a decade, she resigned to attend the Oberlin Conservatory of Music. A year later she returned to Atlanta where she worked as an assistant principal in the local school system. Shortly after assuming this position she resigned to marry Henry Lincoln Johnson, an Atlanta attorney, on September 28, 1903.[31] In 1910 she and Henry Sr. relocated in Washington, DC, with their two young sons, Henry Lincoln Jr. (1906–c. 1990[32]) and Peter Douglas (1907–1957). In Washington Henry Sr. ("Link") established a law firm. In 1912 President Taft appointed him to a four-year term as the Recorder of Deeds, a position traditionally held by a black man since Frederick Douglass. This appointment securely placed the Johnsons into elite black society.

Although Johnson was circumscribed by middle-class matrimony and maternity, she was not "a conventional housewife" (Shockley, 348). She gave expression to her creative impulses by writing stories, poems, and songs, teaching music, and performing as a church organist. The dining room table, according to her good friend writer Alice Dunbar-Nelson, was routinely cluttered with papers, a typewriter, and literary journals, much to her husband's disapproval.[33] According to Johnson herself, "He thought a woman should take care of her home and her children and be content with that" (quoted in Hull, 167). Even though her husband "tried to discourage" her ambition to write, he seems not to have been a major obstacle. She wrote volumes of poetry. In fact she ironically dedicated her first two collections of verse, *The Heart of a Woman* (1918) and *Bronze* (1922), to her somewhat critical spouse.

Sometime around 1920 Johnson began arranging informal gatherings for writers at her home at 1461 "S" Street, Northwest, in Washington. Johnson's home (which she would later call the "Half Way House") offered a convenient place for comfortable rest and relaxation for her black friends and associates who traveled between the North and the South when segregated public accommodations were the rule. Johnson ritualized these meetings as her literary salon. Publicly documented in Gwendolyn Bennett's "Ebony Flute" columns in *Opportunity*[34] and privately recalled in Dunbar-Nelson's diary entries as well as in the correspondence of Renaissance notables, Johnson's "Saturday Nighters Club" offered the most celebrated black writers of the period a place to share their work and discuss literature. Writers of the young generation—for example, Jean Toomer, Countee Cullen, Anne Spencer, Jessie Fauset, Marita Bonner, Willis Richardson, Montgomery Gregory, and Bruce Nugent as well as Hughes, Thurman, Hurston, and Bennett of *Fire!!*—met in various combinations at Johnson's home with those of the old generation—Du Bois, Dunbar-Nelson, Locke, James Weldon Johnson, Angelina Grimké, and Braithwaite, among others.

Johnson's affectionate rapport with these literary personalities is recorded in their letters to her. For example, Toomer mentions their mutual affinity for music. His appreciation for rhapsody made him an exceptionally sensitive reader of Johnson's love lyrics. In his letter of March 4, 1920, he remarks, "I read your lines and I swear that as love lyrics[,] aiming not at the rhythmic subtleties and virtuosities of the genius but at the true expression of emotion and feeling filtered thru the imagination[,] they come nearer [to] my heart than anything I've read. Send me some more."[35] The exchange of manuscripts, musings, aspirations, ideas, and advice between Johnson and Toomer was typical of the rapport that she developed with many of the writers of the Renaissance. Unfortunately, Toomer's response to Johnson's poetry was less than sincere; unbeknownst to Johnson, he was a patronizing reader of her work. In Toomer's letter to John McClure, editor of the *Double Dealer*, he describes Johnson's verse as having "Too much poetic jargon, too many inhibitions check the flow of what I think to be real (if slender) lyric gift."[36] While there may be other reasons for Toomer's callous disapproval of Johnson's poetry, his criticism calls attention to Johnson's anxiety of authorship engendered by the social constraints that regulated the erotic expression of black bourgeois women.

On September 10, 1925, Henry Sr. died of a stroke. His death ended Johnson's career as the "housewife-writer" and began her life as a wage earner (Hull, 184). As a widow, she had the personal and emotional space to write but little time. From 1925 to around 1934 she had to work outside the home in a series of nine-to-five public service jobs to pay her sons' tuitions and to support herself. Her income enabled Henry Jr. to complete Bowdoin College and Howard University Law School and Peter to finish Dartmouth College and Howard University Medical School.

Despite the demands on her time, Johnson continued to write. In 1926 her one-act play *Blue Blood* won honorable mention in the *Opportunity* contest. The following year *Plumes*, another one-act play, won first prize in the 1927 competition. The *Opportunity* prize marked the peak of Johnson's career. From the perspective of 1927, Johnson undoubtedly believed that her career was in its ascendancy. By 1928, though, the tide was changing. She was unable to secure a commercial publisher for *An Autumn Love Cycle* and as a result published it (just as she had earlier published *The Heart of a Woman* and *Bronze*) at her own expense in 1928. In a 1928 feature article in the Pittsburgh *Courier*, Johnson revealed her rising anxiety about the difficulty of publishing additional works. The article referred to five books that "could, on short notice, be prepared for the publishers if she had the time to do it."[37] I suspect that Johnson used this announcement to invite queries about her work in the hope of attracting a publisher. Most of these works were finished, as she would recall in her "Catalogue of Writings," but they were never published.

Undoubtedly, the stock market crash of 1929 and the ensuing Great Depression further diminished opportunities for Johnson to find publishers for her work. The crash dismantled the patronage that supported the Renaissance and left the New Negro writers struggling to survive. Black artists could no longer afford to visit Washington, DC, with regularity, and their absence caused Johnson's Saturday Nighters Club to disband in the thirties. Without the intense stimulation of first-rate artists, Johnson's writing suffered. She settled into the pattern of recycling old poems in small local magazines and became a closeted fiction writer.

In 1941 Johnson was invited to join The Writers' Club, Inc. of Washington, DC, a group of local black writers, most of whom had connections with Howard University. The club was incorporated on April 16, 1941, and lasted until 1960. According to the club's constitution "this organization exists for the purpose of stimulating more creative writing among those who have had their writings accepted by periodicals or publishers of note."[38] In addition to Johnson, the better-known members were dramatist Owen Dodson, poet and playwright May Miller Sullivan, archivist Dorothy Porter and her artist husband, James, dramatist Willis Richardson, historian-diplomat Merze Tate, and poet-scholar Sterling Brown. Although Johnson's attendance was spotty during the first years of the group, after 1948 she seldom missed a meeting. Dorothy Porter Wesley recalled that Johnson was always "very stiff, still, and quiet" as she sat wrapped in a big fur coat. Not gregarious like her good friend May Miller Sullivan, Johnson read her poetry in a very evenly measured voice that invited listeners but no commentary.[39] Johnson probably knew that her time to mature into a first-rate poet had passed. Therefore, she settled into the role of an antiquated, minor sage.

The minutes of nearly two decades of the triannual meetings of the D.C. Writers' Club preserve a record of Johnson's literary activities and reveal that she remained an enormously energetic woman during the last years of her life. For example, the minutes of the May 19, 1951, meeting report the publication of her serial story in *True Confessions*. This work corroborates Gloria Hull's speculation that Johnson, like Wallace Thurman, supplemented her meager income by writing for "pulp" serials under pseudonyms (203). The minutes also report that Decker Press (Prairie City, IL) published her poetry collection *Friendship Fires* and that her poems appeared in anthologies published in the Netherlands, Czechoslovakia, Sweden, China, Israel, and South America.[40]

Despite her prominence during the Renaissance and her tremendous productivity, Johnson was to witness the publication of a only few short stories and several poems after the twenties. The Boston-based *Challenge* magazine published two stories— "Gesture" and "Tramp Love" in 1936 and 1937 respectively— under the name of Paul Tremaine (a male-narrative appropriation whose significance I shall discuss below). Johnson's serial story in *True Confessions*, noted in the minutes of the Writers' Club, was probably also published under a pen name. These acts of pseudonymous authorship are reminiscent of her submission of *Plumes* to the 1927 *Opportunity* contest under the name of John Temple. The circumstances of publication for these works and probably others during the decade of the 1920s prompted Dunbar-Nelson to write in her "As in a Looking Glass" column of May 13, 1927, that "Georgia Douglas Johnson has as many aliases as Lon Chaney had faces. One is always stumbling upon another nom de plume of hers" (quoted in Hull, 202). Scholars will probably never recover all of her published works because they appear under signatures not associated with Johnson on pages of no longer extant publications.[41] This practice was symptomatic of her intense anxiety of authorship, for she was fully convinced, and rightly so, that her readers would be more likely to treat her works seriously if she disassociated her black and female self from them.

Johnson also wrote a weekly column, "Homely Philosophy," from 1926 to 1932, syndicated to Negro newspapers, including the Pittsburgh *Courier*, Boston *Guardian*, New York *News*, Chicago *Defender*, New York *Amsterdam News*, Philadelphia *Tribune*, and New York *Age*" (Hull, 185). As the titles of representative columns—"Starting All Over Again," "Look Up at the Sky," "The Winner," "Visions," "A Smile on the Lips," and "Find Pleasure in Common Things"—suggest, these somewhat clichéd bits of wisdom were Johnson's attempt "to bring cheer into the homes of Americans during the Great Depression" (Donlon, 641).[42] When juxtaposed to Johnson's M. V. Strong columns on social commentary on such topics as integration, the 1964 Civil Rights Bill, the 1964 presidential campaign, and building character, we can begin to reconstruct Johnson's active public life. Moreover, when Johnson's activism is placed alongside her syndicated "Beauty Hints by Nina Temple" (also published in *The Negro Woman's World*), we can appreciate how Johnson found very pragmatic ways to express all sides of her personality. For example, "Nina Temple" is not concerned with promoting cosmetics for artificial beautification, but rather she advises her readers to "Powder your face with sunshine." In another column she advises her readers to associate the ardor of love with the fullness of life: "Verily this is true. He who loves not, lives not and he who loves most, lives most."[43] Taken together, these columns help us to understand

Johnson's appreciation of love, beauty, and hopefulness as the bases for an existential strategy. She used her delight in sensuality and her selective memory to define the life she endorsed in all of her writings. Furthermore, when we understand that she wrote to sustain her subjectivity and optimistic outlook, it becomes clear how she could be so productive without prospects for publication. Believing that "the greatest mistake is in giving up,"[44] Johnson used writing to define an independent identity for herself and to add purpose and cohesion to her life.

Johnson thrived on talk about all forms of art. She recognized the significance of her salon to literary history. In the early 1940s she shared her plans to publish a book about her literary salon with the members of the Writers' Club. She planned not only to recall dozens of anecdotes but to include letters and original poems of famous Renaissance writers. In a book manuscript Johnson assembled her account of the complex interplay of literary influence that materialized in her living room on Saturday nights. Although the manuscript is no longer extant, a list of the participants, some letters from them, and fragments of their original verse have survived. Almost as tragic as the loss of this manuscript has been the persistence of scholars in fashioning Johnson as a literary hostess rather than as a serious writer in her own right. The role of muse for male ambition diminished the critical appreciation of her talent and fated this enormously energetic and ambitious woman to literary marginality. And yet Johnson is also responsible for her fate. She seems to have deliberately elected the role of muse as a means of maintaining her contact with the most talented artists of the twenties in the hope of expanding the limited alternatives for developing her writing.

Throughout Johnson's declining years she was remarkably vigilant but unfortunately unsuccessful in securing publishers for her post–Renaissance works. Occasionally, she published a poem or a story in black periodicals like *Phylon, Journal of Negro History, Challenge, Negro Digest, Negro Voices, The Observer,* the Baltimore *Afro-American,* and the Washington-based *The Negro Woman's World.* No doubt, remembering her good fortune as the Renaissance's premiere lady poet during the decade of the twenties fortified her resolve not to abandon her ambition. Even after she was forgotten Johnson continued to write lyrical poetry throughout her long life, now and then slipping a poem into correspondence to friends. She also remained active in many political, racial, and cultural organizations, regularly went to the movies, and during the 1940s ran a correspondence club for "[l]onely people all over the world."[45]

Johnson's correspondence club suggests her ingenuity and persistence, as well as her ability to stretch the truth in her claim that "This club has been running successfully for 30 years."[46] Johnson named the club "One World: Washington Social Letter Club, Inc.," and ran it under the name M. Strong primarily during the Second World War. Wartime provided Johnson with an abundance of lonely people as potential members. However, the commanders of DC-area military bases wanted to restrict her epistolary activities. On at least two occasions the commanders asked her not to promote her club among the enlisted men in the interest of national security. No doubt Johnson's venture had two purposes: recreational and financial. Like the people whom she targeted, Johnson longed for a fuller life and the excitement of meeting new people. Moreover, the application fee of two dollars supplemented her dwindling income.

Johnson frequently itemized her writings as a part of her persistent but unsuccessful application to funding agencies. For example, she applied to the Harmon Foundation[47] from 1927 to 1930, to the Guggenheim Foundation in 1929, the Rosenwald Fund in 1942 and 1944, and the John Hay Whitney and the Guggenheim Foundations in 1950. Her age was always a problem. In the 1928 Harmon Foundation application, as Gloria Hull notes, Johnson falsified her birthday. Here she states that she was born in 1888 and therefore was forty-two. As it turns out, she was not forty-seven, as Hull suspected, but actually fifty-one. In the 1950 Whitney application, she attempted to make her maturity work to her benefit by explaining to one respondent that "one would need age in order to qualify for the thing I would do" and by requesting that he refer to her as "the mother of the Negro Poets."[48]

If the letters of recommendation written in her behalf to the Harmon Foundation and the Rosenwald Fund are typical, it is no wonder that Johnson's applications were unsuccessful. For during the cycles of Harmon applications, Braithwaite, Du Bois, Carter G. Woodson, and James Weldon Johnson repeatedly "damned her with faint praise." Johnson's application to the Rosenwald Fund generates the same kind of response from A. Philip Randolph. Although these avid "race men" wrote supportive letters, they could not conceal their belief that writing love poetry was a superfluous endeavor when compared to social activism.[49] Moreover, because all of her advocates with the exception of James Weldon Johnson were generally unfamiliar with or unsympathetic to the aesthetic and critical language of the white literary establishment, they could not describe Johnson's work in terms that the establishment would appreciate. In addition, the more extreme segregation of Washington and Atlanta versus New York City probably conditioned her not to seek the assistance of white mentors. She may also have been afraid of success, like many talented women who accepted their lack of opportunity rather than risk responsibility for their own failure. As a result of all or some of these reasons, Johnson's frequent applications for funding were doomed to failure.

And yet, despite rejection after rejection, somehow Johnson remained hopeful. In a March 2, 1950, letter to Harold Jackman, whom she addresses as "My Dear son," Johnson characterized her perseverance in pursuing funding: "You would be surprised to know how many foundations I have tried, and more surprised to learn that each one, said, 'no,' but *most* surprised, to learn that I have still high hopes—am looking with my heart's bright eyes to the bright tomorrow."[50] This was one of many letters to Jackman in which Johnson preserved her literary ambitions by sharing her ideas, mentioning self-promotional undertakings, and asking for his advice and assistance. Although she was greatly disappointed with each rejection, she continued to apply for funding until the last years of her life. In 1963, three years before her death, as her correspondence reveals, Johnson inquired about Ford Foundation grants.[51]

The letters between Johnson and Jackman, cast with the mutual affection of surrogate mother and son, suggest that she and Jackman were kindred spirits.[52] Although Johnson maintained a similar history of correspondence with Langston Hughes, the relationship with Jackman was more intense. They seem to have written to each other more frequently and over a longer period of time than the other correspondents. With tender affection, he helped Johnson to preserve her literary ambitions and to maintain her ego as a poet. Although she insisted in her letters to Jackman that she was "utterly refusing to grow old" (March 2, 1950), that she was "not dimming out but carrying on with more intensity as the days march!" (March 27, 1951), and that she was still "Hoping with my heart's bright eyes" (December 2, 1952), Johnson knew that her time was running out.[53]

Always anticipating that "bright tomorrow," Johnson prepared her "Catalogue of Writings" in the last years of her life and deposited it in the archive at Atlanta University either in 1963 when she attended the Baccalaureate Services[54] or in 1965 when she returned to her alma mater to receive the honorary degree Doctor of Letters. Her care in safeguarding the survival of the catalogue suggests that she intended for it to serve as a research guide for future literary scholars, as by the 1960s most of her works remained unpublished. Moreover, it was also clear to Johnson that her early success in the New Negro Renaissance was long forgotten. As her letter written to Jackman two decades before would suggest, these circumstances did not seem to burden her unduly. In that letter of August 8, 1944, she writes of her works that it "seems I must go to that last peaceful abode without getting them printed . . . but why should I be worrying, Balzac left forty unpublished books."[55] According to her catalogue, Johnson left behind seventeen books.

This well-organized directory seems to be Johnson's effort to convince her posterity of her former literary prominence and continued productivity despite the neglect she suffered. She concludes the catalogue by summarizing statements in recognition of her early renown. In this last section, entitled "Reviews and Tributes," Johnson cites references to herself as "the modern Sappho" (John White of the *Washington Times*-Herald), "the foremost woman poet of her race" (Braithwaite), and "one of the finest and most distinctive voices in the renaissance of American Poetry" (Clement Wood[56]). But more important than these accolades, the catalogue lists her unpublished books:

1. "Little Eagles," a book of inspirational thought for "aspiring youth"

2. "Bridge to Brotherhood," a collection of seventy-seven poems

3. "Little Philosophies," several booklets for inspiring human progress

4. "My Bible," a collection of "heartwarming, heartlifting thoughts"

5. "Homely Philosophies," a collection of vignettes on common-place wisdom

6. "One and One Makes Three," a novel about the life of a child born to parents much like Johnson and her husband

7. "The Black Cabinet," a biography of her husband, Henry Lincoln Johnson, cast against the history of the Republican politics[57]

8. a book of seventeen short stories, related to her by a real or fictitious person named Gypsy Drago

9. "Literary Salon," the story of the literary meetings at her home on "S" Street

10. a collection of twenty-one short stories

11. a collection of ten short-short stories

12. three one-act black historical plays

13. four primitive life plays ("Plumes," "Blue Blood," "Red Shoes," and "Well-Diggers")

14. three stories of "average Negro life"

15. six plays of "average Negro life"

16. eleven lynching plays

17. twenty-four copyrighted songs

Despite Johnson's inability to find publishers for these works, she made plans for new books, which she lists in her private papers as "Glittering Fire," "Ride Atilt," "Sundry," "Destiny's Darling," "Psychological," "My Anthology," "Prefaces," and "Lovelight."[58] Johnson wrote in numerous genres and formats; nevertheless, it was undoubtedly poetry that sustained her artistic life and vigor. For Johnson, writing poetry was a way of intensely experiencing life. For this reason it is not surprising that she was still publishing poetry up until her death and entering literary contests during her last decade. Sometimes her efforts met with success. She won a prize for poetry awarded by *Flame Magazine* (Avalon, TX) in 1959.[59] Her poems appeared in poetry journals like *Poetry Digest* (Milldale, CT) and *New Athenaeum* (Crescent City, FL). In 1962, four years before her death, Johnson published her last poetry collection, *Share My World*.

Johnson's literary ambition and her identity as a writer were very important to her. As she lay dying at Howard University's Freedman's Hospital on May 14, 1966, her close friend May Miller Sullivan comforted her by sitting "by her bedside stroking her hand and repeating quietly over and over 'Poet Georgia Douglas Johnson.'"[60] Remembering that she had been a poet seems to have greatly consoled her in her final hours. After Johnson's death Miller Sullivan, probably responding to Johnson's deathbed request, beseeched Henry Jr. "to preserve the barrels of papers that his mother kept at home," but to no avail (Fletcher, 163).

Johnson correctly anticipated her own literary recovery. Not only did she deposit her "Catalogue" at Atlanta University, she also labeled her letters and annotated the carbon copies of individual poems with publication information. Sadly, she overestimated her family's appreciation for the mildewed manuscripts, rotting in the basement of her home. Henry Jr. undoubtedly did not realize their value, for immediately after the funeral, according to Owen Dodson, her manuscripts were treated as so much rubbish:

> I do know that she had a great deal of unpublished material—novels, poems, essays, memoirs, remembrances, all kinds of things. But as the car stopped in front of her house, the men were cleaning out the cellar, and I clearly saw manuscripts thrown into the garbage. I said, "A lifetime to the sanitation department!"[61]

Perhaps Dodson was too overcome with grief to offer the sanitation workers a few dollars in order to salvage Johnson's papers for posterity. An opportunity forever lost.

Like the other scholars of Johnson's life and works, I too believed that all of her manuscripts and personal papers were forever lost, until I learned that on January 6, 1992, the Manuscript Division of Howard University retrieved enough documents from the attic of Johnson's "S" Street House to fill four large boxes.

Among an assortment of miscellaneous items are included fragments of many of the unpublished works, unpublished poetry, old photographs, correspondence, newspaper clippings, issues of old journals, typescripts of her syndicated columns, and information about her correspondence club. Fortunately, all was not lost.

THE LYRICAL LADY

A member of the old guard of Negro writers by birth, Georgia Douglas Johnson was a woman and a poet who understood feminine gender conventions. They stipulated that women could be muses for male ambition, but they were not to harbor similar ambitions for themselves. As Johnson's poem "Woman" (which she published rather late in her career in *Opportunity* in 1947[62]) indicates, she was well aware of the protocol that prescribed woman's sanctioned relation to man:

> UNSELFISH, silent potently
> Behind each man of history
> A woman stands, upon whose strength
> He leans to cast his shadow's length.
>
> She is his stairway to the sky,
> His bow of hope, his inward eye,
> His rhythm, yea his very breath
> That plays betwixt his lips and death.
>
> Aye, some brave woman without crown
> Behind each male-throne huddles down,
> A sentinel to guard his sleep,
> A bosom where he kneels to weep.
>
> To woman then! whose urge to live
> Is summed within the right to give,
> To merge her own identity
> Into another's entity!

While this poem commemorates the conventional wisdom that behind every successful man there is a woman, it harbors a feminist reproach inscribed in her critique of masculine dependency on feminine strength and talent. The tension signaled by the punctuation of the final line insinuates a cynicism that interrogates the conventional wisdom of the very virtues that the poem purportedly salutes. Had Johnson written more poems like this one and published them in small women's journals like *The Negro Woman's World*, there would have been a significant feminist record in which to place her writings. Instead of persistently pursuing this course, Johnson seems to have tried to fit her poetic sensibility to the vicissitudes of a conservative marketplace. She maintained her posture as "the lady poet," recycled old poems, and wrote what she thought would see print, rather than develop her work by exploring the complex critical sensibility that shaped her own life and vision. Even when her writing ventured beyond the routine she masked her efforts behind pseudonymous names. Without a circle of supportive and yet critical colleagues, Johnson was not able to focus her writing on the complicated social and sexual life she lived, except in a few furtive works.

Johnson's public persona would only allow the feminist in her to peek out from behind the veil of the lady. She seems only to have nurtured her feminist critique in her unpublished works and in her pseudonymously and posthumously published stories. What becomes immediately apparent on examining Johnson's life is that she did not make her complicated social and sexual attitudes the explicit focus of her writing. Neither did she allow her extensive circle of gay, lesbian, and bisexual black artists to inform her writing.[63] She seems to have possessed what late-twentieth-century scholarship defines as a feminist sensibility and sensuality. She refused to subscribe to a patriarchal sexuality that designated women as male property and that condemned homoeroticism as immoral, although she reined in these transgressive attitudes in her writing within a Victorian ethos.

Johnson undoubtedly understood the consequences of abandoning the posture of the lady for she knew that black women writers who dared to follow their literary aspirations were hampered by the double burden of bourgeois respectability in a black patriarchal order. Not only were black writers of Johnson's epoch expected to observe the anachronistic artistic customs of the post–Reconstruction period (1885–1915) that defined art as the measure of civilization, black women writers were also expected to prove to both white and black America, by self-consciously endorsing chaste literary conventions, that they did not remotely resemble the Jezebel stereotype. Hence early twentieth-century black women's writing was generally refined with a vengeance. Johnson knew she faced a different battle than that commonly associated with the Harlem Renaissance. While Hughes and Schuyler debated over whether poets who happened to be black were poets or black poets, Johnson understood the gendered politics of art. Much to the detriment of her writing, Johnson also seems also to have sought flattery rather than candid constructive criticism of her work. She might have swayed from convention, but she didn't visibly rock the boat.

For Johnson the contest was not whether she was a poet or a black poet but whether she could secure recognition as a poet during an age that inherently understood poetry as a masculine art form. Despite this obstacle, Johnson did have one advantage; poetry was the dominant genre of the New Negro Renaissance, and it was anthologized in a plethora of poetry collections. The most prominent of these include *The Book of American Negro Poetry* (1922), edited by James Weldon Johnson; *Negro Poets and Their Poems* (1923), edited by Robert T. Kerlin; *An Anthology of Verse by American Negroes* (1924), edited by Newman I. White and Walter C. Jackson; *Caroling Dusk* (1927), edited by Countee Cullen; and *Ebony and Topaz* (1927), edited by Charles S. Johnson. Each of these works accorded Johnson a prominent place in the Renaissance.

I suspect, though, she guaranteed her place by electing the feminine role of the lady poet and muse and by appealing to friends rather than daring the originality she was capable of voicing. Had she dared to fulfill her potential, the literary politics of the Renaissance might have regarded her as an aberration and accorded her little or no recognition. No doubt Johnson calculated her odds and placed her bet where she had the greatest chance for winning recognition. The results of such conservative politicking were short-lived at best. By the 1960s and 1970s anthologies of African-American literature either mention Johnson as a "minor" writer or omit her altogether.[64] During the 1980s, the second decade of the resurgence of the women's movement, Johnson's identity as a literary *woman* activates her partial recovery. And now in the 1990s the scholarly focus on understanding how race, gender, class, and sexuality mediate artistic subjectivity, production, and reception has enhanced her presence in an increasingly more complex rendering of the United States literary landscape.[65]

However, the changing scholarly ethos does not fully explain how Johnson managed to secure recognition during the New Negro Renaissance only to be "lost" and recovered during successive literary ages. Did she achieve her reputation as "the lady poet" of the Renaissance by writing volumes of poetry alone? Or did she assure her recognition by fashioning herself for this role? I offer the following analogy as an answer to these questions.

During a visit with Johnson and her husband, Alice Dunbar-Nelson recalls (on October 1, 1921) in her diary that Henry Sr. was more impressed with her teaching Johnson "how to put on hats" than with their discussion of the "manuscript of her new book."[66] If knowing "how to put on hats" was publicly sanctioned feminine knowledge, the mature Johnson learned her lesson well. She was seldom seen in public without a hat, as her numerous photographs reveal. I suspect that like the properly dressed lady wearing a stylish hat, Johnson's feminine comportment in both appearance and writing was the basis of her construction of self-confidence and insured as well her acceptance as a (woman) poet of the Renaissance.

While her contemporary Zora Neale Hurston also wrote about subjects that addressed the female domain, Hurston's now legendary manner and immodest commentary emphatically challenged masculine authority. Georgia Douglas Johnson did not ostensibly challenge the gender conventions of her age. In fact, critics frequently remark on how ladylike she was. For example, the Pittsburgh *Courier* columnist Geraldyn Dismond provides the following impression of Johnson: "From the place [Johnson] occupies in the Negro renaissance, I had expected to see a brusque, cold-blooded individual whose efficiency and belief in sex equality would be fairly jumping at one. I imagined she was engrossed in herself and work, sophisticated and self-sufficient."[67] Contrary to her expectation, Dismond explains that Johnson "is very sensitive, retiring and absolutely feminine." Johnson's work is a synecdoche of this feminine persona. For as Dismond remarks, Johnson's writing reflects "the charm of her quiet dignity and tender sympathy" (8).

During the early stages of her career Johnson had looked to William Stanley Braithwaite to provide her with a poetic model. In an autobiographical sketch that she wrote for Countee Cullen's *Caroling Dusk*, Johnson recalls Braithwaite's influence by describing herself as "a little yellow girl in Atlanta, Georgia, [who, many years ago] came across a poem in a current paper that told of a rose struggling to bloom in a window in New York City. A child tended this flower and her whole life was wrapt [*sic*] up in its fate. This poem was written by William Stanley Braithwaite."[68] This critic and editor of the *Anthology of Magazine Verse* from 1913 to 1929, and himself author of several volumes of verse, objected to having his poems "classified indiscriminately as 'Negro' poetry," as Sterling Brown has recalled, for "he is concerned nowhere in his poems with race but wishes them to be 'art for art's sake.'" According to Brown Braithwaite's "lines are graceful; at their best, exquisite," though "the substance is thin."[69] This description of Braithwaite's verse ostensibly fits Johnson's poetry. However, when Locke wrote about Johnson, he did not compare her to Braithwaite but to another American minor woman poet—Sara Teasdale (1884–1933)—who also wrote compact, conventional romantic lyrics about melancholic introspection and intuition and published several of them in Braithwaite's editions of *Anthology of Magazine Verse*.

From a late-twentieth-century perspective, Locke's invocation of Teasdale's poetry to characterize Johnson's verse might seem a ready comparison, governed by gender conventions that aligned women writers only with other women. Nevertheless, there are many important similarities between the two women. Teasdale was the first woman poet to achieve a national reputation for voicing a woman's point of view and emotions as well as the first to compile an anthology, *Love Songs* (1917), organized around a coherent view of women's attitudes on love.[70] This was Teasdale's most popular work, and it probably influenced Johnson's *The Heart of a Woman* (1918). In addition, Teasdale's favorite poem, "Arcturus in Autumn" (1922), lyricizes a midlife, eroticized melancholy that would also dominate Johnson's *An Autumn Love Cycle* (Drake, 213). Whereas Teasdale was divided between self-fulfillment and Victorian moral imperatives, Johnson seems to have been a freer spirit, who eroticized despair but not self-destruction.

Johnson and Teasdale were popular among their respective constituencies. However, unlike Johnson, Teasdale's large readership translated into tangible rewards of cash prizes and royalties. Most important, for the upper, white middle class, love poetry was not an extraneous concern; it reinforced the gender roles to which this class subscribed. But for the black population, mired in racism, bigotry, and poverty, lyrical expressions of genteel love must have seemed superfluous when compared to art with an explicit political agenda. Though they shared the erotic milieu, both women suffered from their failure to attend to the changing expectations for poetry. Rather than consistently focus their verse on the complexity of the self and the world, they relied on genteel formulas of sedate feminine reflection. As a result, they were not entirely innocent victims of a modern(ist) influence. Johnson slipped into obscurity when the Renaissance was inscribed into literary history as an inherently masculine aesthetic movement,[71] and Teasdale became marginalized when the new critics canonized modernist poetry.

In the mid-twenties, though, Johnson was a mature woman, who undoubtedly saw that her effort to bloom as a poet had much in common with the tenement rose in Braithwaite's poem. In her autobiographical sketch in *Caroling Dusk,* Johnson revealed that his languishing rose provided her with a metaphor for her persona that enabled her to reconcile her ambition to be a prominent poet with the gender conventions of black bourgeois aesthetics. This figurative model allowed her to veil her aspirations and disguise her grievances, and, unfortunately, retarded the development of her verse.

In another autobiographical sketch, published in the *Opportunity* "Contest Spotlight" in 1927, she relied on caprice, rather than frailty, to invite assistance: "If I might ask of some fairy godmother special favors, one would sure be for a clearing space, elbow room, in which to think and write and live beyond the reach of the Wolf's fingers."[72] Rather than presume to develop her art and risk revealing her disappointment, Johnson concealed her desperate petition for assistance behind the mask of guileless, feminine whimsy. In striking contrast to Johnson's calculated caprice, in the same article Arna Bontemps assertively expressed his gratitude to the *Opportunity* judges for awarding him "the Pushkin award again" by claiming, "At least it would seem that matrimony and fatherhood do not especially shorten one's luck" ("Spotlight," 204). I have to wonder what Johnson might have thought when she read his comment, for matrimony and mother-hood habitually circumscribed her possibilities, despite her effort to recast her roles as wife, widow, and mother to her advantage.

Johnson's preoccupation with the emotional tenor of the female domain suggests that she used *The Heart of a Woman* and her projection of feminine comportment to solicit the appellation and role of "the lady poet" for herself in the unfolding drama of the New Negro Renaissance. Because she laid claim to the feminine domain of poetic expression from the vantage point of the lyrical wife and mother, and because she wrote more poetry than her black female contemporaries—Anne Spencer, Jessie Fauset, Helene Johnson, and Alice Dunbar-Nelson—Johnson gained recognition as the premier woman poet of the New Negro Renaissance. Unfortunately, this self-selected domain offered her little opportunity to develop her verse outside its parameters. Johnson's emphatically self-determined feminine voice, subject matter, and demeanor also invited early anthologists to regard her work as feminine effusion and to segregate the work of other women writers similarly. By appropriating "the heart of a woman" as the domain of female poetic expression, Johnson handed anthologists a gendered category that reified the segregation of male and female writers in anthologies as distinctive gendered voices throughout most of the twentieth century.

While anthologists of the twenties did not regularly adhere to sex segregation in their volumes, by the thirties, when the Renaissance was beginning to be inscribed into literary history, the women writers' section was a standard feature of anthologies and critical texts. For example, the 1935 edition of Robert Kerlin's *The Negro and His Poetry*, originally published in 1923, represented the poetry of the Renaissance in two chapters. One chapter, entitled "The Present Renaissance of the Negro," was composed entirely of male poets. Its complementary chapter, entitled "The Heart of Negro Womanhood," contained the works of Miss Eva A. Jessye, Mrs. J. W. Hammond, Mrs. Alice Dunbar-Nelson, Mrs. Georgia Douglas Johnson, Miss Angelina W. Grimké, Mrs. Anne Spencer, and Miss Jessie Fauset. While a few women poets were dispersed throughout the other six chapters, the overwhelming proportion of the poets were male, and most of the women were catalogued in the women's section with their marital status marked by the polite title—Miss and Mrs. It was not long before male scholars unquestioningly leaped from the assumption that feminine emotion was the subject of women's art to simply discussing their lives and not their works, that is, if they addressed women writers at all.[73]

Before we late-twentieth-century readers censure Johnson for inviting the emotional platitudes that trivialized her works, we should be mindful that the choices for Johnson may very well have been to be a "lady poet" or to receive no recognition at all. I suspect that her self-conscious adoption of an intensely feminine authorial posture was a calculated risk. For she seems to have gone out of her way to align her small poems with the feminine poetic imagination and to please Braithwaite by entitling her first collection of poetry *The Heart of a Woman*.[74] Before examining Johnson's major collections of poetry, I refer to their forewords to characterize their reception.

Braithwaite's foreword to *The Heart of a Woman*, published in 1918, sets the tone for the reception of this work and those that follow. He writes that the

> poems in this book are intensely feminine and for me this means more than anything else that they are deeply human. We are yet scarcely aware, in spite of our boasted twentieth-century progress, of what lies deeply hidden, of mystery and passion, of domestic love and joy and sorrow, of romantic visions and practical ambitions, in the heart of a woman.[75]

As Gloria T. Hull, Johnson's biographer, astutely notes, Braithwaite broaches the possibility that Johnson could speak for humankind rather than only for women before backing off with clichés "about the secrets of a woman's nature," as Locke was also to do in his foreword to *Autumn*, discussed above (Hull, 157; Braithwaite, ix). In 1922 James Weldon Johnson similarly acknowledges *The Heart of a Woman* in *The Book of American Negro Poetry*. "It may be," he writes here, "that her verse possesses effectiveness precisely because it is at the pole opposite to adroitness, sophistication, and a jejune pretension to metaphysics. Her poems are songs of the heart, written to appeal to the heart" (181). James Weldon Johnson praises her for being "neither afraid nor ashamed of her emotions" and adds that "the principal theme of Mrs. Johnson's poems is the secret dread down in every woman's heart, the dread of the passing of youth and beauty, and with them love" (xliv). Moreover, he exalts "her ingenuously wrought verses," which "through sheer simplicity and spontaneousness" exude "a note of pathos or passion that will not fail to waken a response, except in those too sophisticated or cynical to respond to natural impulses" (*The Book*, xliv). Thus, in self-consciously gendered praise he appreciates her verse by regarding it not as art but as natural, transparent, feminine self-expression, in contrast to cultivated artistic creation, which is by implication to be associated with masculine expression.

In the foreword to *Bronze*, published in 1922, W. E. B. Du Bois racializes James Weldon Johnson's gendered response. In this rather short introduction, Du Bois describes the volume by explaining that it reveals "what it means to be a colored woman in 1922—and to know it not so much in fact as in feeling, apprehension, unrest and delicate yet stern thought." He concludes by hoping that "Mrs. Johnson will have [a] wide reading. . . . Her word is simple, sometimes trite, but it is singularly sincere and true, and as a revelation of the soul struggle of the women of a race it is invaluable."[76]

Gloria Hull asks why Johnson would permit "such a bald, condescending statement to be printed" and concludes that she must have felt that any word from Du Bois "was a boon" (Hull, 163). I suspect that Johnson had locked herself into the consequences of a bad decision by following Braithwaite's recommendation to ask

Du Bois to write this foreword.[77] Even when Du Bois uses more flattering language in the foreword, like "stern thought," his failure to elaborate on this, among other passing remarks, makes the entire foreword fade into clichés about femininity. Six years later Alain Locke's foreword to *An Autumn Love Cycle* seals this typecasting. Even though Locke momentarily departs from the predictable tributes, he nevertheless settles on proclaiming that Johnson "has set herself" to the task of "documenting the feminine heart" (xv). These somewhat flattering and reductive readings of feminine sensibility would restrict a broader appreciation of Johnson's poetic imagination and entice her into duplicating worn lyrical strategies.

The Heart of a Woman and Other Poems has been labeled by anthologists and scholars alike as "a book of tidy lyrics" that voices "the love-longing of a feminine sensibility" (Hull, 157). However, beneath Johnson's ostensible concern with the "intensely feminine" "secrets of a woman's nature" (Braithwaite, vii and ix) is her persistent depiction of a soaring human imagination, her own. Despite disappointment and an unrelenting awareness of mortality, despite the confinement of convention, Johnson records moments of intense introspection and sensuality in lyrics characterized by their evanescence. As Gloria Hull has also noted, the dreams, dead hopes, sympathy, and pain depicted in this and the other collections of Johnson's verse are not simply lyrical monuments dedicated to universal feelings but "masked autobiographical utterances of the author herself" about unfulfilled desire (158).

Heart begins with Johnson's most anthologized poem—"The Heart of a Woman":

> The heart of a woman goes forth with dawn,
> As a lone bird, soft winging, so restlessly on,
> Afar o'er life's turrets and vales does it roam
> In the wake of those echoes the heart calls home.
>
> The heart of a woman falls back with the night,
> And enters some alien cage in its plight,
> And tries to forget it has dreamed of the stars
> While it breaks, breaks, breaks on the sheltering bars.

If one fails to heed the figuration of this woman's heart, as did the male critics of the Renaissance, this heart is presumed to be defined by feminine pathos. A close reading of this poem, however, reveals that Johnson portrays this female heart not as pulsating corporeality, seeking physical love, but as the classic incarnation of the unfettered imagination—the soaring bird—found in Romantic poems like Wordsworth's "To a Skylark." Hence, by identifying this heart with a bird, "soft winging, so restlessly on," Johnson associates a woman's heart with the traditional image of the poetic imagination, probably with the hope that feminine heart and poetic imagination would appear not simply as complements but as synecdoches for one another.

By caging this bird in the last stanza, Johnson clearly invokes the caged bird of Paul Laurence Dunbar's "Sympathy." While Dunbar's birdlike poetic spirit "beats his bars and would be free," Johnson's spirit, burdened with sentiment and obligation, "tries to forget it has dreamed of the stars" and surrenders to "the sheltering bars." Dunbar's influence on her writing is evident, but no one seems to have noticed the allusion, no doubt because Dunbar was depicting the limitations of race, while Johnson addressed gender confinement. And yet both of them would agree that "the world was an affair of masks."[78]

"The Dreams of the Dreamer," the second poem in *Heart*, repeats the cry of despair that will reverberate throughout this collection. In this poem Johnson depicts the predicament of the imagination as inevitable disappointment; for mortality ends all dreams:

> The dreams of the dreamer
> Are life-drops that pass
> The break in the heart
> To the soul's hour-glass
> The songs of the singer
> Are tones that repeat
> The cry of the heart
> 'Till it ceases to beat.

Weary despair, caused by frequent loss, is the recurring theme of the collection. Although the persona recalls in "Pendulum" that she has "swung to the uttermost reaches of pain" to "rebound to the limits of bliss,/ On the rapturous swing of an infinite kiss," death is her ultimate lover: "O shadows! take me to your breast/ For I am tired—I would rest" ("Tired"). In "Smothered Fires" Johnson portrays her persona as "A woman with a burning flame/ Deep covered through the years/ With ashes," who utters "a sigh of victory/She breathed a soft—good-night!" During the Renaissance her readers assumed that the flame referred to the ardor of physical love and the vigor of youth. This flame was never associated with burning female ambition. Moreover, her contemporaneous critics assumed that her persona voiced the plight of an overly emotional woman rather than an idealized consciousness, struggling to recover lost hope by means of passionate conviction, imagination, and fantasy. Such reductive readings would help to seal Johnson's literary marginality.

Several poems in *Heart* depict marriage as another event for summoning "plaintive melod[ies]" of "shattered hopes that lie/ As relics of a bygone sky" ("Dead Leaves"). Here marriage is emblematic of other dreams unfulfilled. In these poems there is no promise of sexual embrace, companionate unity, but only the painful separation of death. Erlene Stetson has detected the subtle subversion in *Heart* by observing that its poems "are iconoclastic romantic deconstructions of male fantasy."[79] The recurring theme of romantic disillusionment in *Heart* has caused Gloria Hull to underscore Stetson's observation by adding that *Heart* is "quietly seditious" (157). Undoubtedly, these feminist scholars are responding to Johnson's insistence that a woman's life is not circumscribed by romantic rapture and domestic reward (contrary to traditional sexual ideology) but rather conditioned by the same blighting despair that mars all who live with unfulfilled aspirations.

Current feminist scholarship, as Hull and Stetson illustrate, has the tools to analyze what Johnson's contemporaneous critics were unable to recognize as her deconstruction of romantic love. For example in "Foredoom," Johnson laments that "Her life was dwarfed, and wed to blight,/ Her very days were shades of night,/ Her every dream was born entombed,/ Her soul, a bud,—that never bloomed." Because the critics of her day were distracted by conventional beliefs that a woman's life was circumscribed by the domestic consequences of romantic love, they buried the poetic lamentations of Johnson's first collection under platitudes about "the secret dread down in every woman's heart" of not being loved (James Weldon Johnson, *The Book*, xliv).

Bronze, Johnson's second collection of verse, seems a more hopeful work than *Heart* because her persona is not engaged in tragic introspection but absorbed in social dialogue with self-affirmed racial confidence. Du Bois's foreword calls attention to this message, which gives him the occasion to celebrate the book as an "invaluable" "revelation of the soul struggle of the women of the race" (7). Alain Locke observes in his *Crisis* review that there is "a certain fresh breeze of faith and courage" in this collection.[80] According to him *Bronze*'s "healthy, humanistic optimism" about "the saving grace of mother-heart" is "insinuated between the lines of her poems" (161). For Locke these features meant that "Mrs. Johnson has at last come to her own—if not also in a peculiar way into her own" (161). Three decades later Cedric Dover would explain that the subject of *Bronze* "is the heart of a colored woman aware of her social problem."[81] More recently Erlene Stetson has claimed that *Bronze* is "unabashedly racial and strident"; for Johnson is no longer engaged in "the task of documenting the feminine heart" (29). Despite all of these emphatic proclamations of the racial significance of *Bronze*, the work continues to mourn a woman's languishing ambition. However, these themes are now masked behind the mantle of racial restrictions.

In *Bronze*, Johnson turned to the trope of race rather than love to commemorate her self-awareness. *Bronze* was not the first occasion for Johnson to address race in her poetry. As early as 1917 she was writing racial verse, as her correspondence to Arthur Schomburg indicates.[82] However, *Bronze* was to be her only collection of racial poetry. In the author's note to this work, Johnson explains that "This book is the child of a bitter earth-wound. I sit on the earth and sing—sing out, and of, my sorrow." Johnson goes on to racialize and aggregate her sorrow by exhorting that "God's sun shall one day shine upon a perfected and unhampered people" (3). In this way Johnson conceals her own personal despair behind the suffering of her race. Just as the commentators on *Heart* were distracted by the title of the collection, its title poem, and excessive effusion of female commiseration, *Bronze* distracts its readers with the standard racial fare. For the opening section of Bronze, entitled "Exhortation," persuaded her critics, anthologists, and readers to see that "[p]ractically all the poems are racial in theme."[83] However, a close reading of the collection reveals that a third of the poems are not expressly racial but rather the traditional romantic lyrics on love, lost dreams, and sorrow. Another third repeats these themes, but Johnson marks them slightly with racial signifiers like "veil," "sable strain," and "dusky child." And the final third of the collection either depicts typical situations of racial oppression or celebrates advocates of the race in commemorative verse.

Bronze was probably Johnson's most commercially successful book because it was packaged as a work of strong racial awareness. It is not my intention to question in any way Johnson's feelings of racial solidarity. It *is* my intention, however, to suggest that the success of this work is directly related to her readers' enthusiastic recognition that she was depicting the racial oppression and optimism that they shared. Nevertheless, personal cries of impending despair ("Let Me Not Lose My Dream," "Calling Dreams," and "Sorrow Singers," for example) are prominent features of *Bronze*, which make the collection reminiscent of *Heart*.

These cries of desperation dominate Johnson's third collection, *An Autumn Love Cycle* (1928). This collection of love poems is divided into five sections with titles that allude to a musical arrangement: The Cycle, Contemplation, Intermezzi, Penseroso, Cadence. In the already mentioned foreword, Alain Locke writes that with "maturing power and courage of expression," Johnson returns to "the task which she has set [for] herself—documenting the feminine heart." Locke attempts to open space for Johnson's topic beyond the "time-old" and "hackneyed" sentiments of male privilege (xv), but then retreats to the safety of maternal banality. Although respectful of Johnson and her subject, Locke, like the reviewers of *Heart*, still regards the female heart alien to poetic imagination in *Autumn*. He finds that Johnson expresses the "yearning of woman for candid self-expression" presumably about love in "a simple, declarative style"; the collection's ingenuity lies in its candor, naivety, and unsophistication (xvii–xviii).

Although *Autumn* received favorable reviews, gender conventions sharply polarized what is presumed to define the feminine and masculine sensibility. Each reviewer still regarded the collection as a document of a woman's heart rather than of her imagination. What made this book more gratifying for readers than *Heart* is Johnson's poetic treatment of poignant narrative events that focus the emotional response. Nevertheless, insofar as Cedric Dover was concerned, Johnson's return "to the personal notes of her first poems," diminished rather than enlarged her vision. According to him, "The poet is again overwhelmed by herself" (634). And yet, this collection reflects Johnson's profound self-reflection and subtle poetic expression. Perhaps Dover was disheartened by what he saw in *Autumn* as Johnson's "politics of wait and accommodation" (Stetson, 33). Johnson's female contemporary Anne Spencer made a similar comment about its accommodationist tenor. She observed that in *Autumn* "the author has come to terms with life, signed the valiant compromise, the Medean alternative, delivering her awareness over to pain."[84] Blanche Watson's review of *Autumn* in the *Chicago Defender* repeated similar observations but concluded by claiming that "altogether it is a soul-satisfying book."[85]

In contrast to these general accolades, Alice Dunbar-Nelson speculates that the power of *Autumn* is more directly tied to remembered pleasure than accommodation and pain. Writing in her journal, Dunbar-Nelson concedes that "You might call it poetic inspiration, if you will, but it looks suspiciously to me as if Georgia had an affair, and it had been a source of inspiration to her" (quoted in Hull, 175). One of Johnson's last published poems, "Magdalen," in *Share My World*, as well as an unpublished poem entitled "You," raises this question again. In "You" the speaker proclaims, "I'd mount the cross of thorns for you/ And hold the feat sublime/ If, as I go you whisper love/ 'I loved you all the time.'" And in "Magdalen" the speaker "stand[s] at the judgment bar" imploring God's grace: "I have kept the commandments with never a pause/ Save the one You see written there,/ But You are my Judge and I hope You can find/ Some grace for a flaw so grim/ For I loved a mortal far more than my life/ And forfeited heaven for him."

When Dunbar-Nelson's speculation and these two poems are juxtaposed to two love letters written to Johnson, I am led to suspect that Johnson had several affairs. One such letter is probably the only extant erotic letter (written in Moscow on ** 17, 1926) authored by Du Bois. Here he writes, "I'm thinking of you. I'd like to have you here." He closes the letter by imploring her to "Please come down [to * * *] half-dressed with pretty stockings. I shall kiss you." In the fragment of another letter addressed to "My darling, sweet Georgia," Maxwell Hayson chides his "literary pet" on her unreadable penmanship.[86] These letters in concert with "Magdalen" and "You" as well as other poems suggest that Johnson's eroticism was not confined to the intensity of poetic expression in *Autumn*.

The confidence that Anne Spencer associates with Johnson's Medean self-awareness greets us in the opening poem of *Autumn*— "I Closed My Shutters Fast Last Night." Here the persona brings her ". . . heart forlorn,/ Restoring it with calm caress/ Unto its sheltered bower,/ While whispering: 'Àwait, await/ Your golden, perfect hour.'" Unlike in "The Heart of a Woman," the persona's forlorn heart need not break on the "sheltering bars" of "some alien cage" but can rest comfortably with the expectation of fulfillment. Even though this collection embraces rather than yearns for love's satisfaction, the moment of satiation is fleeting: "Oh night of love, your groves of strange content/ project a thralldom over coming days" ("Oh Night of Love"). Rather than mourn the impossibility of satisfaction as in *Heart*, in *Autumn* Johnson uses memory to mystify gratification by returning once again to love as the trope for envisioning delight and time as the promise of its fruition:

> How my heart sinks when I beheld the sad reflection of my face,
> A wan and wistful wound, with oh, such meager grace;
> How can you hold me dear withal and conjure charms withdrawn.
> Or does Autumn twilight hold a charm unknown to dawn?
>
> ("How My Heart Sinks")

Johnson was a modern romantic,[87] who believed that her imagination held the power to perceive the hidden knowledge of daily experience, and this knowledge had the power to transform her sensibility. Because she followed her own inspiration, which did not entirely adhere to the New Negro aesthetic, critics defined her verse as excessively personal. However, when her verse is associated with the carpe diem tradition of seventeenth-century love poetry, it achieves fresh insight and humanistic appeal. This tradition casts desire in a cautionary tale, according to Andrew Marvell, to

> . . . roll all our strength and all
> Our sweetness up into one ball,
> And tear our pleasures with rough strife
> Through the iron gates of life:
> Thus, though we cannot make our sun
> Stand still, yet we will make him run.
>
> (from "To His Coy Mistress")

But from Johnson's point of view, her persona is no longer like Marvell's young, innocent mistress, implicated by the word "we," but an experienced and mature woman, longing once again to savor past delight. This is the recurring theme of *Autumn*. For example, the persona of "Le Soir" speculates that age holds a residual of the bounty of youth: ". . . Hope's blossoms spray/ In lush profusion/ P'er the edge of Day." In "Welt" the persona imagines meeting her young self as one would meet a lover:

> Would I might mend the fabric of my youth
> Which daily flaunts its tatters to my eyes,
> Would I might compromise awhile with truth
> Until love's moon, now waxing, wanes and dies.
>
> For I would go a further while with you
> And drain this Cup of Joy so passing fair,
> Which meets my parching lips like cooling dew
> 'Ere time has brushed cold fingers through my hair.

Indeed, throughout this third collection, the beloved self is figured as the youthful gleam in the Other's aged eye.

Poetry that idealized nature, the individual, and romantic love liberated Johnson by offering her an opportunity to represent her humanity without accentuating her double, indeed triple consciousness as a black American woman. These traditional themes provided her with the means to construct an identity that countered the familiar stereotypes about black women. For Johnson, a broad conceptualization of love not as maternal or connubial devotion nor finite sexual ardor but rather as a metaphysical eroticism was the means for transcending one's human limitations and experiencing the sublime. However, Johnson's modernist impulses made the sublime not a state realized but one sustained by desire. Also typical of the modernist poet, religious faith is tinged in her verse with skepticism, and death is depicted as the ultimate reality that "the timeless and transcendental space" of the lyric cannot alter.[88] Johnson then seems poised at the crossroads of two traditions. She was a modernist in her close attention to metaphoric detail of the fleeting moment of sublime awareness, and she was a Victorian in her refusal to abandon poetic conventions of form and beauty as the last vestiges of permanence.

JOHNSON'S PLAYS

Johnson captured the arrested moment of personal awareness not only in her verse but in her plays as well. During the twenties, while Johnson was writing poetry and hosting her salon on "S" Street, she turned to playwriting with her unique version of Negro folk drama. Although she wrote dozens of one-act plays, only four were published during her lifetime: *Blue Blood* and *Plumes* in 1927 and *Ellen and William Craft* and *Frederick Douglass* in 1935. *Blue Blood* and *Plumes* were reprinted in Locke's *Plays of Negro Life* (1927). *A Sunday Morning in the South, Safe,* and *Blue-Eyed Black Boy* (written circa 1926, 1929, and 1930, respectively) were published posthumously.[89] Two of Johnson's unpublished plays are included here—*Starting Point* (circa 1931), which is a part of the Langston Hughes file in the Beinecke Rare Book and Manuscript Library at Yale University, and *Paupaulekejo* (circa 1926), which surfaced in Johnson's papers at Howard University.

The folk Negro as dramatic subject was a spinoff of the American folk drama movement, influenced by the plays of John Millington Synge and the tour of the Abbey Players in 1911.[90] In 1917 Ridgely Torrence's New York production of *Three Plays for Negro Theatre* stimulated the interest of white artists in black subject matter. In rapid succession the productions of Eugene O'Neill's *The Dreamy Kid* in 1919, *The Emperor Jones* in 1920, and *All God's Chillum Got Wings* in 1924, Paul Green's *In Abraham's Bosom* in 1926, for which he won a 1927 Pulitzer Prize, and Marc Connelly's *The Green Pastures* in 1930 defined the Negro as prime dramatic material. However, white playwrights (even those who were sympathetic) focused on the primitivism and exoticism of black culture and thereby shaped Negro characters to fit familiar stereotypes.

In response to these stilted roles, black playwrights assumed authority for the authentic presentation of black culture. Dramatist Montgomery Gregory, who was a frequent patron of Johnson's salon, probably best expressed this endeavor when he claimed in Locke's *The New Negro* that the Negro "alone can truly express the soul of his people."[91] Gregory organized and directed the Howard Players of Howard University between 1919 and 1924. He also issued the call for "a national Negro Theater where the Negro playwright, musician, actor, dancer, and artist in concert shall fashion a drama that will merit the respect and admiration of America" (Locke, 159). Gregory insisted that "the only avenue of genuine achievement in American drama for the Negro lies in the development of the rich veins of folk-tradition of the past and in the portrayal of the authentic life of the Negro masses of to-day" (Locke, 159). When Du Bois established the Krigwa Little Theatre Movement in 1926 in the basement of the 135th Street Library in Harlem, he repeated the call for self-defined Negro drama. Insofar as Du Bois was concerned, authentic Negro theatre was by, about, for, and near black people.[92]

Several black women responded to these calls for artistic action. In addition to Johnson, Dunbar-Nelson, May Miller Sullivan, Marita Bonner, Mary Burrill, and Eulalie Spence provided dozens of mostly one-act plays about the experiences of black people, particularly those of black women. Almost all of these women were connected with the N.A.A.C.P. Drama Committee, and following Du Bois's manifesto they wrote for church congregations, students, and lodges rather than Broadway. Their plays synthesize social protest (especially protest against lynching), genteel propriety, black history, religion, fantasy, and feminism in various combinations.[93] Unfortunately, until the advent of feminist scholarship, they were routinely erased from literary history.[94]

Like Johnson's racial verse, writing plays about Negro life allowed her to abandon the lyrical monologue of the forlorn self and to engage the polyvocality of social discourse. She took to playwriting just as she had to poetry and wrote about twenty plays, making her one of the most prolific black women playwrights of the Renaissance. Two were powerful antilynching plays. *Safe* (reminiscent of Angelina Grimké's 1919 short story "The Closing Door") dramatizes the utter desperation of a black mother who strangles her newborn son to free him from the future threat of lynchers. And *A Sunday Morning in the South*, which foreshadows Gwendolyn Brooks's 1960 epic poem lamenting the lynching of Emmett Till—"A Bronzeville Mother Loiters in Mississippi. Meanwhile, a Mississippi Mother Burns Bacon"—in the *Bean Eater*, depicts the lynching of an innocent young black man.

Johnson also published two historical plays probably written for school production: *William and Ellen Craft* and *Frederick Douglass*. Interestingly, these two plays focus on intimate moments in the lives of these runaway slaves that were effaced in abolitionist documents. *William and Ellen Craft* recreates the Crafts' summoning their mutual conviction in love as they prepare to escape. *Frederick Douglass* reconstructs Douglass's last visit with his future first wife, Anne Murray, before his escape to Massachusetts. While these plays reveal Johnson's efforts to recover aspects of a black heroic past through drama, *Blue Blood* and *Plumes* earned her her reputation as a playwright.

Blue Blood and *Blue-Eyed Black Boy* are about miscegenation, a theme to which Johnson had a special affinity because of her own mixed-blood heritage. In these works Johnson reveals how tangled were the racial strains of citizens of a country that purportedly upheld strict separation of the races. *Blue Blood*, which won honorable mention in the 1926 *Opportunity* play competition, was produced that year by the Krigwa Players of New York City with May Miller Sullivan and Frank S. Horne in the principal roles (Smith, 581). The success of *Blue Blood* anticipates that of *Plumes*.

Plumes is Johnson's most celebrated play. It recalls a poor black mother trying to decide whether to allow a doctor to operate on her daughter and possibly save her life or to reserve the doctor's fee for her elaborate funeral, complete with plumed horses. Before the woman can decide, the child dies. While scholars have read *Plumes* as an indictment on poverty and superstition, I suggest that the play, like *Autumn*, also represents the inevitability of death and Johnson's steadfast conviction that only love can preserve human dignity. Thus the mother's final display of love for her daughter is more important than trying to postpone the certainty of death.

Starting Point dramatizes the failure of youth to live up to its potential. Thus, like death, failure seems inevitable. By setting the play in Charleston, South Carolina, and referring to Cat Fish Row, Johnson offered her commentary on the very popular *Porgy*,[95] staged by DuBose and Dorothy Heyward in 1927. Rather than subscribe to the "happy darky" plot sanctioned by the white literati, Johnson critiqued that story with another about an old black couple, Martha and Henry Robinson, who attempt to live out their ambition through their son, Tom. They work and scrape to send Tom to a northern medical school. The opening scene foreshadows Tom's fate. Here his parents share the trouble of a friend, whose son has become involved in the numbers racket. When Tom unexpectedly visits his parents with Belle, his new, blues-singing wife, the old couple expect the worst. At this point in the plot Johnson complicates the anticipated ending. While Belle's name, manner, and singing suggest a tawdry woman whom the old couple regard as inappropriate for their ambitious son, she proves to be kind and sincere by insisting that Tom tell his parents about his involvement in the numbers racket. Moreover, she insists that he quit the hustling life and relieve his parents by assuming his father's menial job. As in Johnson's other plays, the title and ironic ending make her point with poignant economy. The Robinsons are representative of ambitious black families who in spite of their labor find themselves never getting beyond the "starting point." The play is also a poignant statement about Johnson's own failure to live up to her potential.

Johnson's *Paupaulekejo: A Three-Act Play* is penned under the name of John Tremaine. Like the stories "Tramp Love" and "Gesture," discussed below, Johnson's use of this nom de plume signals sexual content she evidently thought needed to be masked with masculine authority.[96] This is a miscegenation play set in Africa. Rather than relying on the often forced sexual pairing of white men and black women, which was the staple of American miscegenation stories, Johnson reverses the racial and sexual identities of the couple and depicts a story of probable miscegenation by consent.

The principal action concerns the devout effort of Claire, a white missionary's daughter, to teach Paupaulekejo, the half-caste son of the chief, about Christian love. Depending on the reader's racial ideology, Paupaulekejo either learns the lesson too well or fails to learn it at all. He falls in love with Claire, and she evidently loves him. However, Claire's father convinces her that she's been bewitched and arranges for her to leave. At their farewell, Paupaulekejo embraces her and then "plunges [a] knife into Claire's heart and then into his own. They fall on [a] couch." Despite Paupaulekejo's belief that in death they can be together, as the curtain falls the black maid, perhaps out of jealousy, endorses the racial hegemony by separating the lovers and embracing the dead Paupaulekejo herself. Again, Johnson relies on the ironic ending to make her point: convention rivals even fateful intention.

JOHNSON'S SHORT STORIES

The dramatic irony that distinguished Johnson's plays can also be found in her extant stories. As in the plays, Johnson focuses on poignant moments to present the subtlety and utter paradox of complex motives and conflicted awareness. Such complexity often results in indeterminate meaning but always in the protagonist's acceptance of the finality of fate with resignation. "Free" was originally a part of her Harmon application and recently posthumously published.[97] "The Smile" surfaced in her papers at Howard University. As mentioned, "Gesture" and "Tramp Love" were originally published in *Challenge: A Literary Quarterly* in 1936 and 1937, respectively, under the name of Paul Tremaine.

"Free," recalled in third-person narrative, recounts the unconventional resolution of a love triangle after the funeral of the principal agent, elderly Dr. Paul Ryan. His wife, Martha, expects finally to be "free" of the young nurse Rose Delaney, whom the doctor invited to share their home for twenty-five years as their alleged daughter. While Martha waits to hear the reading of his will, she muses, "At last, boss in her own house, and out [Rose]'d go! Her friends had taunted her long enough[;] she'd show them how she'd handle the situation." Martha is dumbfounded when the will names both women as equal beneficiaries. However, Rose volunteers to leave, announcing that "'anything Mrs. Ryan suggests will be all right with me.'" As Rose starts to leave, Martha is suddenly aware that Rose is no longer a young woman but old like herself. She realizes that over the years in spite of her determination, she had grown attached to Rose's attending to her needs and keeping her unobtrusive company. At the threshold of their parting, the two women embrace: "Mrs. Ryan flung open her arms and cried brokenly, 'Rose!'"

The title and the early plot of the story invite us to anticipate the wife's liberation from an adulterous marriage, then complicates that possibility. However, the resulting tension turns to irony as "free" takes on another meaning—freedom from the patriarchal conventions that define women as antagonistic contestants for male affection to acknowledge their own mutual dependence and affection. Johnson complicates even this meaning in her masterful ending, for she goes yet one step farther to reveal how custom condemns women to share complicity in their own oppression. She has Martha initiate the display of the women's mutual affection at the end of the story. But Johnson leaves the story's outcome uncertain. She refuses to disclose whether Martha has the strength of her own conviction to thwart public opinion and invite Rose to live with her.

"The Smile" is a more conventional story about unrequited love, which, like all of Johnson's plots, draws on irony to reveal how the capriciousness of life defeats best intentions. The story is about Florence Rowe, a woman of thirty-five, who longs for a "smart, sophisticated, modern romance," like the ones she reads about in serials. When she inherits a small legacy from her aunt, Florence resigns from her teaching position to travel to the French Riviera. No sooner does she arrive than she is involved in an accident that disfigures her face. Facial reconstruction and a series of events transform the plain Florence into the beautiful, literary sophisticate Flordé, whose lips are forever frozen into "a faint, skeptical, cynical smile." When she meets Gene, the "most brilliant and cynical of the younger writers, they are drawn to each other. . . . The fact that she was ten years older than he ceased to matter."[98] After the death of his mother, she lovingly consoles him, and he begins to return her affection. But on gazing into her face, he becomes full of loathing and retreats in horror. Unable to understand what prompted his behavior, she catches "a glimpse of herself in a mirror—smiling, aloof, cool."

"Gesture"[99] is the first of Johnson's two "on the road" stories. Cast in third-person, presumably masculine narration, "Gesture" recalls the refusal of a young man, tramping across an Arizona desert, to accept a condescending offer for a ride from a rich woman. Here Johnson seems to be experimenting with a masculine perspective to project on the one hand, spontaneity, leisure, and impulsiveness routinely forbidden to women, and on the other hand, freedom constructed as mobility typically ascribed only to whites. Moreover, this masculine mask allowed Johnson to claim "an authority of experience," as scholar Thadious M. Davis explains in another context, for sexual topics "usually denied to the female, especially to one who surveyed them without moral commentary."[100] The nameless young man can "lay flat on his back gazing up into the dusty skies" and then yawn and stretch "luxuriously" without the threat of a white vigilante carting him off to jail to protect the virtue of white women. He is "free, white, and twenty-one." Johnson uses him to construct the "courtesy of the road" of the West, which is not dependent on class position, in contrast to the rigid social proprieties of the East.

Johnson is more comfortable with constructing her male persona in the second "on the road story"—"Tramp Love."[101] Here Johnson returns to her conventional first-person narrative position to dramatize the brief encounter between a tramp and a female hitchhiker during the Great Depression. Again, Johnson frees her story from the well-known sexual stereotypes associated with black women by implying that her narrator is a white man. Unlike "Free," the plot of "Tramp Love" requires little delineation because the plot of the one night stand is so familiar. However, Johnson reverses the conventional sexual responses of the male and female characters to liberate the latter from sexual prescription even while she relies on stock devices to portray them. For instance, the young woman has "very blond" hair and she wears "white slacks and seem[s] quite neat and trim." Her comment on paying for a ride "the only way a poor girl could pay" concedes her rather cavalier acceptance of the sexual protocol of the road. "At first," she admits, "it was rather hard to take, but one learns it doesn't matter. A bath in the morning, and one forgets the bad taste. . . . I keep going and going. Doing the best I can. . . . hoping and dreamin' that a day will come when I can get a break, a good guy, a fairy prince." As she and the tramp talk, she realizes that he's not like the others who have tried to lay claim to her body. She likes the tramp and asserts that "We're alike." Believing that she can make him happy at least momentarily, she propositions him. The tramp refuses, realizing that a night of pleasure would make him even more unhappy after she left. Rather than spend the night with him, she hitches a ride, determined to get to another town that night, and the tramp jumps a freight car. As the girl leaves, she "turn[s] and look[s] back" and "[doesn't] wave," gestures suggesting her capturing the moment for future savoring. "Tramp Love" repeats another theme central to Johnson's canon: disappointment finds solace in recalling arrested desire.

JOHNSON'S POETIC FINALE

Share My World, published in 1962, is Johnson's last collection of verse. Like *The Heart of a Woman, Bronze: A Book of Verse*, and *An Autumn Love Cycle*, Johnson arranged to have *Share* published at her own expense. This fourth collection is the most modest in size, number of poems, and appearance. The cover sketch of *Share* by Effie Newsome repeats the theme of her frontispiece sketch for *Autumn*. Both sketches feature the same female face. However, *Autumn*'s cover foregrounds the woman's enlarged heart, droplets (rain or tears), and falling leaves, while *Share*'s cover replaces the heart, droplets, and leaves with the globe of the Earth, planets, and stars. In *Autumn* the erotic object is reflected as the Other, and the persona savors the sensual and, indeed, transformative power of love, while mourning the passage of youth. But in *Share* a lifetime of experiences has taught the persona life's ultimate wisdom: she learns that love's object is the desiring self. The erotic object then is not so much another person but her own subjectivity, conditioned by earthly existence: "the bubble of life's joy" caught "Within my eager fingers/ A fragile, fairy meteor/ That never, never lingers" ("The Bubble"). Thus, rather than reflected onto another, the erotic object in *Share* is *desire* itself. And for Johnson poetry was both a metaphor and a metonymy for desire.

Share is Johnson's last major tribute to her erotic subjectivity. In the opening poem, entitled "Share My World," she proclaims the power of faith, prayer, and love, mediated by her poetic imagination, to "rebuild [her] shattered world." In "Your World" Johnson invokes the trope of the soaring bird of her most famous poem, "The Heart of a Woman," to acknowledge that her persona "used to abide/ In the narrowest nest in a corner/ My wings pressing close to my side./ But I sighted the distant horizon/ Where the sky-line encircled the sea/ And I throbbed with a burning desire/ To travel this immensity." The persona's "burning desire" to go to the horizon is reminiscent of Zora Neale Hurston's Janie in *Their Eyes Were Watching God* (1937). Like Janie, Johnson's persona commemorates her persistence in pursuing lifelong dreams, even though they are seldom realized. In "I Gaze into the Sun" the persona explains the preservation of desire as the blinding and exhilarating experience of daring "To look at life aflame." In "The Gift of Years" the lines—"The mellow years have brought to me/ Many a precious thing,/ The infinite peace of forgetting,/ The joy of remembering"—are again reminiscent of *Their Eyes Were Watching God*. On the opening page of the novel the narrator remarks on how "women forget all those things they don't want to remember, and remember everything they don't want to forget. The dream is the truth."[102] For Johnson's persona the dream is to preserve and cultivate desire.

"The Audacious" is the final poem of *Share My World* and Johnson's tribute to a daring life of creative possibility. Whether she actually fulfilled this ambition is difficult to determine. By what standards do we measure her literary aspirations, assess her talent, and place her in literary history? Johnson believed that the seventeen unpublished works left in the basement of her "S" Street home would distinguish her achievement and secure her reputation, but they are no longer extant. Yet, a close examination of Johnson's extant writings (most of which are assembled here for the first time) reveals the emotional complexity, the artistic sophistication, and verbal acuity typically associated with highly respected writers. Not only do these characteristics demand that we reevaluate Johnson's writings, but when they are appreciated in the context of a problematized analysis of her life, we can also begin to understand how race, gender, and class have delimited a black woman's artistic endeavors.

Women writers of the New Negro Renaissance faced basically two choices. If they wanted an exceptional career, they had to step beyond the conventional feminine roles and risk social censure. Or if they were unwilling to challenge these conventions, they had to learn to accept the label of "minor" permanently affixed before their endeavors. The pragmatic Johnson tried to consolidate these choices with predicable results. Although her persistence in pursuing her writing career was exceptional, her dependency on the appreciation of Braithwaite, Locke, Du Bois, and others like them underdeveloped her talent. In addition, without a sustained, first-rate literary community, Johnson could not dispel her authorial anxiety and publicly risk venturing beyond the accepted lyrical mode. She needed supportive and competent criticism rather than polite flattery. And she certainly needed the time that financial assistance could provide to test her ability.

Johnson realized that she should invest her talent in more substantial literary forms than modest love lyrics if she were to garner sustained critical attention. By the time Johnson won the *Opportunity* contest for *Plumes*, she was a single parent, who found it necessary to work a full-time job to maintain her "S" Street home and to finance the completion of her sons' educations. Hence, during the formative period of her career, finding enough time to devote to her writing became a serious problem. Longer works demanded greater commitments of her time and concentration; nevertheless, in addition to poetry Johnson also wrote impressive amounts of fiction, drama, and exposition. But publishers were not interested in these longer works. Consequently, she concentrated on publishing tidy lyrics in the hope of keeping her public reputation alive. Unfortunately, that reputation was confined to the minor role of the lady poet of the New Negro Renaissance. This was the only uncontested position available to her, and she chose a nonoppositional stance for herself.

The circumstances of Johnson's personal life also dictated the literary risks she was and was not willing to take. Unlike Zora Neale Hurston, who rejected the posture of the lady, renounced social acceptance, and spent her talent pursuing her own aspirations, Johnson chose modest security within social conventions. In addition, like most black literary women of her epoch (Jessie Fauset, Anne Spencer, and Helene Johnson, for example), Johnson generally acquiesced to gender conventions. She was conditioned by the social codes of her age, region, and race to assert and defend her claim to ladyhood. Furthermore, her experience as a wife for over two decades reinforced that conditioning. Thus Johnson learned to mediate female desire within the parameters of a racially contested black patriarchy in which the fair-skinned woman was the esteemed sexual object. These factors shaped her writing and necessitated the masking of her more innovative and transgressive works behind pseudonyms or burying them in the basement of her home.

By contrast, the exceptionally talented Hurston was not acquiescent to the gender conventions of female subordination, and she was neither agent nor object of a "color struck" black society. Moreover, Hurston refused to be reticent and "act like a lady." As a result, she was severely ridiculed, censured, and, in fact, ostracized for her unorthodox behavior. Furthermore, Hurston was ill suited for the role of wife, even though she married at least twice. And whether from fate or choice, she had no children. Instead of the traditional life of gendered convention, Hurston sought intellectual and sexual experience outside the borders of wife and mother.

Rather than risk venturing toward the mythic horizon, like the audacious Hurston, who for her effort left behind an extraordinary literary legacy for scholars to recover and appreciate, Johnson accepted recognition for writing traditional love lyrics and hoped that the large volume of her unpublished works would rescue her reputation. Rather than, like Hurston, hazard expeditions in unfamiliar places, Johnson clipped roses in her own backyard. Hurston's final years in obscurity, sickness, and poverty attest to the high price she paid for her absolute devotion to her career as a writer and folklorist. While Johnson tried "to snatch the stars/ From out the purple blue," as the lines of "The Audacious" report, she stood firmly on the ground. Johnson was prudent, discreet, and dependable. By contrast, Hurston spent her life "jumping at the sun," and she paid exorbitantly for the uncommon undertaking. There is no evidence to suggest that either woman regretted her decision, and in no way do I wish to appear judgmental. My intention is to represent the severe limitations they both experienced as black women writers.

Given the publication date of "The Audacious" in 1962, two years after Hurston's death, we can read it as a more fitting tribute to her than to the more prudent Johnson. Johnson did manage to grasp a few "stars." Equally significant is her vigilance in keeping her literary aspirations at the center of her life for half a century. *Share My World* is Johnson's memorial to that life and the key to understanding her tremendous productivity. Although Johnson wrote for recognition, and during her lifetime was at best trivialized and at worst forgotten, writing allowed her to nourish her imagination, arrest the delight of desire, and endure the insults of time.

NOTES

[1] Alain Locke, Foreword to *An Autumn Love Cycle* by Georgia Douglas Johnson (New York: Harold Vinal, 1928), xvii–xviii.

[2] Audre Lorde, "Uses of the Erotic: The Erotic as Power," in *Sister Outsider* (Trumansburg, NY: Crossing Press, 1984), 56–7.

[3] Undated letter to Theresa Davis and Charles Freeman at Fisk University Special Collections. Davis and Freeman wrote " A Biographical Sketch of Georgia Douglas Johnson and Some of Her Works" (Nashville, TN: Y.M.C.A. Graduate Schools, 1931). References to this letter appear parenthetically as "Davis and Freeman" in the introduction.

[4] Johnson financed the publication of these three collections as well as *Share My World*.

[5] I use the uppercase "R" in "Romantic" to distinguish the conventions of nineteenth-century romanticism from the more reductive tradition of romantic love normally associated with women.

[6] This is Susan Lanser's term.

[7] Jeffrey C. Stewart, "Alain Locke and Georgia Douglas Johnson, Washington Patrons of Afro-American Modernism, *G. W. Washington Studies* 12 (July 1986): 37.

[8] I thank Jeffrey Stewart for sharpening this observation.

[9] The first two quotations are taken from Robert Kerlin's *Negro Poets and Their Poems* (Washington, DC: Associated Publishers, 1923, 1935), 148. The second two quotations are taken from Alain Locke's foreword, xvii–xviii.

[10] "Georgia Douglas Johnson: An Appreciation," written July 20, 1920. This document is a part of the Locke papers at Howard University's Moorland-Spingarn Research Center.

[11] Alain Locke, "Propaganda or Poetry?" *Race* 1 (Summer 1936): 70.

[12] See Robert Bone, *The Negro Novel in America* (New Haven: Yale University Press, 1964).

[13] Nathan I. Huggins, *Harlem Renaissance* (New York: Oxford University Press, 1971), 7.

[14] Alain Locke, "A Decade of Negro Self Expression," An Occasional Paper (Chapel Hill, NC: Trustees of the John F. Slater Fund, 1928), 7.

[15] James Weldon Johnson, *The Book of Negro Poetry*, vii. *An Anthology of Verse by American Negroes*, ed. Newman I. White and Walter C. Jackson (Durham, NC: Trinity College Press, 1924), also shares this perspective:

"It is therefore no longer to be doubted that the Negro will make his contribution to American poetry, if there is any poetry in him to contribute. And whether there is any poetry in him may be partly judged from the quality of what has hitherto been produced" (1–2). This viewpoint is essentially an enlightenment tenet, held over from the post–Reconstruction period. For the formulation of the relationship between art and activist politics, also see my *Domestic Allegories of Political Desire* (New York: Oxford University Press, 1992), 83–87.

[16]Langston Hughes, "In the Twenties," *Saturday Review of Literature* 22 (June 22, 1940): 13. Other founders of *Fire!!* include John Davis, Aaron Douglas, Arthur Huff Fauset, and (Richard) Bruce Nugent.

[17]Alain Locke, "Fire: A Negro Magazine," *The Survey* (August 15–September 15, 1927): 563.

[18]William E. B. Du Bois, "The Criteria of Negro Art" (originally published in *The Crisis* 32 [October 1926]); reprinted in *W. E. B. Du Bois: The Crisis Writings*, ed. Daniel Walden (Greenwich, CT: Fawcett, 1972), 289.

[19]"The Negro in Art, How Shall He Be Portrayed: A Symposium" ran in 1926 in the April (pp. 278–80), May (pp. 35–36), June (pp. 71–73), August (pp. 193–94), September (pp. 238–39), and November (pp. 28–29) issues of *The Crisis*. The seven questions in the survey focused on speculating about the consequences of the recurring negative portrayals of black people in art. Question 7 summarizes Du Bois's concern: "Is there not a real danger that young colored writers will be tempted to follow the popular trend in portraying Negro character[s] in the underworld rather than seeking to paint the truth about themselves and their own social class?" The quotation in the introduction is a paraphrase of question 6, which appears on the first page of the *Crisis* surveys.

[20]Georgia Douglas Johnson's response to the symposium on "The Negro in Art: How Shall He Be Portrayed, *The Crisis* 34 (August 1926): 193.

[21]Georgia Douglas Johnson, "Book Chat," Norfolk *Journal and Guide* (October 4, 1930): 12.

[22]Both letters are a part of Johnson's file at the Moorland-Spingarn Research Center at Howard University.

[23]George S. Schuyler, "The Negro-Art Hokum," *The Nation* 122 (June 16, 1926): 662.

[24]Langston Hughes, "The Negro and the Racial Mountain," *The Nation* 122 (June 23, 1926): 694.

[25]W. E. B. Du Bois, "Returning Soldiers," *The Crisis* 18 (May 1919): 14.

[26]Joan R. Sherman, "Introduction," *Collected Black Women's Poetry*, vol. 2 (New York: Oxford University Press, 1987), xxix. In addition to volume 2, see volumes 3 and 4 for selections of these poets' verse.

[27]Benjamin Brawley, "The Negro Literary Renaissance," *Southern Workman* 56 (1927): 177.

[28]Locke, "A Decade of Negro Self Expression," 7.

[29]The biographical information on Johnson's life is derived from Gloria T. Hull, *Color, Sex and Poetry: Three Women Writers from the Harlem Renaissance* (Bloomington: University of Indiana Press, 1987), 115–211; Winona Fletcher, "Georgia Douglas Johnson" in *Afro-American Writers from the Harlem Renaissance to 1940*, vol. 51; *The Dictionary of Literary Biography*, ed. Trudier Harris (Detroit: Gale, 1987), 153–64; Anne Allen Shockley's *Afro-American Women Writers, 1746–1933: An Anthology and Critical Guide* (Boston: G. K. Hall, 1988), 346–53; Jessie Carney Smith, "Georgia Douglas Johnson," in *Notable Black American Women* (Detroit: Gale, 1992), 578–84; and Jocelyn Hazelwood Donlon, "Georgia Douglas Johnson," in *Black Women in America: An Historical Encyclopedia*, ed. Darlene Clark Hine (Brooklyn, NY: Carlson, 1993), 640–42. Hull and Smith list the repositories of Johnson's papers. References to these works appear parenthetically in the introduction under the author's name. In addition, I gleaned information from Johnson's papers at the Moorland-Spingarn Research Center at Howard University.

[31]It seems that Laura Douglas had a daughter, Elizabeth Douglas, between marriages. After her marriage to Spaulding, she had at least three more children: Henry, Willie (a daughter), and Roy Spaulding. See Johnson's letter of January 5, 1962, to Rev. William Holmes Borders and Roy Spaulding's letter of September 22, 1959, to Johnson. Both letters are in Johnson's file at Howard University.

[31]Henry Sr. received the A.B. degree from Atlanta University (ca. 1888) and the LL.B. from the University of Michigan (ca. 1892).

[32]The code of the District of Columbia restricts access to information concerning the death of its residents not in the public domain; thus 1990 is an approximate date of the death of Henry Lincoln Johnson Jr.

[33]*Give Us Each Day: The Diary of Alice Dunbar-Nelson*, ed. Gloria T. Hull (New York: Norton, 1984), 87.

[34]See, for example, "The Ebony Flute" (July 1927): 212; (October 1926): 322; and (November 1926): 356–58.

[35]Toomer's letter is a part of Johnson's file at Howard University. Gloria T. Hull claims that the literary salon was Toomer's idea. See Hull, *Color, Sex and Poetry*, 165.

[36]See Toomer's letter of October 6, 1922, to John McClure, the editor of *Double Dealer* (a journal published in New Orleans). Toomer's remark is quoted in George B. Hutchinson, "Jean Toomer and the 'New Negroes' of Washington," *American Literature* 63, no. 4 (December 1991): 683. The

McClure letter is a part of the Jean Toomer papers in the Beinecke Rare Book and Manuscript Library at Yale University.

[37]Floyd Calvin, "Georgia Douglas Johnson Fears She Won't Have Time to Complete All of the Work She Has Planned," Pittsburgh *Courier*, 7 July 1928, 6. Quoted in Hull, *Color, Sex and Poetry*, 165.

[38]The records of the Writers' Club, Inc. of Washington, DC, are preserved at the Moorland-Spingarn Research Center at Howard University.

[39]Interview with Dorothy Porter Wesley at her home in Washington, DC, on December 22, 1993.

[40]See the minutes of May 14, 1949, and May 2, 1959, of the Writers' Club at the Moorland-Spingarn Research Center. In Johnson's "Catalogue of Writings" in the Cullen-Jackman Collection at Atlanta University Library, she lists some of these anthologies. They include *Half-Caste*, edited by Cedric Dover in London; *American Authors*, edited by Anna Lenah Elgstrom in 1927 in Sweden; *Black and White Ladyship*, edited by Nancy Cunard in 1931 in London; and *Russian Anthology*, edited by R. Magidoff in 1934 in Russia.

[41]Gloria Hull notes, for example, that in a letter to Harold Jackman, Johnson refers to a magazine (in Fort Worth, TX) publishing her serial story "Double Exile" (203). This story may or may not have been published under her name. In addition, Johnson's papers at Howard University reveal a wealth of information about her likely publishers, which in addition to those listed in the text of the introduction include the Christopher Publishing Company in Boston; Different Press in Corpus Christi, Texas; and *Brief Stories* magazine in Philadelphia. Also, the editor of *Guinea Times* (Accra, Ghana) thanks Johnson for sending her articles. In the absence of the full body of her manuscripts, locating these works is very difficult if not impossible. However, there are fragments of Johnson's manuscripts and published writings in her file at Howard University that suggest that in addition to M. Strong, Mary V. Strong, John Tremaine, Paul Tremaine, and John Temple, Johnson used the names Nina Temple, Ninevah Gladstone, Miriam Nosra, Lorraine Lillith, and Bessie Brent Winston to cloak her authorship. Although Johnson identifies Thomas H. Malone as a poetry-writing friend of her deceased husband, and the mysterious Gypsy Drago as a black man who believed he was white, these probably are additional names appropriated by Johnson.

[42]The first four columns are a part of Johnson's file at Howard University.

[43]The fragments of her manuscripts and newspaper clippings at the Moorland-Spingarn Research Center document that she wrote syndicated columns under the name Mary V. Strong during the 1940s and 1950s. These fragments also suggest that she may have used the names Tom Malone and John Sutton. I suggest that her acquisition of a post office

box—P.O. Box 6345, Washington 9, DC—was to facilitate her correspondence in a variety of names and the management of her correspondence club under the name M. Strong.

[44]This is one of Johnson's "Wise Sayings" that completed each manuscript page of "M. V. Strong Talks" and "Beauty Hints by Nina Temple." See Johnson's file at Howard University.

[45]Jessie Carney Smith lists Johnson as a member of the following organizations: the American Society of African Culture, the (New York City) Civic Club, the District of Columbia Women's Party, the League for Abolition of Capital Punishment, the (District of Columbia) Matrons, the National Women's Party, the Poet Laureate League, the Poets League of Washington, the Republican Club of Washington, the Virginia White Speel Republican Club, and the Writers League Against Lynching. In addition, Johnson was in charge of publicity for the Eastern Area Conference of Negro Republican Women and a member of the First Congregational Church. See Smith, *Notable Black American Women*, p. 582, and her undated letter to James Weldon Johnson in her archive at Fisk University. In her autobiographical sketch, Johnson also identifies her habit of regularly attending the movies.

[46]An application form for the club is a part of Johnson's file at the Moorland-Spingarn Research Center.

[47]Information regarding Johnson's application to the Harmon Foundation was secured from the Harmon Foundation Records in the manuscripts division of the Library of Congress (folder #53).

[48]Correspondence to Robert Weaver (March 14, 1950) in Johnson's papers at Howard University.

[49]Braithwaite writes (June 18, 1927) in response to the question about the quality of her achievement that she has "deep feeling, imaginative substance, to which she has given poignant lyric expression." Woodson writes (September 17, 1928), "She has a bait of poetic genius." Du Bois writes (September 17, 1928, and April 16, 1929, respectively) in response to the same question, "I know that many competent people regard her work very highly," and "Her work has received high praise." In 1928 Du Bois additionally writes, "I think Mrs. Johnson has a real poetic gift and succeeds after work in giving it adequate expression." In 1929 he adds, "Mrs Johnson has an unusually sincere, interesting literary message." James Weldon Johnson's praise was fainter still. In an April 16, 1929, recommendation, he responds to the question about his estimation of the public opinion about her achievement with the single word "Yes." Later he adds that "[s]he has done some very beautiful lyric poetry." See the Harmon Foundation Records in the manuscript division of the Library of Congress. A. Philip Randolph sent a copy of his letter to Johnson, which is among her private papers at Howard University,

[50]Letter to Harold Jackman from Georgia Douglas Johnson (March 2, 1950) in the Countee Cullen-Harold Jackman Collection of the Woodruff Library, Special Collections, of Atlanta University.

Harold Jackman (1901–1961) established the Countee Cullen Collection of Negro Cultural Memorabilia, also known as the Countee Cullen-Harold Jackman Collection of Atlanta University. Described as a Renaissance man by his contemporaries, Jackman was born in London and lived in Harlem for thirty-seven years. He was the associate editor of *Challenge: A Literary Magazine*, contributing editor of *Phylon: Atlanta University Quarterly*, and a member of the executive board of the Negro Actors Guild of America, Inc. For additional biographical information see *Harold Jackman*, compiled by the Harold Jackman Memorial Committee, 1973, at the Moorland-Spingarn Research Center at Howard University, and *Who's Who in Harlem: The 1949–1950 Biographical Register* (New York: Magazine and Periodical Printing and Publishing, 1950).

[51]In response to Johnson's query, Chester Kerr of Yale University Press provides Johnson with the address of the Ford Foundation in his letter dated July 2, 1963.

[52]David Levering Lewis mentions that Johnson "mothered [Bruce Nugent's] neuroses when he returned to Washington in 1924." See Lewis's *When Harlem Was in Vogue*, 196. Gloria Hull also mentions that Johnson had an affinity for mothering a group of homosexual young black men (which in addition to Jackman and Nugent included Glenn Carrington and Wallace Thurman) whom she called her sons. She was also very close to Angela Grimké, Mary Burrill, and Alice Dunbar-Nelson. See *Color, Sex and Poetry*, 187–88. In a letter of May 26, 1958, to Langston Hughes, Johnson mentions that she wants Grimké to recuperate at her home in Washington. Moreover, she informs him that Grimké has written two novels and a book of verse "that should be printed. . . . It would be a great loss if it were not." This letter is a part of Hughes's papers in the Beinecke Library.

[53]These letters are a part of the Cullen-Jackman file in the Woodruff Library at Atlanta University.

[54]A copy of the program is in her papers at the Moorland-Spingarn Research Center at Howard University.

[55]This letter is a part of the Cullen-Jackman file in the Woodruff Library at Atlanta University.

[56]Born in 1888, Clement Wood was a white man from Alabama, who studied at Yale Law School but became a poet. According to *The University of Alabama Alumni News* (May–June 1921), his poem "De Glory Road" possesses "all the musical swing and rhythm" of black America (112). His sociological novel *Nigger*, published in 1922, sympathetically portrayed a

poor black family from slavery in the South to exploitative wage-labor force in the urban North.

[57]A fragment, including the "Author's Word," "Contents," and "Chapter I: A Statesman Is Born," is extant in Johnson's papers at the Moorland-Spingarn Research Center.

[58]Several copies of Johnson's "Catalogue" as well as the table of contents for "Lovelight" appear in Johnson's file at the Moorland-Spingarn Research Center at Howard University.

[59]See Johnson's "Catalogue of Writings" at the Woodruff Library at Atlanta University. Several copies of this document are held by the manuscript division of the Moorland-Spingarn Research Center. Johnson also states that she won first prize for the story "The Skeleton" in a contest sponsored by the *Washington Tribune*.

[60]Quoted in Winona Fletcher, *Georgia Douglas Johnson*, 163. Also see Johnson's obituary in *The Baltimore Afro-American Way* (May 28, 1966): 18.

[61]Gloria T. Hull, *Color, Sex and Poetry*, 210. In the August 1944 letter to Jackman, Johnson mentions that she has "quite a lot of unpublished material from Jean Toomer, Bruce Nugent, etc." The "etc." referred to the young writers who regularly attended her "S" Street salon.

[62]Georgia Douglas Johnson, "Woman," *Opportunity* 25 (January–March 1947): 16.

[63]While Johnson maintained close friendships with many homosexuals, no clear evidence has surfaced to suggest that she was herself homosexual or bisexual. Yet, Johnson did pen three sonnets, signed "G. D. J.," that may suggest a lesbian relationship with Grimké. The sonnets are included in Grimke's papers at Howard University. I thank Barbara Foley for calling my attention to this material. Also see note 52.

[64]During the late 1930s and 1940s Johnson was anthologized in poetry collections and discussed in studies on black literature. For example, Sterling Brown's *Negro Poetry and Drama* (1937; reprint, New York: Atheneum, 1968) includes Johnson in a discussion of women poets from 1914 to 1936. *The Negro Caravan* (1941; reprint, New York: Arno, 1970), ed. Sterling Brown, Arthur Davis, and Ulysses Lee, contains four of Johnson's poems. *The Poetry of the Negro, 1746–1949*, ed. Langston Hughes and Arna Bontemps (New York: Doubleday, 1949), contains eight of her poems.

By the 1960s Johnson's poetic presence begins to fade away in anthologies and literary scholarship. For example, only one poem, "I Want to Die While You Love Me," appears in *Kaleidoscope, Poems by American Negro Poets*, ed. Robert Hayden (New York: Harcourt, Brace, 1967). *Dark Sympathy: Negro Literature in America*, ed. James Emanual and Theodore Gross, (New York: Free Press, 1968), includes one poem each written by two Harlem Renaissance writers, Rudolph Fisher and Eric Walrond and no works of women writers of the Renaissance. Dudley Randall's *The Black Poets* (New York: Bantam, 1971) contains selections from McKay, Toomer, and Tolson but none of Johnson's poems, indeed, no work of women poets of the Renaissance. Randall's *Black Poetry* (Chicago: Broadside, 1969) similarly anthologizes Frank Horne, Hughes, Bontemps, and Cullen. *Cavalcade: Negro American Writings from 1760 to the Present*, ed. Arthur Davis and Saunders Redding, (Boston: Houghton Mifflin, 1971), does not mention Johnson at all. Houston Baker's *Black Literature in America* (New York: McGraw-Hill, 1971) discusses Cullen, Toomer, McKay, Fisher, and Hughes but no woman writer of the Renaissance period. Davis's *From the Dark Tower* (Washington, DC: Howard University Press, 1974) only mentions Johnson in the claim that she was not less talented than Anne Spencer. This scholarship sets the pattern of Johnson's exclusion until the second wave of the women's movement slowly reverses it by focusing on the recovery of women's writings.

[65]For example, see *Shadowed Dreams: Women's Poetry of the Harlem Renaissance*, ed. Maureen Honey (New Brunswick, NJ: Rutgers University Press, 1989).

[66]Gloria T. Hull, ed., *Give Us Each Day: The Diary of Alice Dunbar-Nelson* (New York: Norton, 1984), 87–88.

[67]Geraldyn Dismond, "Through the Lorgnette," Pittsburgh *Courier* 29 October 1927, 8,

[68]Countee Cullen, ed. *Caroling Dusk: An Anthology of Verse by Negro Poets* (New York: Harper, 1927), 74.

[69]Sterling Brown, *Negro Poetry and the Drama* (1937; reprint, New York: Atheneum, 1968), 50.

[70]William Drake, *Sara Teasdale: Woman and Poet* (New York: Harper & Row, 1979).

[71]Thadious Davis explains that the sexual chauvinism of the New Negro Renaissance took a decided turn for the worse after the 1926 *Opportunity* Civil Club dinner. Masked as an occasion to honor Jessie Fauset, who had been touted as the "midwife" of the Renaissance, the dinner was actually a promotional ploy for the magazine. From this moment on, Davis explains, the leadership of the New Negro Renaissance became misogynistic. According to Davis, *Opportunity*'s editor, Charles S. Johnson, used the magazine to counter if not block Fauset's further development as a literary leader by elevating Locke to that position. When Locke became the dean of the New Negro Renaissance, Davis writes, "the unspoken antagonism toward women and the latent sexual rivalry triumphed. Women were largely excluded from decision-making circles, particularly after 1926 when Fauset, seemingly disillusioned both with the turn of events and with her mentor Du Bois, resigned from her position on *Crisis*" to

begin "a year of study in France." See Thadious M. Davis, *Nella Larsen: Novelist of the Harlem Renaissance* (Baton Rouge: Louisiana State University Press, 1994), 159–60.

[72]"The Contest Spotlight," *Opportunity* (July 1927): 204. References to this work appear parenthetically in the introduction as "Spotlight."

[73]See, for example, Hughes's "In the Twenties," mentioned above, in which he refers to Hurston's personality rather than her work, and Darwin Turner's *In Minor Chord: Three Afro-American Writers and Their Search for Identity* (Carbondale: Southern Illinois University Press, 1971), in which he discusses Hurston's life rather than her work.

[74]A September 2, 1917, letter to Arthur Schomburg in which Johnson questions the title suggests that it may have been Braithwaite's choice. This letter is a part of the Schomburg file at the Schomburg Center for Research in Black Culture.

[75]William Stanley Braithwaite, introduction to *The Heart of a Woman and Other Poems* by Georgia Douglas Johnson (1918); reprint (Freeport, NY: Books for Libraries Press, 1971), vii.

[76]See the foreword to *Bronze* (Boston: Brimmer, 1922), 7.

[77]See Braithwaite's letter, dated December 12, 1921, in which he writes, "About the introduction: that is really a thing you would have to decide, but if Mr. Du Bois wrote an introduction there is no doubt it would add to the distinction and appeal of the book." This letter is a part of the William Stanley Braithwaite file in the James Weldon Johnson Collections at the Beinecke Library at Yale.

[78]*The Paul Laurence Dunbar Reader*, ed. Jay Martin and Gossie H. Hudson (New York: Dodd, Mead, 1975), 266.

[79]Erlene Stetson, "Rediscovering the Harlem Renaissance: Georgia Douglas Johnson, 'The New Negro Poet,'" *Obsidian* (Spring/Summer 1979): 28.

[80]Review of *Bronze* by Alain Locke in "Notes on the New Books," *The Crisis* (February 1923): 161.

[81]Cedric Dover, "The Importance of Georgia Douglas Johnson," *The Crisis* 59 (December 1952): 634.

[82]See note 75.

[83]Newman I. White and Walter C. Jackson, eds. *Anthology of Verse by American Negroes* (Durham, NC: Trinity College Press, 1924), 225.

[84]Anne Spencer, "The Browsing Reader," review of *An Autumn Love Cycle*, *The Crisis* 20 (March 1929): 87.

[85]Blanche Watson, "The Bookshelf," review of *An Autumn Love Cycle*, entitled "A Document of a Woman's Heart," *Chicago Defender*, Part 2, 16 March 1929, 1.

[86]Maxwell Hayson is described as a "colored" poet on the card catalogue entry at Howard University's Moorland-Spingarn Research Center. One work of his is on file there, a five-page "An Ode of Welcome to Samuel Coleridge-Taylor," published in 1906. Both letters are in Johnson's file at Howard Unviersity. In addition to Hayson, Toomer and Fauset also comment on Johnson's illegible handwriting.

[87]"Modern romantic" is the label that Ronald Primeau ascribes to Johnson in "Frank Horne and the Second Echelon Poets of the Harlem Renaissance" in *Harlem Renaissance Remembered*, ed. Arna Bontemps (New York: Dodd, Mead, 1972), 265.

[88]Chavina Hosek and Patricia Parker, eds., *Lyric Poetry Beyond New Criticism* (Ithaca, NY: Cornell University Press, 1985), 199. References to this work appear parenthetically in the introduction as *Lyric Poetry*.

[89]Johnson submitted at least five plays of social protest (*Blue-Eyed Black Boy*, *Safe*, *A Sunday Morning in the South*, *Frederick Douglass*, and *William and Ellen Craft*) to the Federal Theatre Project between 1935 and 1939, the project's final year. None were accepted for publication. After reviewing the readers' commentary at the Federal Theatre Project archives at George Mason University, Winona L. Fletcher speculates that Johnson "forsook the writing of drama and concentrated again on writing poetry, which evidently was more acceptable to white publishers." See Winona L. Fletcher, "From Genteel Poet to Revolutionary Playwright: Georgia Douglas Johnson," *The Theatre Annual* 40 (1985): 41–64.

Plumes was originally published by Samuel French (New York, 1927). It was reprinted that year in *Plays of Negro Life: A Source Book of Native American Drama*, ed. Alain Locke and Montgomery Gregory (New York: Harper, 1927). *Blue Blood* was originally published by Appleton-Century (New York, 1927). It was reprinted in *Fifty More Contemporary One-Act Plays*, ed. Frank Shay (New York: Appleton-Century, 1938). *Frederick Douglass* and *William and Ellen Craft* were originally published in *Negro History in Thirteen Plays*, ed. Willis Richardson and May Miller (Washington, DC: Associated Publishers, 1935). *A Sunday Morning in the South* was originally published in *Black Theatre, U.S.A.: Forty-Five Plays by Black American Playwrights, 1847–1974*, ed. James V. Hatch and Ted Shine (New York: Free Press, 1974). *Safe* and *Blue-Eyed Black Boy* were recovered from the Federal Theatre Project research division, Fenwick Library, George Mason University, and published in *Wines in the Wilderness: Plays by African Americans*, ed. Elizabeth Brown-Guillory (New York: Greenwood, 1990).

Johnson's unpublished plays, which apparently are no longer extant, included the following in categories of her designation. Her primitive life plays were *Red Shoes* and *Well-Diggers*. Her plays of average Negro life were *Jungle Love, Little Blue Pigeon, Scapegoat, The New Day: A Brotherhood Play, One Cross Enough, Holiday,* and *Sue Baily.* Her lynching plays were *Safe, A Bill to be Passed, And Still They Paused, Camel-Legs, Miss Bliss, Heritage,* and *Midnight and Dawn.* These works are listed in Johnson's "Catalogue of Writings.For a partial listing see also Perkins, 243–48.

For additional discussions on black theatre during the twenties and women's participation in black drama, see Nellie McKay, "Black Theater and Drama in the 1920s: Years of Growing Pains," *Massachusetts Review* 28 (Winter 1987): 615–26; Nellie McKay, "'What Were They Saying?' Black Women Playwrights of the Harlem Renaissance," in *The Harlem Renaissance Re-Examined,* ed. Victor Kramer (New York: AMS, 1987), 129–47; Doris E. Abramson, "Angela Weld Grimké, Mary T. Burrill, Georgia Douglas Johnson, and Marita O. Bonner: An Analysis of Their Plays," *Sage* 22 (Spring 1985): 9–12; and Jeanne-Marie A. Miller, "Georgia Douglas Johnson and May Miller: Forgotten Playwrights of the New Negro Renaissance," *C.L.A. Journal* 33 (June 1990): 349–86.

[90]See Leslie Catherine Sanders, *The Development of Black Drama: From the Shadows to Selves* (Baton Rouge: Louisiana State University Press, 1988), 8–10, 13–23 for a summary of the relationship of American folk drama and Negro folk drama.

[91]Alain Locke, ed., *The New Negro* (1925; reprint, New York: Atheneum, 1969), 159.

[92]See W. E. B. Du Bois, "Krigwa Little Theatre Movement," *The Crisis* 32 (July 1926): 134. Krigwa was the acronym for the Crisis Guild of Writers and Artists; however, Du Bois changed the "C" to "K." See *Black Female Playwrights,* ed. with an introduction by Kathy A. Perkins (Bloomington: University of Indiana Press, 1989), 5.

[93]Elizabeth Brown-Guillory, *Their Place on the Stage: Black Women Playwrights in America* (Westport, CT: Greenwood, 1988), 5.

[94]For example, Doris Abramson's study *Negro Playwrights in the American Theatre, 1925–1959* (New York: Columbia University Press, 1959) outlines the development of Negro theatre without mentioning any black women playwrights of the New Renaissance era.

[95]The play was based on the 1925 novel *Porgy* by DuBose Heyward.

[96]Under the name Paul Tremaine, Johnson also published a review of Boston mayor James Michael Curley's *I'd Do It Again: A Record of All My Uproarious Years, New Republic* 137 (September 9, 1957): 17–19. Here Johnson clearly appropriates the unquestioned authority of white masculinity to critique not only Curley's book and his political character but to participate in one of the principal organs of hegemonic discourse.

[97]I could not find the manuscript of "Free" in the Harmon file at the manuscript division of the Library of Congress. The story is published in *The Sleeper Wakes: Harlem Renaissance Stories by Women*, ed. Marcy Knopf (New Brunswick, NJ: Rutgers University Press, 1993), 55–59. Johnson's "Catalogue" refers to one apparently nonextant story, "Holiday."

[98]This character seems based on Jean Toomer.

[99]"Gesture" was originally published in *Challenge: A Literary Quarterly* 1, no. 1 (June 1936): 13–17. The quarterly was edited and copyrighted by Dorothy West.

[100]Davis's observation concerns Nella Larsen's adoption of the name Allen Semi for the publication of two stories in *Young's Realistic Stories* magazine. However, Davis's observation fits Johnson and other women writers hampered by Victorian notions about the appropriate topics for women writers. See Davis's *Nella Larsen: Poet of the Harlem Renaissance*, 173.

[101]"Tramp Love" was originally published in *Challenge: A Literary Quarterly* 2, no. 1 (Spring 1937): 3–11.

[102]Zora Neale Hurston, *Their Eyes Were Watching God* (1937; reprint, New York: Harper Perennial, 1990, 1.

ACKNOWLEDGMENTS

Scholarship involves the collaboration of many people. Without the invitation of Henry Louis Gates, Jr., to prepare *The Selected Works of Georgia Douglas Johnson* I probably would not have had the profound experience of reexamining her life and writings. Many people helped me with this project, and I take this opportunity to express my appreciation. A very special thanks goes to Dorothy Porter Wesley (historian and Director Emeritus of the Moorland-Spingarn Research Center), who drew on her remarkable memory to help me reconstruct Johnson. Dorothy also informed me of Johnson's membership in the D.C. Writers' Club and gave me an original copy of Johnson's *Share My World*. I thank May Miller Sullivan, who during a telephone conversation (on the afternoon of December 22, 1993) remembered her good friend Georgia. Both Dorothy and May are now deceased. I thank Nella "Mike" Miller Newman, May Miller's niece, for allowing me to examine May's brother Kelly Miller Jr.'s scrapbook. I thank David Levering Lewis (Martin Luther King Professor of History at Rutgers University) and E. Ethelbert Miller (Director of the Afro-American Resource Center at Howard University) for recalling their interviews with Henry Lincoln Johnson Jr. and for helping me to understand the fate of Johnson's papers that were stored in the basement of her home. I thank Jeffrey C. Stewart for sharing information about Alain Locke and Johnson. I thank Thomas Battle (director), Esme Bhan (former Manuscript Research Associate) and Joellen R. El-Bashir (Senior Manuscript Librarian) all at Moorland-Spingarn Research Center for making the papers of Georgia Douglas Johnson, Alain Locke, and the D.C. Writers' Club available to me. I thank Ann Allen Shockley, Associate Librarian of Special Collections at the Fisk University Library, and Wilson Flemister, Manuscript Librarian of the Robert Woodruff Library at Atlanta University, for making their respective holdings on Johnson available to me. I thank Danielle McClellan, public services assistant at the Beinecke Rare Book and Manuscript Library at Yale University Library, for locating Johnson's "Paupaulekejo: A Three-Act Play" in Langston Hughes's papers. I thank the staff at the manuscripts division at the Library of Congress for access to the files of the Harmon Foundation records. I thank Jennifer Burton of the Afro-American Studies program at Harvard for promptly sending me copies of Johnson's works. I thank theatre professors Kathy A. Perkins and Winona L. Fletcher for information about Johnson's dramatic writings. And I also thank my friends and colleagues—Jeffrey C. Stewart, David Levering Lewis, Dorothy Porter Wesley, Eve Hawthorne, Ann Kelly, Jennifer Jordan, Vicki Arana, Alinda Sumers, and Winona Fletcher—for carefully reading various drafts of this introduction and for generously offering me their criticism. Their perceptive suggestions greatly enhanced this introduction. Its defects are mine.

Extract from letter of W.E.B. Du Bois to Georgia Douglas Johnson found on p. 1v is reprinted by permission of David Graham Du Bois.

POETRY

GEORGIA DOUGLAS JOHNSON

This photograph was part of her application to the Harlem
Foundation. Courtesy of the Manuscript Division of the
Library of Congress.

THE HEART *of a* WOMAN
AND OTHER POEMS

BY

GEORGIA DOUGLAS JOHNSON

WITH AN INTRODUCTION BY
WILLIAM STANLEY BRAITHWAITE

BOSTON
THE CORNHILL COMPANY
1918

TO
H. L. Johnson

INTRODUCTION

The poems in this book are intensely feminine and for me this means more than anything else that they are deeply human. We are yet scarcely aware, in spite of our boasted twentieth-century progress, of what lies deeply hidden, of mystery and passion, of domestic love and joy and sorrow, of romantic visions and practical ambitions, in the heart of a woman. The emancipation of woman is yet to be wholly accomplished; though woman has stamped her image on every age of the world's history, and in the heart of almost every man since time began, it is only a little over half of a century since she has either spoke or acted with a sense of freedom. During this time she has made little more than a start to catch up with man in the wonderful things he has to his credit; and yet all that man has to his credit would scarcely have been achieved except for the devotion and love and inspiring comradeship of woman.

Here, then, is lifted the veil, in these poignant songs and lyrics. To look upon what is revealed is to give one a sense of infinite sympathy; to make one kneel in

spirit to the marvelous patience, the wonderful endurance, the persistent faith, which are
hidden in this nature.

> The heart of a woman falls back with the night,
> And enters some alien cage in its plight,
> And tries to forget it has dreamed of the stars
> While it breaks, breaks, breaks on the sheltering bars.

sings the poet. And

> The songs of the singer
> Are tones that repeat
> The cry of the heart
> Till it ceases to beat.

This verse just quoted is from " The Dreams
of the Dreamer," and with the previous quotation tells us that this woman's heart is keyed
in the plaintive, knows the sorrowful agents
of life and experience which knock and enter
at the door of dreams. But women have
made the saddest songs of the world, Sappho
no less than Elizabeth Barrett Browning,
Ruth the Moabite poetess gleaning in the
fields of Boaz no less than Amy Levy, the
Jewess who broke her heart against the London pavements; and no less does sadness
echo its tender and appealing sigh in these
songs and lyrics of Georgia Douglas Johnson.

[viii]

[8]

But sadness is a kind of felicity with woman, paradoxical as it may seem; and it is so because through this inexplicable felicity *they* touched, intuitionally caress, reality.

So here engaging life at its most reserved sources, whether the form or substance through which it articulates be nature, or the seasons, touch of hands or lips, love, desire, or any of the emotional abstractions which sweep like fire or wind or cooling water through the blood, Mrs. Johnson creates just that reality of woman's heart and experience with astonishing raptures. It is a kind of privilege to know so much about the secrets of woman's nature, a privilege all the more to be cherished when given, as in these poems, with such exquisite utterance, with such a lyric sensibility.

WILLIAM STANLEY BRAITHWAITE.

Cambridge, Massachusetts.

[ix]

CONTENTS

[xi]

[xii]

THE HEART OF A WOMAN

The heart of a woman goes forth with the
    dawn,
As a lone bird, soft winging, so restlessly on,
Afar o'er life's turrets and vales does it roam
In the wake of those echoes the heart calls home.

The heart of a woman falls back with the night,
And enters some alien cage in its plight,
And tries to forget it has dreamed of the stars
While it breaks, breaks, breaks on the sheltering
    bars.

[1]

THE DREAMS OF THE DREAMER

The dreams of the dreamer
  Are life-drops that pass
The break in the heart
  To the soul's hour-glass.

The songs of the singer
  Are tones that repeat
The cry of the heart
  'Till it ceases to beat.

[2]

GOSSAMER

The peerless boon of innocence,
  The first in nature's list,
Is fading, ere the rising sun
  The world awake has kist.

The early dew upon the grass,
  The purity of morn,
The glint that lies in virgin cheek,
  Frail cobwebs — of the dawn.

[3]

SYMPATHY

My joy leaps with your ecstasy,
   In sympathy divine;
The smiles that wreathe upon your lips,
   Find sentinels on mine:

Your lightest sigh I'm echoing,
   I tremble with your pain,
And all your tears are falling
   In my heart like bitter rain.

[4]

CONTEMPLATION

We stand mute!
No words can paint such fragile imagery,
Those prismic gossamers that roll
Beyond the sky-line of the soul;
We stand mute!

[5]

DEAD LEAVES

The breaking dead leaves 'neath my feet
A plaintive melody repeat,
Recalling shattered hopes that lie
As relics of a bygone sky.

Again I thread the mazy past,
Back where the mounds are scattered fast —
Oh! foolish tears, why do you start,
To break of dead leaves in the heart?

[6]

DAWN

Trailing night's sand-sifted stars,
Rainbows sweep, as day unbars,
Fragrant essences of morn,
Bathe humanity — new-born!

[7]

ELEVATION

There are highways in the soul,
  Heights like pyramids that rise
  Far beyond earth-veilèd eyes,
  Sweeping through the barless skies
  O'er the line where daylight dies —
There are highways in the soul!

PEACE

I rest me deep within the wood,
  Drawn by its silent call,
Far from the throbbing crowd of men
  On nature's breast I fall.

My couch is sweet with blossoms fair,
  A bed of fragrant dreams,
And soft upon my ear there falls
  The lullaby of streams.

The tumult of my heart is stilled,
  Within this sheltered spot,
Deep in the bosom of the wood,
  Forgetting, and — forgot!

| 9 |

WHITHER?

Minutes swiftly throb and pass,
  Shadows cross the dial-glass,
Speeding ever to some call,
  Weary world and shadows, all.

Down the closing aisles of day,
  Tramping footsteps die away,
But no tidings thread the gloom,
  From the hushed and silent tomb.

[10]

QUEST

The phantom happiness I sought
  O'er every crag and moor;
I paused at every postern gate,
  And knocked at every door;

In vain I searched the land and sea,
  E'en to the inmost core,
The curtains of eternal night
  Descend — my search is o'er.

[11]

MATE

Our separate winding ways we trod,
Along the highways, unto God,
Unbonded by the clasp of hand,
Without a vow — we understand,
Estranged for aye, the fusing kiss,
Omnipotent, we bide in this —
They need no trammeling of bars
Whose souls were welded with the stars.

EMBLEMS

A wordless kiss, a stifled sigh,
A trembling lip, a downcast eye,
   " Alas," they say,
   " A-day, a-day,"
The cruse has failed, the lamp must die!

[13]

MIRRORED

When lone and solitaire within your chamber,
  With lamp unlit, as evening shades unroll,
If you reveal the trail your thoughts are taking,
  I then may read the riddle of your soul.

For it is then, the tired mind unveiling,
  Drifts stark into the holy after-glow,
Within the hour of quiet meditation,
  The tidal thoughts, like limpid waters, flow.

[14]

REPULSE

Nobody cares when I am glad,
   I beat upon their hearts in glee,
   " Drink, drink joy's brimming cup with me,"
   All echoless, my ecstasy —
Nobody cares when I am glad.

Nobody cares when I am sad,
   Whene'er I seek compassion's breast,
   I falter wounded from my quest
   Back! back into my heart, sore prest —
Nobody cares when I am sad.

QUERY

Is she the sage who will not sip
The cup love presses to her lip?
Or she who drinks the mad cup dry,
And turns with smiling face — to die?

[16]

PENT

The rain is falling steadily
  Upon the thirsty earth,
While dry-eyed, I remain, and calm
  Amid my own heart's dearth.

Break! break! ! ye flood-gates of my tears
  All pent in agony,
Rain, rain! upon my scorching soul
  And flood it as the sea! !

PAGES FROM LIFE

Not for your tender eyes that shine,
Nor for your red lips pulsing wine,
I love you, dear: your soul divine,
In sweet captivity, holds mine!

. . . .

The tender eyes have lost their glow,
The flagons of the lips run low,
The autumn trembles in the air, —
A woman passes solitaire!

[18]

RECALL

Winter — aback sweeps the inward eye,
Fleet o'er the trail to a rose-wreathed sky,
Girt by a cordon of dreams I dwell
Deep in the heart of the old-time spell.

Almost, the tones of your whispered word,
Almost! the thrill that your dear lips stirred,
Almost! ! that wild pulsing throb again —
Almost! ! ! —
        ('Tis winter, the falling rain).

[19]

GETHSEMANE

Into the garden of sorrow,
Some day we all must roam,
If not to-day, then to-morrow,
Bow 'neath its purple dome,
Out from the musk-laden banqueting halls,
Doffing our mirth-spangled vestments like
    thralls,
Softly we wend to Gethsemane,
In the hour that sorrow calls!

[20]

IMPELLED

Athwart the sky the great sun sails,
Through æons thus, the daylight trails,
And man, living breath of the sod
Beholding, in his heart knows God.

Throughout the night's long brooding deep,
Earth's trustful children die-to-sleep,
But with the whisperings of morn
Awake, unto the day, new-born.

The mystery of earth untold,
The great infinite, none behold,
Forge ever new the spiral chain,
Revolving man to God again.

[21]

EVENTIDE

The silence of the brooding night,
Enfolds me with its eerie light;
I lie upon its shadowed breast
A pilgrim, wearying for rest

Nightfall! thy sable curtains steep
My very soul in solace deep,
God sends thee with thy soothing balms,
That I may falter to thy arms.

THRALL

Fragile, tiny, just a sprite,
Holding me a thrall bedight,
Stronger than a giant's wand
Serves the word of your command.

Out from rushing worlds, though low
Should you whisper, I would know,
And would answer, though the breath
Be the gateway unto death.

YOUTH

The dew is on the grasses, dear,
  The blush is on the rose,
And swift across our dial-youth,
  A shifting shadow goes.

The primrose moments, lush with bliss,
  Exhale and fade away,
Life may renew the Autumn time,
  But nevermore the May!

JOY

There's a soft rosy glow o'er the whole world
  to-day,
There's a freshness and fragrance that trembles
  in May,
There's a lilt in the music that vibrates and
  thrills
From the uttermost glades to the tops of the
  hills.

Oh! I am so happy, my heart is so light,
The shades and the shadows have vanished from
  sight,
This wild pulsing gladness throbs like a sweet
  pain —
O soul of me, drink, ere night falleth again!

[25]

POSTHUMOUS

Of what avail the tardy showers,
To the famished summer flowers?
All in vain the rain-drops cry,
Dead things never make reply.

Life's belated cup of bliss,
Woo the weary lips to kiss,
When the singing is a sigh,
Pulses quivering, to die.

[26]

OMEGA

The fragile fabric of our dream
Drifts as a feather down life's stream —
The long defile of empty days
Grim silhouetted, mock my gaze.

Though oft escapes the stifled sigh,
A desert ever broods my eye —
Since you have utterly forgot,
God grant that I remember not!

[27]

TEARS AND KISSES

There are tears sweet, refreshing like dewdrops
    that rise,
There are tears far too deep for the lakes of the
    eyes.

There are kisses like thistledown, fitfully sped,
There are kisses that live in the hearts of the
    dead.

ISOLATION

Alone! yes, evermore alone — isolate each his
    way,
Though hand is echoing to hand vain sophistries
    of clay,
Within that veilèd, mystic place where bides the
    inmost soul,
No twain shall pass while tides shall wax, nor
    changing seasons roll.

Enisled, apart our pilgrimage, despite the arms
    that twine,
Despite the fusing kiss that wields the magic
    charm of wine,
Despite the interplay of sigh, the surge of
    sympathy,
We tread in solitude remote, the trail of destiny !

[29]

WHERE?

I called you through the silent night
  Across the brooding deep,
I sought you in the shadowland
  From out the world — asleep;

No answer echoed to my call,
  And now my way I thread
About the lowly mounds that rise
  Among the silent dead.

Though voiceless, you will hear my call,
  Your soul will heed my cry,
Will rise, and mock the prison where
  Your bones recumbent lie.

TIRED

I'm tired, days and nights to me
Drag on in slow monotony,
With not a single star in sight
To lend a gleam of cheering light.

I'm tired, there are none to care
That I am drifting to despair:
O shadows! take me to your breast
For I am tired — I would rest.

[31]

SMOTHERED FIRES

A woman with a burning flame
  Deep covered through the years
With ashes.   Ah! she hid it deep,
  And smothered it with tears.

Sometimes a baleful light would rise
  From out the dusky bed,
And then the woman hushed it quick
  To slumber on, as dead.

At last the weary war was done
  The tapers were alight,
And with a sigh of victory
  She breathed a soft — good-night!

THE MEASURE

Fierce is the conflict — the battle of eyes,
Sure and unerring, the wordless replies,
Challenges flash from their ambushing caves —
Men, by their glances, are masters or slaves.

INEVITABLY

There's nothing in the world that clings
As does a memory that stings;
While happy hours fade and pass,
Like shadows in a looking-glass.

[34]

MODULATIONS

The petals of the faded rose
    Commingle silently,
One with the atoms of the dust,
    One with the chaliced sea.

The essence of my fleeting youth
    Caught in the web of time,
Exhales within the springing flowers
    Or breathes in love sublime.

[35]

MEMORY

Love's roses I gathered, all dewy, in May,
My heart holds the breath of their attar to-day;
And now, while the blasts of the winter winds
    ring,
I hear not the tempest, I'm dreaming of Spring.

⌊ 36 ⌋

RHYTHM

Oh, my fancy teems with a world of dreams, —
  They revolve in a glittering fire,
How they twirl and go with the tunes that flow
  On the breath of my soul-strung lyre.

[37]

GILEAD

Walk within thy own heart's temple, child, and
    rest,
What you seek abides forever in thy breast,
Closer than thy folded arm
Is the soul-renewing-balm,
Walk within thy own heart's temple, child, and
    rest.

[38]

FOREDOOM

Her life was dwarfed, and wed to blight,
Her very days were shades of night,
Her every dream was born entombed,
Her soul, a bud, — that never bloomed.

[39]

WHENE'ER I LIFT MY EYES TO BLISS

Whene'er I lift my eyes to bliss,
I stagger blind with pain,
Afar into the folding night
The silence, and the rain.

Whene'er I feel the urge of Spring,
A throbbing, unknown woe
Enfolds me; I am desolate
When love is calling low.

[40]

DESPAIR

The curtains of twilight are drawn in the west
    And vespers are sweet on the air,
While I, through my leafless, ungarlanded way
    But pause at the gates of despair.

Good-bye to the hopes that were never fulfilled,
    Good-bye to the fond dreams that failed,
Good-bye to my dead that has never been born,
    Good-bye to love's ship that ne'er sailed.

[41]

WHEN I AM DEAD

When I am dead, withhold, I pray, your bloom-
    ing legacy;
Beneath the willows did I bide, and they should
    cover me;
I longed for light and fragrance, and I sought
    them far and near,
O, it would grieve me utterly, to find them on
    my bier!

[42]

SUPREME

The fairest lips are those we kiss,
With greatest ecstasy and bliss;
The brightest eyes, are those that shine,
Unchangingly through changing time;
The greatest love is that we know,
When life is just an afterglow.

[43]

IN QUEST

With the first blush of morning, my soul is
    awing,
Away o'er the phantom lands free, wandering,
I seek thee in hamlet, in woodland, and hall,
Till night-shades, enfolding my tired heart, fall.

Yet ever and alway, like the thrush in a tree,
My heart lifts its preluding love-song to thee;
I call through the days, through the long weary
    years,
And slumber at night-fall, refreshed by my
    tears.

[44]

RECOMPENSE

Roses after rain,
Pleasure after pain,
Happiness will soothe the sigh,
Smiles await the tear-dimmed eye —
Bloom will follow blight,
Daylight trails the night,
Life is sweeter
Love is deeper
In the heart's twilight!

POETRY

Behold! the living thrilling lines
That course the blood like madd'ning wines,
And leap with scintillating spray
Across the guards of ecstasy.
The flame that lights the lurid spell
Springs from the soul's artesian well,
Its fairy filament of art
Entwines the fragments of a heart.

[46]

WHAT NEED HAVE I FOR MEMORY?

What need have I for memory,
    When not a single flower
Has bloomed within life's desert
    For me, one little hour.

What need have I for memory
    Whose burning eyes have met
The corse of unborn happiness
    Winding the trail regret?

[47]

A FANTASY

I breathe the lyric of my love
    Across the twilit way,
The gentle echoes bear it on
    Beyond the edge of day:

All vibrant is the melody
    The silences repeat,
My song is but my longing heart
    Pulsated with its beat.

It winds amid the dusky ways
    Where far mysteries shine,
To find amid God's trackless space,
    One answering song to mine.

SOUVENIR

A little hour of sunshine,
  A little while of joy,
We winnow in our harvesting
  From all the world's alloy.

None, none, are so benighted,
  Who journey up life's hill,
But have some treasured memory,
  Which lives all vibrant still.

ILLUSIONS

Who hath not built his castles in the free and
    open air?
Who hath not dreamed his rosy dreams, more
    fair than all the fair?
Who hath not seen his castles fall, all scattered
    to the ground?
Who bears his dream unshattered, from the
    dream-land where they're found?

[50]

TRANSPOSITIONS

Smiles do not always echo cheer,
  Nor tear-drops measure grief,
For sorrow seeks a gilded mask,
  And joy in tears, relief.

[51]

THE WILLOW

When life is young, without a care,
  Alone we walk, and free:
The world, a splendid merry round
  Of rhythmic melody.

Before the end, grim sorrow calls
  Into each mortal ear,
When friendship fades to memories,
  And love lies in its bier.

Then, then it is that sympathy
  Is holden close and dear;
Ah, then life's consolation comes
  Commingled with a tear.

DEVASTATION

O love, you have shorn me, and rifled my heart,
You have torn down the shrine from the inner-
    most part,
And through it now rushes a grief, sadly-wild,
That breaks as the plaint of a sorrowing child.

[53]

SPRINGTIDE

All deep there stirs the throb of Spring,
Its vital pulse I'm answering,
Swift to its dominant I merge,
One with its undulating surge;
My heart awakes to virile tone
And breaks — unanswered, and alone.

GLOAMTIDE

The shades of the gloaming around me are
    stealing,
The lure of the dusk through the silences call,
While blossoming incense comes mutely appeal-
    ing,
And choiring wood-voices, vespering, fall.
Immersed in the deep of my dim sylvan-bower,
    Upborne on the breast of its emerald tide,
I drift with the gleam of the vanishing hour
    Afar — where my uttermost longings abide.

[55]

PENDULUM

I have swung to the uttermost reaches of pain,
'Mid the echo of sighs, and a deluge of rain,
But ah! I rebound to the limits of bliss,
On the rapturous swing of an infinite kiss.

[56]

DELUGE

A whisper at twilight, a sigh through the night,
A strain of soft music, a perfume so light,
Will sweep as a feather the bulwark of years,
To surges of rapture, or rivers of tears.

57]

RETROSPECT

Love's kisses spurned so long ago,
Dead as the years, that o'er them flow; —
And now, my gilded treasuries
Would I might give — for memories.

GLAMOUR

O come while youth's bright rosy veil
  Beguiles your eyes and mine,
Let's tread the asphodel of bliss,
  And drink life's magic wine:
Soon time will rend the gossamer,
  To wisdom's cruelty,
While we are blind, my love, be kind,
  For soon, too soon, we see!

THE RETURN

Again we meet — a flashing glance,
And then, to scabbard, goes the lance,
While thoughts troop on in cavalcade
Adown the wide aisles time has made.

Back in the glow of yesterday,
With tender troth you rode away,
The sheen of rainbows in our eyes,
That swept the rim of other skies.

And now a writhing worm am I,
Beneath a doomed love's lensing eye,
Let me but stagger, far from sight,
To hide my anguish, in the night.

LOVE'S TENDRIL

Sweeter far than lyric rune
Is my baby's cooing tune;
Brighter than the butterflies
Are the gleams within her eyes;
Firmer than an iron band
Serves the zephyr of her hand;
Deeper than the ocean's roll
Sounds her heart-beat in my soul.

[61]

MY LITTLE DREAMS

I'm folding up my little dreams
　　Within my heart tonight,
And praying I may soon forget
　　The torture of their sight.

For time's deft fingers scroll my brow
　　With fell relentless art —
I'm folding up my little dreams
　　Tonight, within my heart.

[62]

BRONZE

BRONZE:
A BOOK OF VERSE

BY

GEORGIA DOUGLAS JOHNSON

AUTHOR OF: "THE HEART OF A WOMAN"

"AN AUTUMN LOVE CYCLE," ETC.

WITH AN INTRODUCTION BY

DR. W. E. B. Du BOIS

BOSTON
B . J. BRIMMER COMPANY
1922

[78]

Permission to reprint certain poems in this book has been courteously granted by the editors of *"The Crisis"* and *"The Liberator."* The author wishes to make acknowledgment of the thanks due to Professor Alain Leroy Locke, of Howard University, for helpful criticism.

AUTHOR'S NOTE

This book is the child of a bitter earth-wound. I sit on the earth and sing — sing out, and of, my sorrow. Yet, fully conscious of the potent agencies that silently work in their healing ministries, I know that God's sun shall one day shine upon a perfected and unhampered people.

TO H. L. J.

FOREWORD

Those who know what it means to be a colored woman in 1922—and know it not so much in fact as in feeling, apprehension, unrest and delicate yet stern thought — must read Georgia Douglas Johnson's BRONZE. *Much of it will not touch this reader and that, and some of it will mystify and puzzle them as a sort of reiteration and over-emphasis. But none can fail to be caught here and there by a word — a phrase — a period that tells a life history or even paints the history of a generation. Can you not see that marching of the mantled with*

"VOICES STRANGE TO ECSTASY?"

Have you ever looked on the "twilight faces" of their throngs, or seen the black mother with her son when

"HER HEART IS SANDALING HIS FEET?"

Or can you not conceive that infinite sorrow of a dark child wandering the world:

"SEEKING THE BREAST OF AN UNKNOWN FACE!"

I hope Mrs. Johnson will have wide reading. Her word is simple, sometimes trite, but it is singularly sincere and true , and as a revelation of the soul struggle of the women of a race it is invaluable.

W. E. B. Du BOIS.

New York, August 4, 1922.

7

CONTENTS

9

[87]

10

Exhortation

SONNET TO THE MANTLED

And they shall rise and cast their mantles by,
Erect and strong and visioned, in the day
That rings the knell of Curfew o'er the sway
Of prejudice—who reels with mortal cry
To lift no more her leprous, blinded eye,
Reft of the fetters, far more cursed than they
Which held dominion o'er human clay,
The spirit soars aloft where rainbows lie.

Like joyful exiles swift returning home—
The rhythmic chanson of their eager feet,
While voices strange to ecstasy, long dumb,
Break forth in major rhapsodies, full sweet.
Into the very star-shine, lo! they come
Wearing the bays of victory complete!

SONNET TO THOSE WHO SEE BUT DARKLY

Their gaze uplifting from shoals of despair
Like phantoms groping enswathed from the light
Up from miasmic depths, children of night,
Surge to the piping of Hope's dulcet lay,
Souled like the lily, whose splendors declare
God's mazèd paradox—purged of all blight,
Out from the quagmire, unsullied and fair.

Life holds her arms o'er the festering way,
Smiles, as their faith-sandalled rushes prevail,
Slowly the sun rides the marge of the day,
Wine to the lips sorely anguished and pale;
On, ever on, do the serried ranks sway
Charging the ultimate, rending the veil.

16

BROTHERHOOD

Come, brothers all!
Shall we not wend
The blind-way of our prison-world
By sympathy entwined?
Shall we not make
The bleak way for each other's sake
Less rugged and unkind?
O let each throbbing heart repeat
The faint note of another's beat
To lift a chanson for the feet
That stumble down life's checkered street.

17

Supplication

LET ME NOT LOSE MY DREAM

Let me not lose my dream, e'en though I scan the veil
    with eyes unseeing through their glaze of tears,
Let me not falter, though the rungs of fortune perish
    as I fare above the tumult, praying purer air,
Let me not lose the vision, gird me, Powers that toss
    the worlds, I pray!
Hold me, and guard, lest anguish tear my dreams
    away!

21

LET ME NOT HATE

Let me not hate, although the bruising world decries
    my peace,
Gives me no quarter, hounds me while I sleep;
Would snuff the candles of my soul and sear my inmost
    dreamings.

Let me not hate, though girt by vipers, green and hiss-
    ing through the dark;
I fain must love. God help me keep the altar-gleams
    that flicker wearily, anon,
On down the world's grim night!

22

CALLING DREAMS

The right to make my dreams come true
I ask, nay, I demand of life,
Nor shall fate's deadly contraband
Impede my steps, nor countermand.

Too long my heart against the ground
Has beat the dusty years around,
And now, at length, I rise, I wake!
And stride into the morning-break!

23

DESIRE

Ope! ye everlasting doors, unto my soul's demand,
I would go forward, fare beyond these dusty boule-
    vards,
Faint lights and fair allure me all insistently
And I must stand within the halls resplendent, of my
    dreams.

24

SHADOW

SORROW SINGERS

Hear their viol-voices ringing
   Down the corridor of years,
As they lift their twilight faces
   Through a mist of falling tears!

27

THE CROSS

All day the world's mad mocking strife,
The venomed prick of probing knife,
The baleful, subtle leer of scorn
That rims the world from morn to morn,
While reptile-visions writhe and creep
Into the very arms of sleep
To quench the fitful burnished gleams:
A crucifixion in my dreams!

28

PREJUDICE

These fell miasmic rings of mist, with ghoulish menace
    bound,
Like noose-horizons tightening my little world around,
They still the soaring will to wing, to dance, to speed
    away,
And fling the soul insurgent back into its shell of clay:

Beneath incrusted silences, a seething Etna lies,
The fire of whose furnaces may sleep—*but never dies!*

29

[105]

LAOCOÖN

This spirit-choking atmosphere
  With deadly serpent-coil
Entwines my soaring-upwardness
  And chains me to the soil,
Where'er I seek with eager stride
  To gain yon gleaming height,
These noisesome fetters coil aloft
  And snare my buoyant flight.

O, why these aspirations bold,
  These rigours of desire,
That surge within so ceaselessly
  Like living tongues of fire?
And why these glowing forms of hope
  That scintillate and shine,
If naught of all that burnished dream
  Can evermore be mine?

30

LAOCOÖN

It cannot be, fate does not mock,
And man's untoward decree
Shall not forever thus confine
My life's entirety,
My every fibre fierce rebels
Against this servile role,
And all my being broods to break
This death-grip from my soul!

31

MOODS

My heart is pregnant with a great despair
With much beholding of my people's care,
'Mid blinded prejudice and nurtured wrong,
Exhaling wantonly the days along:
I mark Faith's fragile craft of cheering light
Tossing imperiled on the sea of night,
And then, enanguished, comes my heart's low cry,
"God, God! I crave to learn the reason why!"
Again, in spirit loftily I soar
With wingèd vision through earth's outer door,
In such an hour, it is mine to see,
In frowning fortune smiling destiny!

32

HEGIRA

Oh, black man, why do you northward roam, and leave
all the farm lands bare?
Is your house not warm, tightly thatched from storm,
and a larder replete your share?
And have you not schools, fit with books and tools the
steps of your young to guide?
Then what do you seek, in the north cold and bleak,
'mid the whirl of its teeming tide?

I have toiled in your cornfields, and parched in the sun,
    I have bowed 'neath your load of care,
I have patiently garnered your bright golden grain, in
    season of storm and fair,
With a smile I have answered your glowering gloom,
    while my wounded heart quivering bled,
Trailing mute in your wake, as your rosy dawn breaks,
    while I curtain the mound of my dead.

Though my children are taught in the schools you have
    wrought, they are blind to the sheen of the sky,

33

For the brand of your hand, casts a pall o'er the land,
    that enshadows the gleam of the eye,
My sons, deftly sapped of the brawn-hood of man, self-
    rejected and impotent stand,
My daughters, unhaloed, unhonored, undone, feed the
    lust of a dominant land.

I would not remember, yet could not forget, how the
    hearts beating true to your own,
You've tortured, and wounded, and filtered their blood
    'till a budding Hegira has blown.

Unstrange is the pathway to Calvary's hill, which I
    wend in my dumb agony,
Up its perilous height, in the pale morning light, to
    dissever my own from the tree.

And so I'm away, where the sky-line of day sets the
    arch of its rainbow afar,
To the land of the north, where the symbol of worth
    sets the broad gates of combat ajar!

34

THE PASSING OF THE EX-SLAVE

Swift melting into yesterday,
The tortured hordes of ebon-clay;
No more is heard the plaintive strain,
The rhythmic chaunting of their pain.

Their mounded bodies dimly rise
To fill the gulf of sacrifice,
And o'er their silent hearts below
The mantled millions softly go.

Some few remaining still abide,
Gnarled sentinels of time and tide,
Now mellowed by a chastened glow
Which lighter hearts will never know.

Winding into the silent way,
Spent with the travail of the day,
So royal in their humble might
These uncrowned Pilgrims of the Night!

35

THE OCTOROON

One drop of midnight in the dawn of life's pulsating
    stream
Marks her an alien from her kind, a shade amid its
    gleam;
Forevermore her step she bends insular, strange,
    apart—
And none can read the riddle of her wildly warring
    heart.

The stormy current of her blood beats like a mighty sea
Against the man-wrought iron bars of her captivity.
For refuge, succor, peace and rest, she seeks that
    humble fold
Whose every breath is kindliness, whose hearts are
    purest gold.

36

ALIENS

(To You—Everywhere! Dedicated)

They seem to smile as others smile, the masquerader's
    art
Conceals them, while, in verity, they're eating out their
    heart,
Betwixt the two contending stones of crass humanity
They lie, the fretted fabric of a dual dynasty.

A single drop, a sable strain debars them from their
    own,—
The others—fold them furtively, but God! they are
    alone,
Blown by the fickle winds of fate far from the traveled
    mart
To die, when they have quite consumed the morsel of
    their heart.
When man shall lift his lowered eyes to meet the moon
    of truth,

37

Shall break the shallow shell of pride and wax in ways
    of ruth,
He cannot hate, for love shall reign untrammelled in
    the soul,
While peace shall spread a rainbow o'er the earth from
    pole to pole.

CONCORD

Nor shall I in sorrow repine,
But offer a pæan of praise
To the infinite God of my days
Who marshals the pivoting spheres
Through the intricate maze of the years,
Who loosens the luminous flood
That lightens the purlieus of men,
I shall not in sorrow repine
To break the eternal Amen!

38

Motherhood

THE MOTHER

The mother soothes her mantled child
With incantation sad and wild;
A deep compassion brims her eye
And stills upon her lips, the sigh.

Her thoughts are leaping down the years,
O'er branding bars, through seething tears,
Her heart is sandaling his feet
Adown the world's corroding street.

Then, with a start she dons a smile
His tender yearnings to beguile,
And only God will ever know
The wordless measure of her woe.

41

MATERNITY

Proud?
Perhaps—and yet
I cannot say with surety
That I am happy thus to be
Responsible for this young life's embarking.
Is he not thrall to prevalent conditions?
Does not the day loom dark apace
To weave its cordon of disgrace
Around his lifted throat?
Is not this mezzotint enough and surfeit
For such prescience?
Ah, did I dare
Recall the pulsing life I gave,
And fold him in the kindly grave!

Proud?
Perhaps—could I but ever so faintly scan
The broad horizon of a man
Swept fair for his dominion—
So hesitant and half-afraid
I view this babe of sorrow!

42

BLACK WOMAN

Don't knock at my door, little child,
  I cannot let you in,
You know not what a world this is
  Of cruelty and sin.
Wait in the still eternity
  Until I come to you,
The world is cruel, cruel, child,
  I cannot let you in!

Don't knock at my heart, little one,
  I cannot bear the pain
Of turning deaf-ear to your call
  Time and time again!
You do not know the monster men
  Inhabiting the earth,
Be still, be still, my precious child,
  I must not give you birth!

43

"ONE OF THE LEAST OF THESE, MY LITTLE ONE"

The infant eyes look out amazed upon the frowning
    earth,
A stranger, in a land now strange, child of the mantled-
    birth;

Waxing, he wonders more and more; the scowling grows
    apace;
A world, behind its barring doors, reviles his ebon face:

Yet from this maelstrom issues forth a God-like entity,
That loves a world all loveless, and smiles on Calvary!

44

SHALL I SAY, "MY SON, YOU'RE BRANDED"?

Shall I say, "My son, you're branded in this country's
    pageantry,
By strange subtleties you're tethered, and no forum
    sets you free?"
Shall I mark the young lights fading through your soul-
    enchannelled eye,
As the dusky pall of shadows screen the highway of
    your sky?

Or shall I, with love prophetic, bid you dauntlessly
    arise,
Spurn the handicap that clogs you, taking what the
    world denies,
Bid you storm the sullen fortress wrought by prejudice
    and wrong
With a faith that shall not falter, in your heart and on
    your tongue!

45

MY BOY

I hear you singing happily,
  My boy of tarnished mien,
Lifting your limpid, trustful gaze
  In innocence serene.

A thousand javelins of pain
  Assault my heaving breast
When I behold the storm of years
  That beat without your nest.

O sing, my lark, your matin song
  Of joyous rhapsody,
Distil the sweetness of the hours
  In gladsome ecstasy.

For time awaits your buoyant flight
  Across the bar of years,
Sing, sing your song, my bonny lark,
  Before it melts in tears!

46

GUARDIANSHIP

That dusky child upon your knee
Is breath of God's eternity;
Direct his vision to the height—
Let naught obscure his royal right.

Although the highways to renown
Are iron-barred by fortune's frown,
'Tis his to forge the master-key
That wields the locks of destiny!

47

[123]

UTOPIA

God grant you wider vision, clearer skies, my son,
With morning's rosy kisses on your brow;
May your wild yearnings know repose,
And storm-clouds break to smiles
As you sweep on with spreading wings
Unto a waiting sunset!

48

LITTLE SON

The very acme of my woe,
    The pivot of my pride,
My consolation, and my hope
    Deferred, but not denied.
The substance of my every dream,
    The riddle of my plight,
The very world epitomized
    In turmoil and delight.

49

BENEDICTION

Go forth, my son,
Winged by my heart's desire!
Great reaches, yet unknown,
Await
For your possession.
I may not, if I would,
Retrace the way with you,
My pilgrimage is through,
But life is calling you!
Fare high and far, my son,
A new day has begun,
Thy star-ways must be won!

50

Prescience

CREDO

I believe in the ultimate justice of Fate;
That the races of men front the sun in their turn;
That each soul holds the title to infinite wealth
In fee to the will as it masters itself;
That the heart of humanity sounds the same tone
In impious jungle, or sky-kneeling fane.
I believe that the key to the life-mystery
Lies deeper than reason and further than death.
I believe that the rhythmical conscience within
Is guidance enough for the conduct of men.

53

PROMISE

Through the moil and the gloom they have issued
  To the steps of the upwinding hill,
Where the sweet, dulcet pipes of tomorrow
  In their preluding rhapsodies trill.

With a thud comes a stir in the bosom,
  As there steals on the sight from afar,
Through a break of a cloud's coiling shadow
  The gleam of a bright morning star!

54

THE SUPPLIANT

Long have I beat with timid hands upon life's leaden
     door,
Praying the patient, futile prayer my fathers prayed
     before,
Yet I remain without the close, unheeded and unheard,
And never to my listening ear is borne the waited word.

Soft o'er the threshold of the years there comes this
     counsel cool:
The strong demand, contend, prevail; the beggar is a
     fool!

55

HOPE

Frail children of sorrow, dethroned by a hue,
The shadows are flecked by the rose sifting through,
The world has its motion, all things pass away,
No night is omnipotent, there must be day.

The oak tarries long in the depth of the seed,
But swift is the season of nettle and weed,
Abide yet awhile in the mellowing shade,
And rise with the hour for which you were made.

The cycle of seasons, the tidals of man
Revolve in the orb of an infinite plan,
We move to the rhythm of ages long done,
And each has his hour—to dwell in the sun!

56

Exaltation

COSMOPOLITE

Not wholly this or that,
But wrought
Of alien bloods am I,
A product of the interplay
Of traveled hearts.
Estranged, yet not estranged, I stand
All comprehending;
From my estate
I view earth's frail dilemma;
Scion of fused strength am I,
All understanding,
Nor this nor that
Contains me.

59

FUSION

How deftly does the gardener blend
This rose and that
To bud a new creation,
More gorgeous and more beautiful
Than any parent portion,
And so,
I trace within my warring blood
The tributary sources,
They potently commingle
And sweep
With new-born forces!

60

PERSPECTIVE

Some day
I shall be glad that it was mine to be
A dark fore-runner of a race burgeoning;
I then shall know
The secret of life's Calvary,
And bless the thorns
That wound me!

61

WHEN I RISE UP

When I rise above the earth,
And look down on the things that fetter me,
I beat my wings upon the air,
Or tranquil lie,
Surge after surge of potent strength
Like incense comes to me
When I rise up above the earth
And look down upon the things that fetter me.

62

FAITH

The faint lose faith
When in the tomb their all is laid,
And there returns
No echoing of weal or woe.
The strong hope on,
They see the clods close over head,
The grass grow green,
No word is said,
And yet—
A little world within the world
Are we,
Daily our hearts' high yearnings fade,
Are buried!
New ones are made,—
Are crucified!
And yet—

63

Martial

WE FACE THE FUTURE

The hour is big with sooth and sign, with errant men
    at war,
While blood of alien, friend, and foe imbues the land
    afar,
And we, with sable faces pent, move with the vanguard
    line,
Shod with a faith that Springtime keeps, and all the
    stars opine.

67

SOLDIER

Though I should weep until the judgment,
How would it serve—
Brave men are fighting, women speed them,
'Tis a day
Of crucial conflict!
My son, sometimes it seems I'd rather hold
You safe beneath my heart
Than send you forth!
But lo! The sun is red and weaker children go!
Though I should weep until the judgment,
How would it serve!
I'll close my eyes and smile, O Son of Mine,
Your cause is kingly!
Step proud and confident, worthy your mother;
Be firm and brave, O Son of Mine, be strong,
For terror waxeth,
Speed swift away,
Though I should weep until the judgment . . .

68

HOMING BRAVES

There's music in the measured tread
Of those returning from the dead
Like scattered flowers from a plain
So lately crimson, with the slain.

No more the sound of shuffled feet
Shall mark the poltroon on the street,
Nor shifting, sodden, downcast eye
Reveal the man afraid to die.

They shall have paid full, utterly
The price of peace across the sea,
When, with uplifted glance, they come
To claim a kindly welcome home.

Nor shall the old-time daedal sting
Of prejudice, their manhood wing,
Nor heights, nor depths, nor living streams
Stand in the pathway of their dreams!

69

TAPS

They are embosomed in the sod,
   In still and tranquil leisure,
Their lives they've cast like trifles down,
   To serve their country's pleasure.

Nor bugle call, nor mother's voice,
   Nor moody mob's unreason,
Shall break their solace and repose
   Through swiftly changing season.

O graves of men who lived and died
   Afar from life's high pleasures,
Fold them in tenderly and warm
   With manifold fond measures.

70

PEACE

Peace on a thousand hills and dales,
  Peace in the hearts of men
While kindliness reclaims the soil
  Where bitterness has been.

The night of strife is drifting past,
  The storm of shell has ceased,
Disrupted is the cordon fell,
  Sweet charity released.

Forth from the shadow, swift we come
  Wrought in the flame together,
All men as one beneath the sun
  In brotherhood forever.

71

Random

QUESTION

Where are the brave men, where are the strong men?
Pygmies rise
And spawn the earth.
Weak-kneed, weak-hearted, and afraid,
Afraid to face the counsel of their timid hearts,
Afraid to look men squarely,
Down they gaze—
With fatal fascination
Down, down—
Into the whirling maggot sands
Of prejudice.

75

THE INITIATE

The woes of flesh are naught
To one who knows
The agony of soul!
'Twere but the thud of wind and rain
Upon the roof.
The woes of flesh are naught
To one who knows!

76

BONDAGE

Many cages round me,
Bar on bar
Stand grim, forbidding!
Ghostly pressures
Clutch my heart.
I gaze with eyes unseeing—
Whereunto may I wander free?
Alas, alas!
My garden walks lie inwardly!

77

RESOLUTION

With but one life full certified,
And that of every gleam denied
My portion,
Close to the unrelenting sod,
E'en as my fathers dumbly trod,
I've slumbered;
But now a surging, wild unrest
Uproots the poppies from my breast,
My soul awake, erect! anew!
I stand and face the star-swept blue,
And swear to make my dreams come true!

78

ECLIPSE

Aflounder the uncompassed darkness of doubt
  In search of the path to the goal
That lies at the end of our transient day,
  The ultimate bourne of the soul;
I grasp into nothingness, feebly essay
  To clasp but a willow, a stone,
And grope through the stepless, unechoing gloom
  Unanswered, unsuccored, alone!

79

WHY

The verdure sleeps in winter,
  Awakes with April rain,
The sun swings low—'tis night—ascends,
  And lo! 'tis morn again:
The world spins on triumphant
  Across a trackless sky,
And man seeks evermore in vain
  The primal reason why.

O whither are we rushing?
  And wherefrom were we torn?
We breathe from out the silences,
  And breathless, back are borne.

Deep in the soul are voices
  Returning this reply:
It took a God to make us,
  Only God can answer why!

80

HUSKS

Forever and forevermore,
　　Across the heights, the deeps,
Spurred by an ever-flaming zeal
　　That slumbers not, nor sleeps—
We chase the furtive form of fame
　　Beyond the edge of dusk,
To bear within our arms at length,
　　An empty mocking, husk!

81

THE WATCHER

The long, grim years with iron tread
  Move down the shuttered isle
Of time's unrecking labyrinth
  Paved with forgotten dead.

And I, a feather in their wake,
  Gaze long and tremblingly
Into these sunless corridors,
  Praying the light to break!

82

THE VANISHED ROAD

We're wending the trail of the vanishing road,
With a song and a shout, just to lighten the load,
That lies in the heart, filled with queries and cares,
For never a traveler knows where he fares.

But on with a jest, and rollicksome cheer,
With laughter that leaps, as a veil, for the tear;
The world's weary caravan finds that abode
That lies at the end of the vanishing road.

83

Appreciations

SERVICE

When we count out our gold at the end of the day,
And have filtered the dross that has cumbered the way,
Oh, what were the hold of our treasury then
Save the love we have shown to the children of men?

87

[163]

TO THE MARTYRED

O sacrificial throng whose lives
  Build up the yawning deeps
O'er which we pass reflectively
  To broader lights and sweeps.

Know, that we hold with reverence
  The signal price you paid,
And all our trophies, one by one,
  Upon your bier are laid.

88

TO JOHN BROWN

We lift a song to you across the day
Which bears through travailing the seed you spread
In terror's morning, flung with fingers red
In blood of tyrants, who debarred the way
To Freedom's dawning. Hearken to the lay
Chanted by dusky millions, soft and mellow-keyed,
In minor measure, Martyr of the Freed,
A song of memory across the day.

Truth cannot perish though the earth erase
The royal signals, leaving not a trace,
And time still burgeoneth the fertile seed,
Though he is crucified who wrought the deed:
O Alleghanies, fold him to your breast
Until`the judgment! Sentinel his rest!

89

TO ABRAHAM LINCOLN

Within the temple of our heart
Your sacred memory dwells apart,
Where ceaselessly a censor swings
Alight with fragrant offerings;
Nor time, nor tide, nor circumstance
Can dim this grand remembrance,
And all the blood of Afric hue
Beats in one mighty tide—for you!

90

TO WILLIAM STANLEY BRAITHWAITE

When time has rocked the present age to sleep,
And lighter hearts are lilting to the sway
Of rhythmic poesy's enhanced lay,
Recurring sequences shall fitly keep
Your fame eternal, as they lightly sweep
Aside the curtain to that potent day
When you in primal fervor led the way
Unto Apollo's narrow winding steep.

None shall forget your travail, utter, sore,
That oped the golden avenue of song,
When, like a knight, so errantly you bore
The mantled children valiantly along,
Their homage as a rising incense sweet
Shall permeate the heavens at your feet!

91

TO W. E. B. DuBOIS—SCHOLAR

Grandly isolate as the god of day—
Blazing an orbit through the dank and gloom
Of misty morning, far and fair you loom,
Flooding the dimness with your golden ray,—
Cheering the mantled on the thorn-set way,
Teaching of Faith and Hope o'er the tomb,
Where both, though buried, spring to newer bloom—
Strengthened and sweet from the mound of decay.

Soft! strains of Sanctus we lift on the air,
Ere Nunc Dimittus at last shall be sung,
Sing we our Sanctus to fitly declare
Blessings that well up from hearts sorely wrung.

Lead, lead us on o'er the furthermost stair—
Light of our impotence! Joy of our tongue!

92

TO RIDGELY TORRENCE—PLAYWRIGHT

All hail! fair vistas break upon the view,
The gates swing wide and free with clanging sound,
Rejoice! a mighty champion is found,
Son of the morning, prescient and true.
Upon the threshold of a cycle new
He stands, and sentinels its virgin ground,
Seer in his poet-visioning profound,
Presaging vaster reaches—skies more blue.

Lifting their misty glances to the day,
The prismic children pass the erstwhile bars,
Exultant, swiftly, boundingly they stray,
Awhile forgetful of deep, hidden scars
Thus, as a golden legend time shall tell
Of him who wrought so mightily and well!

93

TO RICHARD R. WRIGHT—INSTRUCTOR

Son of a race, whose dusky visage shows
The heel of fortune, those who walk unfree
Though cradled in the hold of liberty,
Whose shackled spirit every gamut knows
Of Hate's cadenza, through whose warm blood flows
The royal ransom of love's dynasty,
Scion of these, he strides to meet his foes.

Erect, unbending, note his sable brow,
The rugged furrows where deep feelings plough,
The step of vigor and the noble air,
The subtle halo of his wintry hair,
Up from the furnace of the Earth's red sea
A man is fashioned for the years to be!

94

TO SAMUEL COLERIDGE TAYLOR, UPON
HEARING HIS

Strange to a sensing motherhood,
Loved as a toy—not understood,
Child of a dusky father, bold;
Frail little captive, exiled, cold.

Oft when the brooding planets sleep,
You through their drowsy empires creep,
Flinging your arms through their empty space,
Seeking the breast of an unknown face.

95

TO EMILIE BIGELOW HAPGOOD —
PHILANTHROPIST

Far from the seried ranks you sway,
    Firm in your own believing
In that frail brotherhood, who stray
    Sore anguishing, sore grieving.
Such hands as yours, adown the years
    Enchain a faith unbroken,
They stay the dreary waste of tears,
    And lift to Hope a token!

96

TO HENRY LINCOLN JOHNSON — LAWYER

Quite firmly did you stand, and unafraid
Before that haughty bar that sought to hold
You fettered, lest you strengthen and grow bold
To break a clearing through that fetid glade
Which their benighted prejudice had made;
They taunted you with darkling hints of gold,
Preferring you were bought as you had sold,
They weaved their webs like spiders in the shade.

But as a giant in the falling night
Of storm, you forged afore with ruthless tread,
To offer up your heart's blood in the fight,
Forgetting self, unmindful, unafraid,
Nor pausing until thrice acclaimed the right
To rally in the tents of those you led.

97

TO MARY CHURCH TERRELL — LECTURER

A pioneer, she blazed a trail of light
Through murky shadows, with a lithesome tread
Unto those forums, where Hope's beams are shed:
Straight through the mighty cordon of the night,
Rapt with a vision, soul-born, clear and bright,
Leaving the South of frigid wrong, she sped
Into the North, where hearts glow warm instead,
A people's tragedy to there recite.

Hope's liquid pipings lift their tender lay,
Morning is waking, flushed with rosy gleam,
Night with its shadow winds with yesterday
Adown the world-way as an inky stream,
Seed time and harvest deftly interplay,
And Life's fruition is its vital dream!

98

TO MAY HOWARD JACKSON — SCULPTOR

You saw the vision in the face of clay,
And fixed it through the magic of a hand
Obedient unto the will's command,
In forms impervious to Time's decay:
Historian of bloods that interplay
Confusedly within a cryptic land,
You've chiseled, and your work of art shall stand
To gem the archives of a better day.

Alone, far from the touch of kindred mind,
You've mounted with a grim, determined zeal,
Despite environment austere, unkind,
Or frozen-fingers clenched to your appeal,
You've held the ardor of your first ideal,
Robed in a queenly majesty, resigned.

99

TO THE MEMORY OF INEZ MILHOLLAND

Folded in silent veils of sleep,
  You calmly rest,
For God hath spoken, should we weep?
  He knoweth best.

But rather let us garner still
  While yet we may,
And meet you in His Holy Hill
  On that Great Day!

100

TO ATLANTA UNIVERSITY — ITS FOUNDERS AND TEACHERS

Pass down the aisle of buried years to-night,
And stand uncovered in that holy place
Where noble structures lift their hallowed height
Beneath a bending Heaven's chaste embrace,
The fruit of those who scorned the path of ease,
To buckle on the armaments of care
Like to the Son of Man Himself, were these
Who gave themselves for brother men — less fair.

Before the blinding footlights of to-day
We man our parts within Life's tragic play,
Full mindful of the earnest love and care
That keeps eternal watch and vigil there;
Nor do they need fair monuments and scrolls —
Their memories are deathless in our souls.

101

AN AUTUMN LOVE CYCLE

An Autumn Love Cycle

From a sketch by
EFFIE LEE NEWSHOLME

AN AUTUMN LOVE CYCLE

Georgia Douglas Johnson

HAROLD VINAL, LIMITED

NEW YORK · MCMXXVIII

[184]

This book is lovingly dedicated to
ZONA GALE
whose appreciation, encouragement
and helpful criticism have
so heartened me

.

Privilege to reprint certain of these poems is through the courtesy of the editors of *The Crisis, The Liberator, Telling Tales, The Sphinx, Music and Poetry, Messenger, Opportunity* and *The Minaret*.

Acknowledgment is made of the very helpful criticism and suggestions from Alain Locke and Clement Wood in the final preparation of this volume.

CONTENTS

FOREWORD

In the title of her first volume, "THE
HEART OF A WOMAN and OTHER POEMS,"
Georgia Douglas Johnson chose with singular felicity, indeed with the felicity of instinct,
her special domain in art. And as she proceeds with maturing power and courage of
expression in this third volume, it becomes all
the more apparent that the task which she has
set herself is the documenting of the feminine
heart. Any poetic expression of life from this
point of view that achieves a genuine authen-
ticity and sincerity of emotion is as welcome as
it is rare. For the emotions of woman, time-old
though they be and hackneyed over as in a sense
they really are, are still but half expressed. They
have yet to be carried beyond the platitudes and
the sentimentalizations of a man-made tradition.
Yet in the wholesome stripping off of mediaeval

xv

brocades and the laces of classic conceits, it has often occurred to us to question whether the imposition of futurist patterns and the cubist cut of the current intellectual modes has given us any more vital or adequate a revelation of the flesh and blood figure of the "eternal feminine." "Clothes are but clothes," as Carlyle would say: modern feminist realism has but overlaid the vitally human with another convention, and interposed another cloak. How long shall we make a sphinx of woman, who herself now yearns to throw off along with the mystery, the psychological vestments of disguise. Our author puts it pointedly in "Paradox,"—

> Alas! you love me better cold
> Strange as the pyramids of old
> Responselessly . . .
> So, like a veil, my poor disguise
> Is draped to save me from your eyes'
> Deep challenges.
> Fain would I fling this robe aside
> And from you, in your bosom hide
> Eternally.

xvi

Voicing this yearning of woman for candid self-expression, Mrs. Johnson invades the province where convention has been most tyrannous and inveterate,—the experiences of love. And here she succeeds where others more doctrinally feminist than she have failed; for they in over-sophistication, in terror of platitudes and the commonplace, have stressed the bizarre, the exceptional, in one way or another have over-intellectualized their message and overleapt the common elemental experience they would nevertheless express. Mrs. Johnson, on the contrary, in a simple declarative style, engages with ingenuous directness the moods and emotions of her themes.

> Through you I entered Heaven and Hell
> Knew rapture and despair.

Here is the requisite touch, certainly for the experiences of the heart. Greater sophistication would spoil the message. Fortunately, to the gift of a lyric style, delicate in touch, rhapsodic in tone, authentic in timbre, there has been added a temperamental endowment of ardent sincerity

xvii

of emotion, ingenuous candor of expression, and, happiest of all for the particular task, a naïve and unsophisticated spirit.

By way of a substantive message, Mrs. Johnson's philosophy of life is simple, unpretentious, but wholesome and spiritually invigorating. On the one hand, she belongs with those who, under the leadership of Sara Teasdale, have been rediscovering the Sapphic cult of love as the ecstasy of life, that cult of enthusiasm which leaps over the dilemma of optimism and pessimism, and accepting the paradoxes, pulses in the immediacies of life and rejoices openly in the glory of experience. In a deeper and somewhat more individual message, upon which she only verges, and which we believe will later be her most mature and original contribution, Mrs. Johnson probes under the experiences of love to the underlying forces of natural instinct which so fatalistically control our lives. [Especially is this evident in her suggestion of the tragic poignancy of Motherhood, where the consummation of love seems also the expiation of passion, and where, between the antagonisms of the dual role of

xviii

Mother and Lover, we may suspect the real dilemma of womanhood to lie.]

Whatever the philosophical yield, however, we are grateful for the prospect of such lyricism. Seeking a pure lyric gold, Mrs. Johnson has gone straight to the mine of the heart. She has dug patiently in the veins of her own subjective experience. What she has gleaned has been treasured for the joy of the search and for its own intrinsic worth, and not exploited for the values of show and applause. Above all, her material has been expressed with a candor that shows that she brings to the poetic field what it lacks most, —the gift of the elemental touch. Few will deny that, with all its other excellences, the poetry of the generation needs just this touch to make it more vitally human and more spontaneously effective.

ALAIN LOCKE.

Washington, D. C.

xix

.

THE CYCLE

I CLOSED MY SHUTTERS FAST LAST NIGHT

I closed my shutters fast last night,
Reluctantly and slow,
So pleading was the purple sky
With all the lights hung low;
I left my lagging heart outside
Within the dark alone,
I heard it singing through the gloom
A wordless, anguished tone.
Upon my sleepless couch I lay
Until the tranquil morn
Came through the silver silences
To bring my heart forlorn,
Restoring it with calm caress
Unto its sheltered bower,
While whispering: "Await, await
Your golden, perfect hour."

3

FOOTSTEPS

Passing ever, early, late,
No fond footsteps seek my gate,
But down the winding road they wend
To some other journey's end.

Yet,—I would not have them wait
Here within my guarded gate,
Certain footsteps I shall know,
And for them I listen low!

4

OH NIGHT OF LOVE

Oh night of love, your rapt ecstatic hours
Were mine, the languor of their pale perfume
Pervades me, kisses in a fountain-fire,
Surround me,—fetter and consume.

Oh night of love, your groves of strange content
Project a thralldom over coming days;
Exalted, derelict, and blind I wend
Unmindfully along Life's misty ways.

5

AUTUMN

Believe me—when I say
That love like yours, at this belated hour,
Overwhelms me,—
Stills the fount of thought!
I move as one new-born—
And strange to swift transitions
As from my prison door
I gaze
Into a blinding sunlight!

6

THRALLDOM

Your voice keeps ringing down the day
    In accents soft and mild,
    With which you have beguiled
    And wooed me as a child.

Your presence bounds my every way
    And thrills me in its fold
    With phantom hands that hold
    Like cherished chains of gold.

7

SEPARATION

Within your pulsing day
There must be little space
For visions of my face
To lure your thoughts away.

Yet, I would have it so,
To bear alone the pain
That saddens love's refrain.
Pray God you never know!

8

LOVE'S MIRACLE

So like a boundless, soundless sea
The miracle of love to me,
With all the world a rosy dream
Sailing upon a silver stream,
While I, a fairy in mid-air,
Am dancing, dancing everywhere.

Hark! do you hear the thunder peal?
I care not what it would reveal,
Tomorrow will be yesterday
When I am shivering and gray:

I will not heed the prompter's ring
Let others answer, I shall sing
And dance the merrier—away!
I'll live and live and live—today!

9

PROVING

Were you a leper bathed in wounds
   And by the world denied,
I'd share your fatal exile
   As a privilege, with pride.

You are the very sun, the moon,
   The starlight of my soul,
The sounding motif of my heart
   Its impetus and goal!

10

INTERIM

The days lie dark between our jeweled meetings
Like wintry burials.

My heart bows low before the cheerless hearth
Until your voice rings through the gloom
And bids me
Wake!
And live!

11

GOOD-BYE

Let's say "Good-bye"
Nor wait Love's latest breath
Poised now so lightly on the wing of Death,
While yet within our eyes one fervent gleam
Remains to hallow this, a passing dream:
Yes, yes "Good-bye,"
For it is best to part
While Love's low light still burns
Within the heart!

12

A PARADOX

I know you love me better cold
Strange as the pyramids of old
Responselessly.
But I am frail, and spent and weak
With surging torrents that bespeak
A living fire.
So, like a veil, my poor disguise
Is draped to save me from your eyes'
Deep challenges.
Fain would I fling this robe aside
And from you, in your bosom hide
Eternally.
Alas! you love me better cold
Like frozen pyramids of old
Unyieldingly?

13

How my heart sinks when I behold the sad reflection of my face,
A wan and wistful wound, with oh, such meagre
grace;
How can you hold me dear withal and conjure
charms withdrawn.
Or does the Autumn twilight hold a charm unknown to dawn?

Hold! Do not speak! some day perchance, I'll
read the message dire
Within the ashes of the flame, the aftermath of
fire,
Ere then perhaps I shall have found the highways
of the soul
Where one may read uncrucified, the blood-
words of the scroll.
Till then, uphold illusion's veil before my gaze
the while
That I may gather strength to fuse from agony,
a smile!

14

TO TIME

Day by day the threads of white
Multiply, Oh! hour-glass!
How passing swift your bright sands pass,
Fain would I hold you,
Linger, bide
Until these surges shall subside,
That sweep me forward unto bliss,
Oh! charging sun, I bid you rest,
Break not your arrow in my breast!

15

Would I might mend the fabric of my youth
Which daily flaunts its tatters to my eyes,
Would I might compromise awhile with truth
Until love's moon, now waxing, wanes and dies.

For I would go a further while with you
And drain this Cup of Joy so passing fair,
Which meets my parching lips like cooling dew
'Ere time has brushed cold fingers through my
    hair.

16

I fear my power impotent
To hold you leal and full content,
Some hapless look or word perchance
Dispels the glamour of romance;
I tremble lest some stranger fair
Arrest you,—cause you to compare
The meagre charms which I possess
With some resplendent loveliness.

How far removed from Youth's command
The trembling sceptre in my hand,
As miserly within the glass
I mark Love's fleeting hours pass.

17

ILLUSION

Oh! for the veils of my far-away youth,
Shielding my heart from the blaze of the truth;
Why did I stray from their foldings and grow
Into the sadness that follows—to know.

Impotent atom with desolate gaze
Treading Life's treacherous, intricate maze—
Oh for the veils, for the veils of my youth,
Shielding my heart from the blaze of the truth!

18

PARODY

You came,
The tapestries of love
Were shining in the sun,
My wishes settled down content
About you as you stood.
I looked into your cryptic eyes
And thought I understood;
But no,—
The splendor of your gaudy robe
Grew dimmer day by day,
I wondered,
Searched within my soul to seize the mystery.
The answer staggered me,
Aghast,
Like one at bay,
I gazed with open eyes of thought upon you,
God! 'twas true—
A mockery, a parody,
Had come to me—in you!

19

DELUSION

You gave me your hand,
I held it to be
The last word, the dear word,
The soul's entity;
I cherished it, treasured it,
Only to find
I held but a gauntlet—
That I had been blind!

20

SUNSET

And now—
As one who closes up the house and goes uncaring
    where
He may forget the scenes of home 'mid foreign
    climes and air,
I bar the chamber of my heart and seal the past
    within
To wander down the city's road amid the whirr
    and din.
The long years seem impassable, the morning has
    no smile,
With naught behind these barring doors and
    nothing else worth while,
Like some lone pilgrim without hope, I stumble
    on my way,
Who lifts no futile plea for sun, but asks for
    clouds less grey.

21

FINIS

I looked death calmly in the face
And placed my hand within his hand
And said:
"Come, come, let us away
For I have lost the magic key
Opening the portals of desire—
My wishes cumber in the dust,
And life is stagnant
           in
              my
                 heart!

22

CONTEMPLATION

IVY

I am a woman
Which means
I am insufficient
I need—
Something to hold me
Or perhaps uphold.
I am a woman.

25

JOY

There's nothing certain, nothing sure
Save sorrow. Fragile happiness
Was never fashioned to endure;
For joy repels the perfect claim
And answers to no certain name;
How furtively we scan the mist
Perchance amid the gloom to find
Some moments rare and rapture-kist

26

ONE DAY

Good-bye dear day of sunshine, rain
    In flooding torrents pours
Its liquid footsteps on my roof,
    Its fingers on my doors.

While I sit tranquilly within
    And tell my beads of joy,
Holding a peace within my heart
    Which nothing can destroy.

27

ATTAR

Fire—tears—
And the torture-chamber,
With the last maddening turn of the screw—
Only thus
Is one precious drop distilled
Of the attar of rose
Of the heart.

28

Oh the sad little dreams of the dim yesteryear
Lying cold, still and stark in the dust of their
    bier,
How the heart hurries back, all the long weary
    way,
Just to bid them good-night at the close of the
    day.

29

I WONDER

I wonder—
      as I see them pass unheeded down the way,
(The women who were once beloved, imperious
       and gay)
Holding with frail, pale hands the cup
Of Life's discarded wine
If memories
Are bliss enough
To make the dregs—divine!

30

VALUES

All the pretty baubles spread
Are not the answer to my need,
These tinseled trappings but beguile
This journeying, while deep within
A want unspeakable resides,
That throbs and throbs unceasingly,—
So hungering,—no banquet spread
Can tempt it, and no golden wine
Make it forget: I balance it—
The world flies upward in the scale!
Always, unsoothed, unquieted,
It aches and aches across the days
And sears the nights that sum my life.

31

ARMAGEDDON

In the silence and the dark
I fought with dragons;
I was battered, beaten sore
But rose again;
On my knees I fought still rising
In my pain:
In the dark I fought with dragons.
Weary tears
Cease your flowing,
Even now the dawn appears!

32

LE SOIR

Mute-lipped—
        unquestioning grim-visaged Fate,
I cleave the shadows toward the Western Gate;
And yet—
        my lagging heart still holds
Mute-arms outstretched
Unto earth's gleaming folds.

Who knows?
        perhaps Hope's blossoms spray
In lush profusion
O'er the edge of day!

33

TREASURE

What matters though love's dream shall pass,
Since from the throbbing hour-glass
One golden-throated moment prest
Its attared incense to my breast.

Since I have known the purple gleam
That lifts above me—can I deem
The way unlighted—when I go
Encircled by love's afterglow?

34

RETROSPECTION

After all—
        mine is the joy
Which naught can lessen or destroy.
For love has led my flying feet
Where immortelles are springing sweet,
And everlasting skies of gold
Are memories, when earth is cold
And though our future paths should lie
Estranged, as star-ways, through the sky,
I shall not look reproof, nor find
Within this pass a charge unkind,
And lightly sorrow shall be met
For I can never know regret.

35

INTERMEZZI

SPRINGTIME

Again it is the vibrant May,
The bursting buds, the leafing trees,
The fragrant, undulating breeze,
Call to my heart in subtlest way:
Come! Come! it is a holiday.

The streamlet with unending song,
Beneath its silver veil of mist
Seems flowing, flowing, to some tryst,
While I—with inner surges strong,
Find incomplete the day, and long.

39

DESTINY

I know my love is seeking me
As restless rivers seek the sea,
Across the nights, across the days
That snare the intervening ways.

I know my love is seeking me
As Time must seek Eternity,
When nights are very still I hear
His footsteps, coming, coming near!

40

ENVOYS

Love calls me tonight
In the beat of the rain
Through the cold little drops
On my bare window-pane;
Calls and calls through the dark
Like a whispered refrain
Tapping soft on my heart
Through the bare window pane.

41

I WANT TO DIE WHILE YOU LOVE ME

I want to die while you love me,
    While yet you hold me fair,
While laughter lies upon my lips
    And lights are in my hair.

I want to die while you love me
    And bear to that still bed
Your kisses—turbulent, unspent,
    To warm me when I'm dead.

I want to die while you love me
    Oh, who would care to live,
'Til love has nothing more to ask
    And nothing more to give.

42

ECSTASY

Not less than this, beloved,
This beaming, highmost ray
That sweeps in royal splendor
Across our perfect day.

Not less than this,—far rather
That we should say "adieu,"
With every rose in Eden
Abloom for me and you.

43

PLEDGE

With kisses I'll awake you love
So tenderly at morn,
The pledges of my fealty
Diurnally reborn.

We'll thread life's way together love,
And when the fading light
Dips softly over western hills
I'll kiss your eyes good-night.

44

YOUR EYES

Your eyes—
Dark pools, so calm and deep,
A thousand ages in them sleep,
A dreaming world within them lies,
And all my hopes
Of paradise!

45

AMOUR

Kiss me!
And let the hours bloom triumphantly
Before life's little sun has set
And I am old.

Love me!
The day is fleet
And I . . .
Am far too passionate
To die!

46

FINALITY

When love's triumphant day is done,
Go forward! leave me to the night
Beneath the coldly staring stars,
The waiting winter and its blight.

For I would never hold the heart
That mutely quivers to be free,
Unfurl your restless wings—away!
And leave the emptiness to me.

47

IN LOVE

I lived in Hell the other day
Its fires wrapt me angrily,
But now their horrors fall and fade
Like ghosts that memory has made.

I lived in Hell even today,
How swift the fierce flames die away—
Submerged with kisses, I forget,
With tears upon my pillows yet.

48

Ah! love!
I shall not seek to penetrate
Your webbed gauze
Nor tease my heart
By queries deep,
But hold you tenderly;
The day is evening,
And I must cull my flowers
'Ere dark.

49

DEAD DAYS

Dead days of rapture and despair
I would your hours exhume,
Renew their wildness once again
Their rigors and perfume.

50

PENSEROSO

BREAK, BREAK MY HEART

Break, break my heart
For love is done,
The pale light trails the dying sun—
And night awaits—no hope—no stars
Darkness
Hide my scars!

53

LITTLE KING

From worshipping I now arise
Stunned and aghast, with open eyes
I see the real, the little you
I thought so gallant, brave and true.

A pity yet is mine, I fear,
Since wherefore comes this falling tear,
For none among your fawning throng
Will love you well, nor love you long.

54

ROMANCE

When I was young
                    I used to say:
Romance *will come* riding by
And I shall surely smile
And play with him awhile.

When I grew older
                    then I said:
Romance *may come* riding by
I wonder shall I smile
And play with him awhile?

But now—
                    Alas! I only say:
Romance *never will* come by
And I shall never smile
He has been dead the while!

55

Confusion, desuetude and gloom,
  The travailing of sound,
Fell desolation in my soul,
  And agony profound;
The gods are falling heavily
  And for all time to be,
And never more my heart shall know
  A shrine to Deity!

56

ARMOR

You cannot hurt me any more
　　For I am armored now
And I can look into your face
　　With cool, unfevered brow.

The tranquil river meets the sea,
　　My life flows on at rest,
Unurged, untorn, but oh, my God!
　　I love the old way best!

57

DIVIDE

Your lightest breath may fan my cheek
Your whisper stir me when you speak,
And yet—
The teeming planets play
Between your heart—and mine
Today.

58

RETURN

Now,
Like the pines intoning
Though some solitary gloom,
My errant thoughts go pattering
About love's ancient tomb,
And though no breath of incense rare
Lies round the shattered cup,
A banquet weird, the fragments
Where the ghost of love
May sup.

59

Just a bit of ashes
Grey, grey ashes—spent—
God! how fierce the fires burned
Down to this content.

Just a bit of ashes,
Not a single spark
Lives in this residuum
Crumbling cold and dark.

Just a bit of ashes—
To the judgment day,
I go with my memories—
Pray, sweet virgin, pray!

60

CELIBACY

Where is the love that might have been
Flung to the four far ends of Earth?
In my body stamping around,
In my body like a hound
Leashed and restless—
Biding time!

61

CADENCE

OFFERING

I seek no token of you dear
   I only ask to give
The purple flower of my heart
   And you will let it live.

I ask no fealty or plight,
   I only pray that you
May find earth's barren places bright
   Perhaps, because it grew.

And when for you the final sun
   Moves toward the darkening West,
I shall be lingering to place
   Love's flower on your breast.

65

ESTRANGEMENT

Some day I shall be dead, and pride
    Which kept me from your feet,
Shall be the burden of the song
    My cold lips shall repeat.

And some day when you too shall find
    A pillow in the sod,
Would you then spurn an hour with me
    Above—where daisies nod?

66

Consider me a memory—a dream
That passed away,
Or yet, a flower that has blown and shattered—
In a day;
For passion sleeps, alas, and keeps no vigil
With the years,
And wakens to no conjuring
Of orison or tears.

Consider me a melody
That served its simple turn,
Or but the residue of fire
That settles in the urn,
For love defies pure reasoning
And undeterred flows
Within—without
The vassal heart!
Its reasoning—
Who knows?

67

SEPULCHRE

I have mounded the corpse of my sorrow
  And wreathed it with roses fair
That none who may pass on the morrow
  May know what lies buried there.

68

CURTAIN

When one has lived
'Tis not so hard
To fold the hands,
To say, "Good-night,"
And creep away
Behind the dark;
But 'tis not strange
The heart rebels
When sounds of night
Ring down the day
That was a weary, joyless way
From early dawn
To setting sun:
How eagerly we trail the light
For crumbs of happiness we fend,
And struggle, struggle—to the end!

69

Through you I entered heaven and hell,
Knew rapture and despair,
I flitted o'er the plains of earth
And scaled each shining stair:
Drank deep the waters of content,
And drained the cup of gall,
Was regal and was impotent,
Was suzerain and thrall.

Now, by Reflection's placid pool
On evening's mellowed brow,
I smile across the backward way
And pledge anew my vow;
For every glancing, golden gleam,
I offer gladly—pain!
And I would give a thousand world
To live it all again!

FINIS

70

THIS BOOK WAS DESIGNED BY ROBERT S. JOSEPHY
AND PRINTED UNDER HIS SUPERVISION AT THE
VAIL-BALLOU PRESS, BINGHAMTON, NEW YORK

Georgia Douglas Johnson

Share My World

A BOOK OF POEMS

By

Georgia Douglas Johnson

MCMLXII

Preface

"She is Sappho and Miriam combined," declared John Millholland, the philanthropist, in describing the poet, Georgia Douglas Johnson. Aside from his own contributions to humanity, he is the father of the sainted Inez, whose statue graces a pedestal in a New York park. This Atlanta Georgia, poet, combining the passion, storm and sweep of Sappho inherits much of the calm of Miriam of Biblical lore.

The definition: "All of the sweet things rolled into one," might well apply here. In short, one may swing to the extreme of intense living with the Attic poet, Sappho, and yet know the tranquility of the nun-like Miriam.

Like Heine, who is distinguished for his concise and condensed quatrain style—this modern Southern poet attains much the same effect in "The Pawn," which is a complete story in miniature:

> The lights are out, the dancers gone
>
> The music with the laughter strays,
>
> Dear was the night, I was the pawn
>
> Oh, endless stretch of weary days!

Michael Victor Strong
January 20, 1962
Washington, D. C.

Author's Word

If it had not been for Schiller, Goethe would never have given us Faust. If it had not been for Lord Este, we would never have had "Jerusalem Delivered." Very often it is through the concern and encouragement of a friend that authors are moved to finish their creations. The applause of a single soul is indeed priceless.

And in this way, *Share My World*, may never have become a reality had it not been for the encouraging help of a person to whom I refer as "My Private Printer." For several years, through the courtesy of N. Wright Cuney, a typographer and printer, I have been able to send a poem each year to my friends and acquaintances. Through his suggestion and his offer to print some of these poems in book form I am able to "Share My World" with you.

CONTENTS

CONTENTS

Dedicated to
DORSEY K. OFFUTT

SHARE MY WORLD

I shall rebuild my world today
Without a sob or sigh,
Assembling and securing it
Ere fleeting time deny.

I shall rebuild my shattered world
More wisely than before,
Shall fashion it with faith and prayer
And love shall be the door.

And when I have rebuilt my world
Uncircumscribed and free
I shall invite all humankind
To share my world with me.

9

OLD LOVE LETTERS

Old love letters
How they bring
Back the tang and glow of spring
Waking with a stab of bliss
Some, almost forgotten, kiss.

Old love letters:
My eyes dim
Through the mist that shadows them
As I read, I know, I know.
I was loved once—long ago.

THE BUBBLE

I catch the bubble of life's joy
Within my eager fingers
A fragile, fairy meteor
That never, never lingers.

A golden globe of glancing gleam
That breaks ere fully fashioned
Which leaves the splashing of a tear,
A fallacy impassioned.

10

I GAZE INTO THE SUN

I gaze into the sun!
I dare
To look at life aflame.
I do not cradle in my arms
The trumpetry of name.

For I was born intense—
Afire
The world my own to hold;
A bouncing ball to spin at will
In answer to my call.

I hold
No brief for foolish fears;
My knees are strangers to the earth
For I was born to move erect,
To travel swift and free
With level look for every man
As God created me . . .
I gaze into the sun!

11

TRIFLE

Against the day of sorrow
Lay by some trifling thing
A smile, a kiss, a flower
For sweet remembering.

Then when the day is darkest
Without one rift of blue
Take out your little trifle
And dream your dream anew.

THE GIFT OF YEARS

The mellow years have brought to me
Many a precious thing,
The infinite peace of forgetting,
The joy of remembering.

A key to earth-born melodies,
A deaf ear to its din
Eyes that see only the beautiful,
And a heart that is young again.

12

COMMON DUST

And who shall separate the dust
Which later we shall be:
Whose keen discerning eye will scan
And solve the mystery?

The high, the low, the rich, the poor,
The black, the white, the red,
And all the chromatique between,
Of whom shall it be said:

Here lies the dust of Africa;
Here are the sons of Rome;
Here lies one unlabelled
The world at large his home!

Can one then separate the dust,
Will mankind lie apart,
When life has settled back again
The same as from the start?

13

READIED

I cannot see beyond the rim
Of this day's dying sun
I'm using all my holdings up
To get this measure done.

And when tomorrow swings her gates
Ajar, the rising sun
Shall find me luggaged, on my way
Before the sands have run.

SOMEBODY LOVED ME

Somebody loved me with all of his heart
Chose me alone, from the whole world apart
For me the love-light shone deep in his eyes,
I was the sun, moon and stars in his skies.

Now, at the end of this earth-weary trek
Worn and neglected, in dreams I go back,
Memory dries every tear at the start—
Somebody loved me with all of his heart.

14

DREAM LIFE

Always the world has ever been
A fairy-land to me.
No road was just a common road
No tree a common tree.

Each road was an enchanted trail
To find a crystal sea
I ran along with skip and jump
At random, fancy-free.

About each tree-trunk hung a spell
Whose pebbles, bits of glass
In hidden nests were images
To bring my dreams to pass.

I never went a-journeying
But that I ended lost,
For I sped down the avenue
A-flame and fancy-tossed.

Ah me! my life has ever been
A fragment from a jest
Torn from the tangled web of dreams
That gossamer my breast.

15

A BIT OF SKY

We search,
We seek unceasingly
A bit of sky
Before we die . . .

Some call it *Peace,*
Some call it *Love,*
All else above.

We search,
We seek eternally
A bit of sky
Before we die . . .

TREASURE

When you count out your gold at the end of
the day,

And have winnowed the dross that has cumbered the way,

Oh, what were the hold of your treasury
then—

Save the love you have shown to the children
of men!

16

MAGDALEN

On the day that the world shall end my dear
I shall stand at the judgment bar
Your name on my lips, your face in my heart
Your love as my guiding star,
And then I shall say to the God above
As he looks through my soul for sin
Only one great fault You will find, dear
    Lord,
Inscribed on the scroll within.

I have tended Your sheep and nurtured Your
    lambs,
I have comforted hearts in despair,
I have kept the commandments with never a
    pause
Save the one You see written there,
But You are my Judge and I hope You can
    find
Some grace for a flaw so grim
For I loved a mortal far more than my life
And forfeited heaven for him.

17

THE POET SPEAKS

How much living have you done?
From it the patterns that you weave
Are imaged:
Your own life is your totem-pole
Your yard of cloth,
Your living.

How much loving have you done?
How full and free your giving?
For living is but loving
And loving only giving.

THE RETURN

The laws of changeless justice bind
Oppressor with oppressed;
As saint and sinner, friend and foe,
We march to God—abreast.

18

I WANT TO DIE WHILE YOU LOVE ME

I want to die while you love me,
While yet you hold me fair,
While laughter lies upon my lips
And lights are in my hair.

I want to die while you love me
I could not bear to see,
The glory of this perfect day,
Grow dim—or cease to be.

I want to die while you love me
Oh! who would care to live
'Till love has nothing more to ask,
And nothing more to give.

I want to die while you love me,
And bear to that still bed
Your kisses, turbulent, unspent,
To warm me when I'm dead.

19

MY HAPPINESS

What is happiness to me?
Fragile, tiny, furtive things,
Gossamers, with fairy wings
Held with my heart a breath,
Just a memory, until death.

What is happiness, who knows?
Whence it comes and where it goes,
Just a whispering, so brief,
Like the falling of a leaf.

BUT NOW

I shall be lonely in my grave
Where willows cast their slender shade
Above me.
But now I crave
Response for which my heart was made.

For I shall cease to sing some day
But now I want to leap and dance
And in some wild-wood lose my way
And leave destiny to chance.

20

YOUR WORLD

Your world is as big as you make it
I know, for I used to abide
In the narrowest nest in a corner
My wings pressing close to my side.

But I sighted the distant horizon
Where the sky-line encircled the sea
And I throbbed with a burning desire
To travel this immensity.

I battered the cordons around me
And cradled my wings on the breeze
Then soared to the uttermost reaches
With rapture, with power, with ease!

21

CRYPTIC

In your deep autumnal eyes
Mystery's dark shadow lies—
None may pass unchallenged there,
Something vestal,
Something rare
Stays the plunging pagan tread—
I hesitate,
And bow my head.

UNFORGETTABLE

A triumph sweet
With every wonderment of youth,
Your eyes, your lips,
Your very tread
Shall thrill the sod when I am dead.

Unforgot!
You'll never know
I live because I love you so . . .
That every tryst my heart shall keep
Will be wherever you may sleep.

22

MATE

Out of the countless teeming throng
Of women sweetly fair
Is one, just one alone, who stands
Undimmed and shining there.

There may have been no lover's tryst
No touch of pulsing hand
But there are surges in the soul
The heart may understand.

Perhaps you saw her in the rush
Of by-gone yesterday . . .
In each man's life one woman is
A haunting memory.

23

BROTHERHOOD

Come, Brothers, All! shall we not wend
The blind way of our prison-world
By sympathy entwined?
Shall we not make the bleak way for each
  other's sake
Less rugged and unkind?

O, let each throbbing heart repeat
The faint note of another's beat
To lift a chanson for the feet
That stumble down life's checkered street

GOAL

I travel! My pilgrimage hither-ward lies
Beyond these proud barriers neath fairer
  skies,
Away from these purlieus that throttle the
  soul
On, on to the bounds of my utter-most goal.
No power that moves in the land or the sea
Can curtail or capture the vision in me,
I follow a lode-star, I can, and I must!
My forehead to God, my feet in the dust.

24

THE MAN TO BE

I ride a-tilt because
Life charges through my veins—
Mixed forces guide the reins
And I must on.

Astride the universe
I go, nor pause nor rest,
With sharp swords at my breast
To lean upon.

These fierce contending bloods
Churn in the depths of me;
Merged in a mighty sea
They urge me on.

O White Men, Black and Red
Look through God's lens and see
This fused intensity—
The man to be,
Your son!

25

NOT LESS THAN THIS

Not less than this beloved,
This beaming sky-tall ray
That sweeps in royal splendor
Across our perfect day.

Not less than this, far rather
That we should say *adieu*
With every rose in Eden
Blooming for me and you.

LOVE IS SO SMALL A THING

Love is so small a thing, you say
So brief a passage in the day,
So fraught with conflict, grief and strife
And yet without it, what is life?

26

CREDO

I believe in the ultimate justice of Fate;

That the races of men front the sun in their turn;

That each soul holds the leaven of infinite wealth

In fee to the will as it masters itself,

That the heart of humanity sounds the same chord

In impious jungle, or sky-kneeling fane.

I believe that the key to the life-mystery

Lies deeper than reason and further than death.

I believe that the rhythmical conscience within

Were adequate guide for the conduct of men.

27

A DIM DOORWAY

Forty years rolled back the curtain;
Standing at a fragrant door
I'm a child, with bright hopes laden
Lush with love and life once more.

Forty years, the days unravel
Softly, evenly as though
I were gazing in a doorway
Where I stood long, long ago.

Just a simple fragrance brought me
Back, where all my dreams belong
Just a fragrance, and my heart found
Laughter I had lost so long.

I WANT TO LIVE

I shall be all too still some day
But now I choose an equal chance
To strum the scale of ecstasy
And sound the gamut of romance.

I seek no cushioned way to love
I want to suffer, if I must
To be consumed, and then to give
My bit of ashes to the dust.

28

ONE LIVES TOO LONG

One lives too long
The days grow pale
And endless creep the nights
One lives too long.

Once, how I laughed and lightly cried
I'd live forever if I could . . .
But now I know the gift of death
Is merciful—when understood.

Within my vaulted empty heart
No echo lives of olden song—
Just softly sandalled, vanished feet . . .
One lives too long!

29

SAVORING THE PAST

I am savoring the past
Sitting-in with long ago,
Breathing of its perfumed air
Dreaming dreams I used to know . . .

I am savoring of the past—
Bitter-sweet the pulsing pain,
Yet I hold it tenderly
As it breaks my heart again.

RESOLUTION

With but one life full certified,
And that of every gleam denied
My portion,
Close to the unrelenting sod,
Just as my fathers dumbly trod
I've slumbered.
But now a surging, wild unrest
Uproots the poppies from my breast,
I stand and face the star-swept blue!
And swear to make my dreams come true!

30

INEVITABLY

Inevitably we must share our bread
Or lose it crumb by crumb,
We must learn to care,
We must learn to share,
Or be forever undone.

LOVELIGHT

Strange atoms we unto ourselves
Soaring a strange demesne
With life and death the darkened doors
And love the light between.

PRIDE

To Pride, upon its altar, what priceless offerings we bring,

The one thing needful—fondest hopes, the
cup of fragile joy,

The price of all the world—it's core, fanati-
cally we give

To satisfy an inward lift—a sloganed, formal pose

Sheathed in the mantle of disguise,

We strive to still the heart's low cries.

31

THE AUDACIOUS

Only the audacious fly
The heaven, with their dreams.
They tempt the Gods, they dare the fates
And ride hopes fitful gleams.

Only the audacious snatch the stars
From out the purple blue
For they, and they alone will dare
To make their dreams come true.

32

PLAYS

BLUE BLOOD

A PLAY

BY GEORGIA DOUGLAS JOHNSON

CHARACTERS

MAY BUSH
MRS. BUSH
JOHN TEMPLE
MRS. TEMPLE
RANDOLPH STRONG
These characters are negroes.
PLACE: *Georgia.*
TIME: *Shortly after Civil War.*

[SCENE: *Large kitchen and dining-room combined of frame cottage, showing one door leading into back yard. One other door (right side of room facing stage) leading into hall. One back window, neatly curtained. Steps on right side of room leading upstairs.*
Enter Randolph Strong with large bunch of white roses and a package. He places the package, unnoticed, on the table—still holding the roses.]

RANDOLPH STRONG. How is my dear Mother Bush?

MRS. BUSH. Feeling like a sixteen-year-old! That's right, you come right on back here with me. [Notices roses.] Oh! what pretty roses! Snow white!

RANDOLPH STRONG. Like um? Thought you would. . . . May likes this kind!

MRS. BUSH. She sho'ly do. Pore chile! She's turning her back on the best fellow in this town, when she turned you down. I knows a good man when I see one.

RANDOLPH STRONG. You are always kind to me, Mother Bush. I feel like the lost sheep to-night, the one hundredth one, out in the cold, separated by iron bars from the ninety and nine! Bah! what am I doing? The milk's spilt! [*Arranging flowers.*] Put these in here?

MRS. BUSH. Sure! My, but they look grand. There ain't many young doctors so handy-like!

RANDOLPH STRONG [*half to himself*]. The first time I saw her she wore a white rose in her hair. . . .

MRS. BUSH. Jest listen! May's plum blind! Oh! if she'd a only listened to me, she'd be marrying you to-night, instead of that stuck up John Temple. I never did believe in two "lights" marrying, nohow, it's onlucky. They're jest exactly the same color . . . hair . . . and eyes alike too. Now you . . . you is jest right for my May. "Dark should marry light." You'd be a perfect match.

RANDOLPH STRONG [*groans*]. Hold, hold for goodness sake! Why didn't you lend that little blind girl of yours your two good eyes?

MRS. BUSH. Humph! She wouldn't hear me. [*Goes up to him, speaking confidentially.*] 'Tween you and me, I shorely do wish she'd a said "yes" when you popped the question las' Christmas. I hates to see her tying up with this highfalutin' nothing. She'll re'lize some day that money ain't everything, and that a poor man's love is a whole sight better than a stiff-necked, good-looking dude.

RANDOLPH STRONG. It can't be helped now, Mother Bush. If she's happy, that's the main thing!

MRS. BUSH. But is she going to be happy . . . that's jest it!

RANDOLPH STRONG. Let us hope so! And yet, sometimes I think—do you know, Mother Bush, [*lowering his voice*] sometimes I think May cares for me.

MRS. BUSH [*confidently*]. Do you know, honey, somehow, sometimes I do too!

RANDOLPH STRONG [*excitedly*]. You do too!! Oh, if I could fully believe that—even now—at the last minute—[*Snaps his finger.*] Oh, what's the use? [*Constrainedly.*] Is everything ready?

MRS. BUSH. You bet! I'm all dressed under this apron. [*Swings it back and discloses a brilliant and much decorated gown. Then with a start.*] Lord save us! That Lyddie Smith ain't brought that my'nase dressing yet. Vowed she'd have it here by eight sharp, if she was alive. What time you got?

RANDOLPH STRONG [*looking at his watch*]. Eight thirty.

MRS. BUSH. Eight thirty? Good gracious!

RANDOLPH STRONG. I'll run over and get it for you.

MRS. BUSH. Oh yes, honey! Do hurry. Oh, what a son-in-law you would'a' made!

RANDOLPH STRONG. Good joke . . . but I can't laugh!

[*He goes. Mrs. Bush busies herself with the table arrangements and finally notices a package that had been left by Strong; she opens it and discloses a beautiful vase and reads aloud the card attached.*]

MRS. BUSH [*reading*]. For May and her husband, with best wishes for your happiness, Randolph. [*She sets it aside without saying a word—only wiping her eyes—thinks a while; shakes her head; picks up the vase again and calls toward the stairway:*] May! May! run down here a minute. I've got something to show you. [*Mrs. Bush polishes the vase with her apron and holds her head to one side looking at it admiringly. Enter May in negligee. Mrs. Bush—with vase held behind her:*] Not dressed yet? . . . Gracious! There . . . look . . . Randolph brought it!

MAY BUSH. Oh! . . . did he? [*Reads card.*] Randolph is a dear!

[*Fondles vase and looks sad.*]

MRS. BUSH. He brought these roses, too . . . said you liked this kind.

[*May Bush takes roses and buries her face in them, then thoughtfully changes them into Randolph's vase; looks at it with head one side, then breaks off one rose, fondles it, places it in her hair.*]

MRS. BUSH. May—May—are you happy!

MAY BUSH. Why—why—[*dashing something like a tear from her eye*] of course I am.

MRS. BUSH. Maybe you is . . . May . . . but, somehow, I don't feel satisfied.

MAY BUSH [*kisses her mother*]. Oh, Ma, everything is all right! Just wait until you see me dressed. [*Noise at door.*] Oh, somebody's coming in here!

[*May retreats partly up the stairway.*
Enter Mrs. Temple, talking. Voices and commotion heard as if coming from the front of the house, where heated argument is

going on at front door, Mrs. Temple's muffled voice being heard.
Hall kitchen door opens suddenly. Enter Mrs. Temple, excitedly.]

MRS. TEMPLE. Heavens! They tried to keep me from coming out here! The very idea of her talking that way to me—the groom's own mother! Who is that little upstart that let me in at the front door? I told her I was coming right out here in the kitchen, for even though we have not called on each other in the past, moving around—as you know—in somewhat different social circles, and, of course, not being thrown very closely together, yet *now*, at this particular time, Mrs. Bush, since our two children are determined to marry, I feel that my place to-night is right back here with you! [*Glancing upward, Mrs. Temple discovers May upon the stairway.*] Why, May, are you not dressed yet! You'll have to do better than that when you are Mrs. John Temple!

MRS. BUSH. Don't you worry 'bout May; she'll be ready. Where's John! Is he here?

MRS. TEMPLE. Sure—he brought me in his car, but the fellows captured him and said they were going to keep him out driving until the last minute. [*Again glancing upward toward May.*] Better hurry, May; you mustn't keep John waiting.

MAY BUSH [*slowly walking upstairs*]. Oh, John, will get used to waiting on me.

[*Exit May.*]

MRS. TEMPLE. [*to Mrs. Bush*]. What's this . . . chicken salad? Is it finished?

MRS. BUSH. No, it ain't. The my'nase ain't come yet. I sent Randolph for it. I jest got tired waiting on Lyddie Smith to fetch it.

MRS. TEMPLE. My gracious . . . give me the things and I'll make the dressing for you in a jiffy.

[*Mrs. Temple removes her white gloves and gets ready for her new role in the kitchen. Without waiting for Mrs. Bush's consent, she rapidly walks over to wooden peg on wall, takes down extra gingham apron and removes her hat and lightweight coat, hanging both upon the peg.*]

MRS. BUSH [*remonstratingly*]. I'm 'fraid you'll git yo'self spoiled doing kitchen work. Sich folks as you'd better go 'long in the parlor.

MRS. TEMPLE. Oh, no indeed. This is my son's wedding and I'm here to do a mother's part. Besides—he is a Temple and everything must be right.

MRS. BUSH [*Takes materials for making the mayonnaise from kitchen safe and reluctantly places them before Mrs. Temple*]. You needn't worry 'bout this wedding bein' right. It's my daughter's wedding—and I'll see to that!

MRS. TEMPLE [*breaking and stirring eggs for the dressing*]. You'll have to admit that the girls will envy May marrying my boy John.

MRS. BUSH [*stopping her work suddenly, and with arms akimbo*]. Envy MAY!!! Envy MAY!!! They'd better envy JOHN!!! You don't know who May is; she's got blue blood in her veins.

MRS. TEMPLE [*laughing sarcastically*]. You amuse me. I'll admit May's sweet and pretty, but she is no match for John.

MRS. BUSH [*irately*]. She's not, eh? If I told you something about my May—who she is—you'd be struck dumb.

MRS. TEMPLE [*nervously stirring the mayonnaise, replies in a falsetto or raised tone, denoting sarcasm*]. Remarkable . . . but I am curious!

MRS. BUSH [*proudly*]. I bet you is—you'd fall flat if I told you who she is.

MRS. TEMPLE [*suspending the operation of the mayonnaise and curiously assuming a soft, confidential tone*]. Pray, Mrs. Bush, tell me then. Who is May?

MRS. BUSH. Who is May? Huh! [*Proudly tossing her head.*] Who is May? [*Lowering her voice, confidentially.*] Why . . . do you know Cap'n WINFIELD McCALLISTER, the biggest banker in this town, and who's got money 'vested in banks all over Georgia? That 'ristocrat uv 'ristocrats . . . that Peachtree Street blue blood—CAP'N McCALLISTER—don't you know him?

MRS. TEMPLE [*starts at the mention of the name but recovers herself in a moment*]. Y—e—s, I've heard of him.

MRS. BUSH [*like a shot out of a gun*]. Well, I'd have you to know—he's May's daddy!

MRS. TEMPLE [*agitatedly*]. W-h-y . . . I . . . I . . . I can't believe it!

MRS. BUSH [*flauntingly*]. Believe it or not, it's the bounden truth so help me God! Ain't you never seed him strut? Well, look at May. Walks jest like him—throws her head like him—an' she's got eyes, nose and mouth jest like him. She's his living image.

MRS. TEMPLE [*almost collapsing, speaking softly and excitedly*]. You . . . you terrify me. Mrs. Bush . . . Captain McCallister can't be May's father!

MRS. BUSH. Can't be May's father! Well, I reckon I ought to know who May's father is! Whut do you know 'bout it anyhow? Whut do you know 'bout Cap'n McCallister?

MRS. TEMPLE. Do you mean to tell—

MRS. BUSH [*interrupting*]. I mean jest whut I said. I'm telling you that my daughter—May Bush—has got the bluest blood in America in her veins. Jest put that in your pipe and smoke it! [*Mrs. Bush here proudly flaunts herself around the kitchen, talking half at Mrs. Temple and half to herself.*] Huh! Talkin' 'bout May not bein' a match fur John. I should say they don't come no finer than May, anywhere.

MRS. TEMPLE [*again collecting herself and speaking in a soft, strained, pleading voice*]. Mrs. Bush, Mrs. Bush, I have something to say to you and it must be said right now! Oh, where can I begin? Let me think—

MRS. BUSH. This ain't no time to think, I'm going to act! [*Takes mayonnaise from Mrs. Temple's apathetic hands.*] My chile's gotter get married and get married right. I . . .

MRS. TEMPLE [*breaking in*]. Please, please, be still a minute for heaven's sake! You'll drive me mad!

MRS. BUSH. Drive you mad! The devil I will. [*Abruptly runs and stands in a belligerent attitude in front of Mrs. Temple.*] Say, look here, Miss High-and-Mighty, what's you up to? Git out of here, you ain't going to start no trouble here.

[*Tries to force Mrs. Temple toward the door.*]

MRS. TEMPLE [*breaking down in tears and reaching for Mrs. Bush's hands*]. Please, please, Mrs. Bush, you don't understand, and how can I tell you—what a day!

MRS. BUSH [*standing squarely in front of Mrs. Temple*]. Look here, is you crazy? or just a fool?

MRS. TEMPLE. Neither, Mrs. Bush, I'm just a broken-hearted mother and you must help me, help me, for May's sake, if not for mine!

MRS. BUSH. For May's sake! 'Splain yourself! This is a pretty come off. For May's sake.

[*Sarcastically.*]

MRS. TEMPLE. It's a long story, but I'll tell you in a few words. Oh, oh, how I've tried to forget it!

MRS. BUSH. Forget what! Look here, what time is it?

[*Mrs. Temple looks at her watch.*]

MRS. TEMPLE. A quarter of nine.

MRS. BUSH [*excitedly*]. Lord, woman, we ain't got no time fur story telling. I've got to hustle!

MRS. TEMPLE [*hysterically*]. You must hear me, you must, you must!

MRS. BUSH. Well, of all things, what *is* the matter with you?

MRS. TEMPLE. Be quiet, just one minute, and let me tell you.

MRS. BUSH. You'd better hurry up.

MRS. TEMPLE. Once . . . I taught a country school in Georgia. I was engaged to Paul Temple . . . I was only nineteen. I had worked hard to make enough to pay for my wedding things . . . it was going to be in the early fall—our wedding. I put my money in the bank. One day, in that bank, I met a man. He helped me. And then I see he wanted his pay for it. He kept on—kept writing to me. He didn't sign his letters, though. I wouldn't answer. I tried to keep away. One night he came to the place where I boarded. The woman where I boarded—she helped him—he bribed her. He came into my room—

MRS. BUSH. The dirty devil!

MRS. TEMPLE [*continuing her story*]. I cried out. There wasn't any one there that cared enough to help me, and you know yourself, Mrs. Bush, what little chance there is for women like us, in the South, to get justice or redress when these things happen!

MRS. BUSH. Sure, honey, I do know!

MRS. TEMPLE. Mother knew—there wasn't any use trying to punish him. She said I'd be the one . . . that would suffer.

MRS. BUSH. You done right . . . and whut your ma told you is the God's truth.

MRS. TEMPLE. I told Paul Temple—the one I was engaged to—the whole story, only I didn't tell him who. I knew he would have tried to kill him, and then they'd have killed him.

MRS. BUSH [*interrupting*]. That was good sense.

MRS. TEMPLE. He understood the whole thing—and he married me. He knew why I wouldn't tell him the man's name—not even when—when that man's son was born to me.

MRS. BUSH. You don't mean John?

MRS. TEMPLE. Yes . . . John. And his father. . . .

MRS. BUSH. Oh no . . . no . . .

MRS. TEMPLE. Yes. [*With a groan.*] Winfield McCallister . . . is John's father, too.

313

MRS. BUSH [*clasping her hands excitedly*]. My God! My God!
[*Whimpering, between sobs.*] Whut kin we do? Just think of my
poor, dear chile, May, upstairs there—all dressed up jest lak a
bride—'spectin' to git married—and all them people from everywhere—in the parlor—waiting for the seymoaney! Oh whut kin
we tell her . . . whut kin we tell them?

MRS. TEMPLE [*looking at watch. Gets up, walks up and down
excitedly.*] Yes . . . we've got to think and act quickly! We can't
tell the world why the children didn't marry . . . and cause a
scandal. . . . I'd be ruined!

MRS. BUSH [*getting irate*]. So far as you is consarned . . . I ain't
bothered, 'bout your being ruined. May'll be ruined if we don't
tell. Why—folks'll all be saying John jilted her, and you can bet
your sweet life I won't stand fur that. No siree! I don't keer who
it hurts . . . I'm not agoin' see May suffer . . . not ef I kin help it!

MRS. TEMPLE. [*bursting into tears*]. Oh! oh! we must do something!

[*Enter Randolph Strong, breathlessly, with mayonnaise dressing
from Lyddie Smith's—placing large glass jar of mayonnaise on
kitchen table.*]

RANDOLPH STRONG. Good evening, Mrs. Temple. I'm a little late,
Mrs. Bush, but here's what you sent me for. [*He notices Mrs.
Temple in tears.*] My, my, why, what's wrong?

MRS. BUSH. Randolph, my dear boy. . . .

RANDOLPH STRONG. What's the matter? What's happened since I
left you awhile ago?

MRS. BUSH [*slowly and feelingly*]. Sump'n . . . sump'n turrible!

RANDOLPH STRONG. Has anything happened to May?

MRS. BUSH. Not only to her—to all of us!

RANDOLPH STRONG. All! Heavens!

MRS. BUSH. Listen, Randolph, and help us, for God's sake! May and
John can't get married!

RANDOLPH STRONG [*turning to Mrs. Temple*]. Can't get married!
Why?

MRS. TEMPLE. It's a long story. I've told—I've explained everything
to Mrs. Bush. She—she understands.

RANDOLPH STRONG. You can trust me. I'm like one of the family.
You both know that I have always cared for May.

MRS. BUSH [*to Mrs. Temple*]. Kin I tell him? [*Mrs. Temple silently
and tearfully nods her assent.*] May mus' know it too—right
away. Let's call her down. May! May! Oh, May! My dear chile

314

come down here a minute—quick—right away! My poor chile . . . my poor chile!

MRS. TEMPLE. What a day! What a day!

MAY'S VOICE. Coming, Ma! [*Enter May Bush, coming downstairs in her wedding gown.*] Am I late? [*Noting Randolph.*] The roses are beautiful. See. [*Points to one in her hair.*]

MRS. BUSH. Randolph . . . Randolph remembered the kind you like, honey.

MAY BUSH [*to Randolph*]. Just like you!

RANDOLPH STRONG. How sweet of you to wear one!

MAY BUSH [*proudly walking across room toward Mrs. Bush*]. How do I look, Ma?

MRS. BUSH [*tenderly kissing her daughter several times*]. Beautiful, my darlin' [*adding softly*], poor chile!

MAY BUSH [*walking toward and kissing Mrs. Temple*]. How do you like me—my other mama?

MRS. TEMPLE. Charming—God protect you, my dear!

MAY BUSH [*noticing the sad expression on the faces of both mothers*]. My, you all look so sad; why so doleful? What is the matter with them, Randolph?

RANDOLPH STRONG. Why . . . I'm wounded, but smiling. The ladies
. . .

MRS. BUSH [*impatiently interrupting*]. Oh, children—don't waste this precious time. We've called you together to tell you sump'n . . . [*stuttering*] we've got sump'n to tell you, and we got to tell you right now!

[*Mrs. Bush drews May aside toward Mrs. Temple, hastily and cautiously locking kitchen hall door.*]

MRS. BUSH [*continuing*]. Listen, May. Come here, come here, Randolph, for I feel that both of you are my children. May, you got to be strong—for if ever you needed wits, now's the time to use 'em. May God forgive me—and Mrs. Temple there, both of us—I just got to tell you 'bout it quick—for all them folks are in the parlor and if we don't do something quick, right now, this whole town will be rippin' us to pieces—all of us, you and me—Mrs. Temple—and—and—the las' one of us! There ain't time to tell you the whole story—but—May—my poor chile—I know you kin trus' your own, dear ma that far?

MAY BUSH [*excitedly*]. Yes, Ma, yes, but what is it?

MRS. BUSH. May, you and John can't marry—you jest can't marry!!

315

MAY BUSH [*aghast*]. Can't marry! Can't marry!

MRS. BUSH. No, never!

MAY BUSH. But why—why!

MRS. BUSH. Your father, and John's father—is—is—

MAY BUSH. You don't mean . . .

MRS. TEMPLE. Yes, May. John's father is your father.

MAY BUSH [*wrings her hands*]. Oh, I'd rather die—I'd rather die than face this. . . .

MRS. BUSH [*crooning*]. I know, honey . . . I know . . . God forgive me . . . God forgive that man. Oh, no . . . I don't want Him to forgive him.

MAY BUSH. Oh why, why did this have to happen to me—oh!! I wish I were dead!

RANDOLPH STRONG. May—don't say that. You mustn't say that.

MAY BUSH. I do. Oh, God—I've kept out of their clutches myself, but now it's through you, Ma, that they've got me anyway. Oh, what's the use . . .

RANDOLPH STRONG. May!

MAY BUSH. The whole world will be pointing at me . . .

MRS. BUSH. Ah, honey, honey, I'll be loving you. . . .

MAY BUSH. I wish I could die right now.

RANDOLPH STRONG. Will you listen to me, now, May?

MAY BUSH. Those people in there—they'll be laughing . . .

[*Knocking is heard.*]

MRS. TEMPLE. It's John. We can't let him come in here now. He mustn't know. . . .

MRS. BUSH. No. We can't let him know or he'll kill his own father. . . .

MRS. TEMPLE. What are you going to do, May?

MRS. BUSH. Yes, May—what are you going to do?

RANDOLPH STRONG. We are going to run away and get married, aren't we, May? Say yes, May—say yes!

MAY BUSH. John . . .

[*The knocking is heard again.*]

MRS. BUSH. Keep it from him. It's the black women that have got to protect their men from the white men by not telling on 'em.

MRS. TEMPLE. God knows that's the truth.

RANDOLPH STRONG. May! Come with me *now*!

MAY BUSH. Randolph—do you want me?

RANDOLPH STRONG. I want you like I've always wanted you.

MAY BUSH [*shyly*]. But—I don't love you.

RANDOLPH STRONG. You think you don't. . . .

MAY BUSH. Do you want me now?

RANDOLPH STRONG. I want you now.

MAY BUSH. Ma, oh, Ma!

MRS. BUSH [*in tears*]. Quick, darlin'—tell him.

MAY BUSH. My coat.

MRS. BUSH. I'll get your coat, honey.

MRS. TEMPLE. Here, May, take *my* coat!

MRS. BUSH. What we going to tell John—and all the people?

MAY BUSH. Tell 'em—Oh God, we can't tell 'em the—truth?

RANDOLPH STRONG. Mother Bush—just tell them the bride was stolen by Randolph Strong!

[*Strong puts the coat around her and they go out of the door, leaving the others staring at them.*]

[*CURTAIN.*]

PLUMES

A FOLK TRAGEDY

By

GEORGIA DOUGLAS JOHNSON

OPPORTUNITY PRIZE PLAY, FIRST DRAMA PRIZE,
1927

*Reprinted by special permission of the author
and Opportunity, Journal of Negro Life*

CHARACTERS

CHARITY BROWN, the mother
EMMERLINE BROWN, the daughter
TILDY, the friend
DOCTOR SCOTT, physician

Scene: A poor cottage in the South.
Time: Contemporary.

PLUMES

SCENE: THE KITCHEN *of a two-room cottage. A window overlooking the street. A door leading to street, one leading to the back yard and one to the inner room. A stove, a table with shelf over it, a washtub. A rocking-chair, a cane-bottom chair. Needle, thread, scissors, etc. on table.*

Scene opens with CHARITY BROWN *heating a poultice over the stove. A groaning is heard from the inner room.*

CHARITY. Yes, honey, mamma is fixing somethin' to do you good. Yes, my baby, jus' you wait—I'm a-coming. (*Knock is heard at door. It is gently pushed open and* TILDY *comes in cautiously.*)

TILDY. (*Whispering*) How is she?

CHARITY. Poorly, poorly. Didn't rest last night none hardly. Move that dress and set in th' rocker. I been trying to snatch a minute to finish it but don't seem like I can. She won't have nothing to wear if she—she ——

TILDY. I understands. How near done is it?

CHARITY. Ain't so much more to do.

TILDY. (*Takes up dress from chair; looks at it*) I'll do some on it.

CHARITY. Thank you, sister Tildy. Whip that torshon on and turn down the hem in the skirt.

TILDY. (*Measuring dress against herself*) How deep?

CHARITY. Let me see, now (*Studies a minute with finger*

289

against lip) I tell you—jus' baste it, 'cause you see—
she wears 'em short, but—it might be —— (*Stops.*)

TILDY. (*Bowing her head comprehendingly*) Huh-uh, I see
exzackly. (*Sighs*) You'd want it long—over her feet—
then.

CHARITY. That's it, sister Tildy. (*Listening*) She's some
easy now! (*Stirring poultice*) Jest can't get this poltis'
hot enough somehow this morning.

TILDY. Put some red pepper in it. Got any?

CHARITY. Yes. There ought to be some in one of them
boxes on the shelf there. (*Points.*)

TILDY. (*Goes to shelf, looks about and gets the pepper*)
Here, put a-plenty of this in.

CHARITY. (*Groans are heard from the next room*) Good
Lord, them pains got her again. She suffers so, when
she's 'wake.

TILDY. Poor little thing. How old is she now, sister Charity?

CHARITY. Turning fourteen this coming July.

TILDY. (*Shaking her head dubiously*) I sho' hope she'll be
mended by then.

CHARITY. It don't look much like it, but I trusts so ——
(*Looking worried*) That doctor's mighty late this
morning.

TILDY. I expects he'll be 'long in no time. Doctors is mighty
onconcerned here lately.

CHARITY. (*Going toward inner room with poultice*) They
surely is and I don't have too much confidence in none of
'em. (*You can hear her soothing the child.*)

TILDY. (*Listening*) Want me to help you put it on, sister
Charity?

CHARITY. (*From inner room*) No, I can fix it. (*Coming
back from sick room shaking her head rather deject-
edly.*)

TILDY. How is she, sister Charity?

CHARITY. Mighty feeble. Gone back to sleep now. My poor little baby. (*Bracing herself*) I'm going to put on some coffee now.

TILDY. I'm sho' glad. I feel kinder low-spirited.

CHARITY. It's me that low-sperited. The doctor said last time he was here he might have to oparate—said, she mought have a chance then. But I tell you the truth, I've got no faith a-tall in 'em. They takes all your money for nothing.

TILDY. They sho' do and don't leave a cent for putting you away decent.

CHARITY. That's jest it. They takes all you got and then you dies jest the same. It ain't like they was sure.

TILDY. No, they ain't sure. That's it exzactly. But they takes your money jest the same, and leaves you flat.

CHARITY. I been thinking 'bout Zeke these last few days— how he was put away——

TILDY. I wouldn't worry 'bout him now. He's out of his troubles.

CHARITY. I know. But it worries me when I think about how he was put away . . . that ugly pine coffin, jest one shabby old hack and nothing else to show—to show —what we thought about him.

TILDY. Hush, sister! Don't you worry over him. He's happy now, anyhow.

CHARITY. I can't help it! Then little Bessie. We all jest scrooged in one hack and took her little coffin in our lap all the way out to the graveyard. (*Breaks out crying.*)

TILDY. Do hush, sister Charity. You done the best you could. Poor folks got to make the best of it. The Lord understands——

CHARITY. I know that—but I made up my mind the time
Bessie went that the next one of us what died would
have a shore nuff funeral, everything grand,—with
plumes!—I saved and saved and now—this yah doctor ——

TILDY. All they think about is cuttin' and killing and taking
your money. I got nothin' to put 'em doing.

CHARITY. (*Goes over to washtub and rubs on clothes*) Me
neither. These clothes got to get out somehow, J needs
every cent.

TILDY. How much that washing bring you?

CHARITY. Dollar and a half. It's worth a whole lot more.
But what can you do?

TILDY. You can't do nothing—Look there, sister Charity,
ain't that coffee boiling?

CHARITY. (*Wipes hands on apron and goes to stove*) Yes
it's boiling good fashioned. Come on, drink some.

TILDY. There ain't nothing I'd rather have than a good
strong cup of coffee. (CHARITY *pours* TILDY'S *cup.*)
(*Sweetening and stirring hers*) Pour you some. (CHAR-
ITY *pours her own cup*) I'd been dead, too, long ago if
it hadn't a been for my coffee.

CHARITY. I love it, but it don't love me—gives me the short-
ness of breath.

TILDY. (*Finishing her cup, taking up sugar with spoon*)
Don't hurt me. I could drink a barrel.

CHARITY. (*Drinking more slowly—reaching for coffeepot*)
Here, drink another cup.

TILDY. I shore will, that cup done me a lot of good.

CHARITY. (*Looking into her empty cup thoughtfully*) I
wish Dinah Morris would drop in now. I'd ask her
what these grounds mean.

TILDY. I can read 'em a little myself.

CHARITY. You can? Well, for the Lord's sake, look here and tell me what this cup says! (*Offers cup to* TILDY. TILDY *wards it off.*)

TILDY. You got to turn it 'round in your saucer three times first.

CHARITY. Yes, that's right, I forgot. (*Turns cup 'round, counting*) One, two, three. (*Starts to pick it up.*)

TILDY. Huhudh. (*Meaning no*) Let it set a minute. It might be watery. (*After a minute, while she finishes her own cup*) Now let me see. (*Takes cup and examines it very scrutinizingly.*)

CHARITY. What you see?

TILDY. (*Hesitatingly*) I ain't seen a cup like this one for many a year. Not since—not since ——

CHARITY. When?

TILDY. Not since jest before ma died. I looked in the cup then and saw things and—I stopped looking . . .

CHARITY. Tell me what you see, I want to know.

TILDY. I don't like to tell no bad news ——

CHARITY. Go on. I can stan' anything after all I been thru'.

TILDY. Since you're bound to know I'll tell you. (CHARITY *draws nearer*) I sees a big gethering!

CHARITY. Gethering, you say?

TILDY. Yes, a big gethering. People all crowded together. Then I see 'em going one by one and two by two. Long line stretching out and out and out!

CHARITY. (*In a whisper*) What you think it is?

TILDY. (*Awed like*) Looks like (Hesitates) a possession!

CHARITY. (*Shouting*) You sure!

TILDY. I know it is. (*Just then the toll of a church bell is heard and then the steady and slow tramp, tramp, of horses' hoofs. Both women look at each other.*)

TILDY. (*In a hushed voice*) That must be Bell Gibson's funeral coming 'way from Mt. Zion. (*Gets up and goes to window*) Yes, it sho' is.

CHARITY. (*Looking out of the window also*) Poor Bell suffered many a year; she's out of her pain now.

TILDY. Look, here comes the hearse now!

CHARITY. My Lord! ain't it grand! Look at them horses—look at their heads—plumes—how they shake 'em! Land o' mighty! It's a fine sight, sister Tildy.

TILDY. That must be Jer'miah in that first carriage, bending over like; he shorely is putting her away grand.

CHARITY. No mistake about it. That's Pickett's best funeral turnout he's got.

TILDY. I'll bet it cost a lot.

CHARITY. Fifty dollars, so Matilda Jenkins told me. She had it for Bud. The plumes is what cost.

TILDY. Look at the hacks—— (*Counts*) I believe to my soul there's eight.

CHARITY. Got somebody in all of 'em too—and flowers— She shore got a lot of 'em. (*Both women's eyes follow the tail end of the procession, horses' hoofs die away as they turn away from window. The two women look at each other significantly.*)

TILDY. (*Significantly*) Well!—— (*They look at each other without speaking for a minute.* CHARITY *goes to the washtub*) Want these cups washed up?

CHARITY. No don't mind 'em. I'd rather you get that dress done. I got to get these clothes out.

TILDY. (*Picking up dress*) Shore, there ain't so much more to do on it now. (*Knock is heard on the door.* CHARITY *answers knock and admits Dr. Scott.*)

DR. SCOTT. Good morning. How's the patient today?

CHARITY. Not so good, doctor. When she ain't 'sleep she suffers so; but she sleeps mostly.

DR. SCOTT. Well, let's see, let's see. Just hand me a pan of warm water and I'll soon find out just what's what.

CHARITY. All right, doctor. I'll bring it to you right away. (*Bustles about fixing water—looking toward dress* TILDY *is working oñ*) Poor little Emmerline's been wanting a white dress trimmed with torshon a long time —now she's got it and it looks like—well—— (*Hesitates*) t'warn't made to wear.

TILDY. Don't take on so, sister Charity—The Lord giveth and the Lord taketh.

CHARITY. I know—but it's hard—hard—— (*Goes into inner room with water. You can hear her talking with the doctor after a minute and the doctor expostulating with her—in a minute she appears at the door, being led from the room by the doctor.*)

DR. SCOTT. No, my dear Mrs. Brown. It will be much better for you to remain outside.

CHARITY. But, doctor——

DR. SCOTT. NO. You stay outside and get your mind on something else. You can't possibly be of any service. Now be calm, will you?

CHARITY. I'll try, doctor.

TILDY. The doctor's right. You can't do no good in there.

CHARITY. I knows, but I thought I could hold the pan or somethin'. (*Lowering her voice*) Says he got to see if her heart is all right or somethin'. I tell you—nowadays——

TILDY. I know.

CHARITY. (*Softly to* TILDY) Hope he won't come out here saying he got to operate. (*Goes to washtub.*)

TILDY. I hope so, too. Won't it cost a lot?

CHARITY. That's jest it. It would take all I got saved up.

TILDY. Of course, if he's goin' to get her up—but I don't believe in 'em. I don't believe in 'em.

CHARITY. He didn't promise tho'—even if he did, he said maybe it wouldn't do no good.

TILDY. I'd think a long time before I'd let him operate on my chile. Taking all yuh money, promising nothing and ten to one killing her to boot.

CHARITY. This is a hard world.

TILDY. Don't you trus' him. Coffee grounds don't lie!

CHARITY. I don't trust him. I jest want to do what's right by her. I ought to put these clothes on the line while you're settin' in here, but I jes hate to go outdoors while he's in there.

TILDY. (*Getting up*) I'll hang 'em out. You stay here. Where your clothespins at?

CHARITY. Hanging right there by the back door in the bag. They ought to dry before dark and then I can iron to-night.

TILDY. (*Picking up tub*) They ought to blow dry in no time. (*Goes toward back door.*)

CHARITY. Then I can shore rub 'em over to-night. Say, sister Tildy, hist 'em up with that long saplin' prop leaning in the fence corner.

TILDY. (*Going out*) All right.

CHARITY. (*Standing by the table beating nervously on it with her fingers—listens—and then starts to bustling about the kitchen*) (*Enter DOCTOR from inner room.*)

DR. SCOTT. Well, Mrs. Brown, I've decided I'll have to operate.

CHARITY. MY Lord! Doctor—don't say that!

DR. SCOTT. It's the only chance.

CHARITY. You mean she'll get well if you do?

DR. SCOTT. No, I can't say that ——— It's just a chance ———
a last chance. And I'll do just what I said, cut the
price of the operation down to fifty dollars. I'm willing to do that for you. (CHARITY *throws up her hands
in dismay.*)

CHARITY. Doctor, I was so in hopes you wouldn't operate—
I—I——— And yo' say you ain't a bit sure she'll get
well—even then?

DR. SCOTT. No. I can't be sure. We'll just have to take
the chance. But I'm sure you want to do everything———

CHARITY. Sure, doctor, I do want to—do—everything I can
do to—to——— Doctor, look at this cup. (*Picks up
fortune cup and shows the doctor*) My fortune 's jes'
been told this very morning—look at these grounds—
they says——— (*Softly*) it ain't no use, no use a-tall.

DR. SCOTT. Why, my good woman, don't you believe in such
senseless things! That cup of grounds can't show you
anything. Wash them out and forget it.

CHARITY. I can't forget it. I feel like it ain't no use; I'd
just be spendin' the money that I needs—for nothing—
nothing.

DR. SCOTT. But you won't though ——— You'll have a clear
conscience. You'd know that you did everything you
could.

CHARITY. I know that, doctor. But there's things you don't
know 'bout—there's other things I got to think about.
If she goes—if she must go . . . I had plans—I been
getting ready—now ——— Oh, doctor, I jest can't see
how I can have this operation—you say you can't promise—nothing?

DR. SCOTT. I didn't think you'd hesitate about it—I imagined your love for your child———

CHARITY. (*Breaking in*) I do love my child. My God, I do love my child. You don't understand . . . but . . . but—can't I have a little time to think about it, doctor? It means so much—to her—and—me!

DR. SCOTT. I tell you. I'll go on over to the office. I'd have to get my— (*Hesitates*) my things, anyhow. And as soon as you make up your mind, get one of the neighbors to run over and tell me. I'll come right back. But don't waste any time now, Mrs. Brown, every minute counts.

CHARITY. Thank you, doctor, thank you. I'll shore send you word as soon as I can. I'm so upset and worried I'm half crazy.

DR. SCOTT. I know you are . . . but don't take too long to make up your mind. . . . It ought to be done to-day. Remember—it may save her. (*Exits.*)

CHARITY. (*Goes to door of sick room—looks inside for a few minutes, then starts walking up and down the little kitchen, first holding a hand up to her head and then wringing them. Enter* TILDY *from yard with tub under her arm.*)

TILDY. Well, they're all out, sister Charity—— (*Stops*) Why, what's the matter?

CHARITY. The doctor wants to operate.

TILDY. (*Softly*) Where he—gone?

CHARITY. Yes—he's gone, but he's coming back—if I send for him.

TILDY. You going to? (*Puts down tub and picks up white dress and begins sewing.*)

CHARITY. I dunno—I got to think.

TILDY. I can't see what's the use myself. He can't save her with no operation—— Coffee grounds don't lie.

CHARITY. It would take all the money I got for the opera-

tion and then what about puttin' her away? He can't
save her—don't even promise ter. I know he can't—I
feel it . . . I feel it . . .

TILDY. It's in the air. . . . (*Both women sit tense in the
silence.* TILDY *has commenced sewing again. Just then
a strange, strangling noise comes from the inner room.*)

TILDY. What's that?

CHARITY. (*Running toward and into inner room*) Oh, my
God! (*From inside*) Sister Tildy—Come here—No,—
Some water, quick. (TILDY *with dress in hand starts
toward inner room. Stops at door, sighs and then goes
hurriedly back for the water pitcher.* CHARITY *is heard
moaning softly in the next room, then she appears at
doorway and leans against jamb of door*) Rip the hem
out, sister Tildy.

CURTAIN

FREDERICK DOUGLASS

A One-Act Play

BY

Georgia Douglas Johnson

FREDERICK DOUGLASS

CHARACTERS

FRED DOUGLASS, *young slave man.*

ANN, *his sweetheart freewoman.*

BUD, *Ann's brother.*

JAKE, *an old slave.*

TIME: SLAVERY DAYS.

PLACE: BALTIMORE, MD.

Permission for the performance of this play must be obtained from
the author, Georgia Douglas Johnson, 1461 S St., N. W., Washington, D. C.

FREDERICK DOUGLASS

*A kitchen in an humble two-room hut at the corner of a street
in the poor section of the city near the railroad, the
home of* ANN *and her brother* BUD, *both free. There is
an open door leading to the front room and another
door leading to the backyard and street. There is a small
window with a calico curtain before it on the side-street
side. Against the wall between the window and door is
a table with a red checked cloth covering one-half of it.
On the uncovered side are a water bucket and yellow
bowl. Near the bucket is a gourd, and hanging on the
wall are a towel and a small piece of broken-looking
glass. On a shelf nearby are a plate, knife, mugs, spoons,
a can of molasses. Near the back door is a small iron
cook stove; on it is a tea-kettle; and a half-knitted sock
is seen over the edge of the sewing box.*

ANN *is seen stooping as she pushes a pan of ginger bread
into the oven to bake. She straightens up, goes to the
table and with a finger wipes around the bowl and tastes
ginger-cake batter.*

ANN

Eugh—good.
> (*She goes to window and looks up and down the street
> expectantly. She then goes to the bit of looking glass,
> stands before it and primps her hair. A knock
> sounds at the door of the front room. She gives her
> hair another pull or two, calling out as she does so.*)

All right!
> (*She hurries through the open door to the front door
> and voices are heard in the next room. She immediate-*

145

ly returns running to the kitchen with DOUGLASS *in pursuit. He tries to kiss her but she eludes him. He puts some papers he brought in with him on the table cloth.)*

No kissin' tell we're married. I promised Ma.

FRED

I can wait—you're worth it. Won't be long now. Look a-here!

(He takes a handful of silver from his trouser pocket and shows it to ANN.)

ANN

Whooee—how much?

FRED

Seventeen dollars and fifty cents—most enough for me to steal away to freedom an' marry with up North.

(Chuckling to himself.)

Honey, do you know something funny happened tonight? When I give Marse Tom his ten dollars I worked an' made fur him this week, he was tickled to death an' said, "Here, Fred, take this here quarter an' buy yourself somethin'." He ain't got no idea how much extra money I picks up during the week. You see I'm a-workin' for freedom an' you.

ANN

(Shyly.)

Oh, Fred! I hopes he don't fin' out 'bout it 'fore we gits away.

FRED

I'm scareful. I hides my money an' just brought it along tonight to show you how I'm a-doin'.

ANN

How many mo' Saddays 'fore you goin' to have enouf fur us to go on?

FRED

Mebbe four more, an' then, little honey,
  (*He snaps his finger exultantly.*)
I'm a-goin' to that free country, learn all I can an' then
I'm a-goin' to help the rest of my poor down-trodden people
to get out from under this yoke.

ANN

You sho look grand when you talk like that.
  (*Hesitatingly.*)
You won't want me then, I speck.

FRED

  (*Putting his arms about her fondly.*)
Oh my little honey, I'm goin' to love you all my life. We
goin' to work together, you an' me, in that great big free
country up North.

ANN

Free country!
  (*She stands with hands clasped as though she saw a
  vision, then, as if dropping back to earth, continues.*)
But look, I got somethin' good fur you.
  (*Advancing toward the stove.*)
Guess whut?

FRED

  (*Advancing a step or two behind her.*)
Not gingy bread, now?

ANN

  (*Opening stove door with her apron.*)
Course 'tis—you done smelled it.

FRED

  (*Peeping in stove from behind her and making noise of
  whiffing spicy flavor.*)
My, that spice sholy smells good—like, like singin' in the

meetin' house! I want you to make a gingy bread for us when we get married, honey.

ANN

I'm a gonner mek one with white icing fur that.

FRED

(*Pensively.*)

Here I am a talkin' 'bout marryin' an' cake an' such like an' me just a poor slave!

(*Sighs deeply and then goes over to table and starts putting down sums for the lessons.*)

ANN

(*Going over to him consolingly.*)

Tain't fur long, Fred, you boun' to be free—I feels it— you got them big free ways.

FRED

(*Caressingly.*)

Honey, you jes' like a rock in a weary land . . . weary land

(*Drops his head into his hands and repeats softly.*)

weary land!

(*A train whistle blows and the sound of a train passing is heard. Both listen.*)

ANN

(*Moving toward the window.*)

The South boun'! Come look at the lights from the train winders.

FRED

(*Following her to window, shaking his head.*)

She's headed the wrong way—South!

ANN

(*Thoughtfully.*)

Yes, she sho is.

(*Goes over to stove to look at ginger bread and turn it around.*)

FRED

(*Facing room observantly.*)
Ann, this here little bit of kitchen of yours is the nearest I ever been to heaven since I been born.
(*Going over to table where papers are, starts putting down sums again.*)

ANN

(*Reprovingly.*)
You forgittin' your own Ma's cook kitchen, ain't you?
(*Quickly.*)
I mean the white folkses' kitchen what owned her?

FRED

(*Sadly.*)
I never saw it—I never saw my own Ma but one time in my whole life.

ANN

Jes' one time; Good Lawd!

FRED

'Twas when I was around six years old. I remember wakin' up long about midnight. . . . I never will forget it. She was huggin' and kissin' me an' her tears was fallin' all down in my face like rain. She said "My poor baby . . . my poor baby . . . I'm your ma, honey," an' she went on callin' me sweet names an' cryin'; then all sudden like, she almost throwed me down on the palatte an' darted out through the door like mad!

ANN

I wonder why she done that?

FRED

I found out from Aunt Dinah that my Ma had to walk forty miles goin' an' comin' that night just to see me. She had

to be back to her new master's plantation before sun-up . . . I
never seen her since.

ANN

Lawd! Lawd!

(*Going up to him and patting him on the shoulder.*)
Don't you fret. We goin' to fin' her one uv these days an'
tell you do I'm a gointer make it all up to you—I'll be yore
wife an' ma all rolled into one.

FRED

(*Thoughtfully.*)
You look like she did that night—your eyes—but come on
an' get some lessons now; we won't wait for Bud. His boat
in yet?

ANN

(*Moving over toward the stove.*)
Yes, it's in. I heard her blow at the dock before you come in.
    (*Taking ginger bread from oven and putting it on top
    of stove.*)
You cummon an' eat a piece uv cake an' mebbe by then
Bud'll be here.
    (*Cuts a piece and hands it to him, leaving cake on back
    of stove.*)

FRED

(*Going over to stove near her.*)
Sure! But what you reckin' is keeping Bud so late; he knows
Sadday night is lesson night.
    (*Takes cake and tastes it.*)
Good!

ANN

(*Beaming appreciatively.*)
He must er stopped down there in some uv them saloons
an' got a drink er two. He sho worries me most to death.
I promised Ma 'fore she died that I would keep him
straight, but Lawd!

FRED

When I get away from here up North I'll take charge of
Bud for he'll hafter live with you an' me, you know!

ANN

Oh, Fred, you so good, teachin' me an' Bud to read an'
figger an' ev'rything. Whuts more, Bud likes you an' you
know he don't like nobody much—he jes' loved Ma and
that's all!

FRED

Bud loves you, Ann.

ANN

Oh jes' since Ma's been dead he kinder hankers after me,
but he aint loved nobody relly but Ma. I do everythin' for
him now. Let me finish this sock while we's waitin' for him.
        (*She picks up sock.*)

FRED

But I want you to do some sums now.
        (*Pulls her on over to the table.*)
You got to learn a lot cause you got to help me when we
get way, honey.

ANN

Let me finish this sock while we's waitin' an' you go on an'
tell me how 'twas you got all that book learnin'. Slaves
roun' here can't read nothin', even down to free ones don't
know nothin'. Look at me an' Bud!

FRED

        (*Still holding pencil and absently tapping the paper
        on the table.*)
Well, you see I use to play with young Marse Tom. We
both was around eight an' old Miss would read to us an'
teach us, but old Marse got mad when he found out about
it an' stopped her.

ANN

He did!

(*She stops knitting a minute in her excitement.*)

FRED

Yes. But that didn't stop me; I'd got a start an' I kept right on—picked up scraps of printin' from the streets an' wet gutters, dried 'em, hid 'em an' kept a-learnin'.

ANN

But sho'ly you couldn't read an' learn all by yoreself!

FRED

I didn't. When I got hold of hard words I couldn't spell, I'd say to some one of the white boys when I'd meet one on the street—"Say, I bet you can't read this here word," an' I'd show it to him. He would always spell it out jest to show off. I played lots of tricks like that to get more learnin'.

ANN

But want you skeered they'd ketch you an' beat you?

FRED

They caught me an' nearly killed me many a time. They took all my papers away, but pshaw! I whirled right around an' found some more an' learned harder than I ever had. Something inside of me just drove me to it!

ANN

I bleve you. You aint like nobody round here. You so— so wonderful like. I'll sho be glad when you git to git away, free!

FRED

It won't be long now till . . .

(*A cautious knock is heard at the back door of the kitchen.*)

ANN

Who at that back door, you reckin? I ain't spectin' nobody
but Bud.
(*She goes over to the door and calls.*)
Who dere?

VOICE

It's me, Jake, open de door.

ANN

(*To* FRED.)
It's Jake.

JAKE

(*Comes in panting as if he'd been running.*)
Look here, Fred, I heered somethin' tonight you ought to
know.

FRED

(*Excitedly.*)
What, Jake?

JAKE

Marse Tom's brother, Marse George, come in on dat las'
boat, an' he swore at Marse Tom an' said he wus a gonner
take you back wid him in de morning down on de Eastern
Shore agin. Sed he was gonner put you back in de field an'
break yo damn sperrit!

FRED

But he give me to Marse Tom.

JAKE

He screeched at Marse Tom, "Youser spilin him, youser
spilin him lettin' him work out fer wages—Fore long you
won't have him, he'll run away."

FRED

He's damn right!
(*Then agitatedly.*)

But what can I do?
(*Slaps his hand to his forehead.*)
In the mornin'. . . . In the mornin'. . . . I got to do
something before mornin'.

JAKE

You sho is.

ANN

Whut *kin* you do?

FRED

I don't know, I don't know but I got to get away . . . got to!

JAKE

You mout hide in de woods tell you could git away, mebbe!

FRED

Yes, but there ain't no safe places to hide in roundabouts!

ANN

(*Excitedly.*)
You got money to ride the train, ain't you?

FRED

(*Thoughtfully.*)
That's so!
(*Then shakes his head despondently.*)
But I can't ride the train without a pass.

JAKE

Dat's so. Now where could you git one?

ANN

(*With sudden animation.*)
Bud's got one!

FRED

(*Brightly.*)
That's so!

(*Then rather colorlessly.*)
But he wouldn't let me take it away.

ANN

For me he would.

JAKE

But where is Bud? You got to git it now—tonight!

ANN

He'll be lon' soon. His boats done docked long time ago.
(*Then with sinking spirits.*)
I hopes he's sober.

FRED

We can't reason with him if he's drunk, but we got to
somehow!

ANN

Yes, we got to.

FRED

(*Excitedly striking his forehead with his hand.*)
I just thought of something. I got to have a sailor's suit.

JAKE

Whut fer?

FRED

They tell me that you get by easy when you're a sailor, the
white folks don't bother them a-tall. I got to have a suit!
(*To* JAKE.)
Jake, you take this dollar an' go down by the docks an' rent
me one quick. Somebody'll let you have one for a few
days. I'll send it back to Ann here with the pass, if I get it.
(*Hands* JAKE *the money and pushes him toward the
door.*)

JAKE

I'll do my bes'. You'se lak a son to me, boy!

FRED

(*Emotionally.*)

Thankee, thankee, Jake. Hurry!

JAKE

(*Poking his head back in at the back door.*)

You'll better lay low cause Marse might be lookin' down here fur you. All de niggers knows you come down here on Sadday night!

(*Door closes.*)

FRED

He's right, Ann, we'd better fix that window an' move that light.

ANN

(*Nervously.*)

All right, Fred.

(*They quickly close the curtains and take the lamp from the table and set it in a corner on the floor.*)

FRED

That's better.

ANN

(*Anxiously.*)

Bud's mighty late! Lawd! I hopes he's sober.

(*Goes to stove and pokes at the fire.*)

FRED

(*Nervously walking up and down.*)

If he is an' we can't get it, I'll have to take to the woods I reckon!

(*A noise is heard at the door as if some one fumbling with the latch. Both start.*)

ANN

(*Excitedly rushing toward the door.*)

That's him now!

(BUD *stumbles in.*)

FRED

Hello, Bud! Too late for your lessons tonight.

BUD

(*Thickly.*)
Eughn nhu.
(*Meaning no.*)
Sor-i-e, Fred.
(*Falls heavily into a chair.*)

FRED

It's all right.

ANN

(*Going over to stove and cutting a piece of ginger bread.*)
Eat a piece of gingy bread, Bud, it's hot yet.
(*Comes over to him with a piece.*)

BUD

(*Drawlingly.*)
I ain't hungry.
(*Slouches down lower on chair.*)
I wanna sleep.

ANN

(*Hands cake to* FRED, *looks at him significantly and pats* BUD *on shoulder coaxingly.*)
Oh, Bud, I want you to do somethin' fur me.
(*He doesn't answer.*)
Hear me, lissen, I wants you to lemme have yore pass fur a little while. Lemme see it. Where is it, Bud?

BUD

(*Fretfully.*)
G'on.

(*Shakes her off.*)
Lemme lone!
> (ANN *looks helplessly at* FRED. FRED *shakes his head despondently.*)

FRED

I reckon I'll have to take the woods.
(*Looks resigned.*)

ANN

(*Droopingly.*)
Ef he wan't drunk he'd be all right.
> (*Then brightening up sudden as if struck with an idea.*)
I know . . . I know . . . I'll make some tea!

FRED

(*Repeats rather absently.*)
Tea?

ANN

(*To* FRED *in a stage whisper.*)
It sobers him! See ef the kittle's boilin'.
> (FRED *goes to stove, looks in kettle.* ANN *goes to table, gets tea and puts some leaves in small saucepan, goes to stove with it.*)

FRED

(*Motioning toward kettle.*)
It's hot.

ANN

(*Putting saucepan on stove.*)
Pour on some.
(*She stirs it.*)
Git a mug.
> (FRED *goes to table and gets mug.*)
> (*While they are fixing tea a noise is heard at back door.* JAKE *enters cautiously with bundle under left arm.*)

JAKE

(*With bated breath.*)
I got 'em! Got de p . . . .

FRED

Sh' . . .
> (*Stopping him, points to* BUD *slouched on chair, and in
> lower voice.*)

He won't.

JAKE

(*Understandingly.*)
Oh!
> (*Gives* FRED *bundle.*)

FRED

Thanks, Jake.
> (FRED *takes bundle listlessly and drops it on the cot
> carelessly.*)

JAKE

> (*Following* FRED *to cot.*)

What you gonner do?

FRED

Ann's givin' him tea to sober him an' then . . . maybe . . .
> (JAKE *goes into a deep study.*)

ANN

> (*Coaxingly holding mug for* BUD.)

Drink this tea, Bud, it's strong an' hot.
> (*Holds it close to his nose.*)

Don't it smell good?

BUD

> (*Smelling.*)

Gimme!
> (*Drinks and brightens at once.*)

JAKE

> (*Excitedly to* FRED.)

Yaw'll wait, I kin git it, watch me!

(*Goes over close to* BUD.)

Got any leaves in dat mug, Bud?

(FRED *beckons to* ANN *and explains to her in pantomime
what* JAKE *is trying to do.*)

BUD

(*Looking inside.*)

Yeah!

JAKE

Wamme to talk wid de sperrits in yore leaves?

BUD

(*With interest.*)

Y-e-a-h! Reckin you could talk wid Ma?

JAKE

(*Taking mug.*)

Lemme see!

(*Looks in mug as if seeing something, then softly and
confidentially to* BUD.)

Yes, Bud, yore Ma's sperrit is here. She got a message fur
you. You ready, Bud?

BUD

(*Hitching his chair closer to* JAKE, *eagerly.*)

Yeah, go on.

(FRED *and* ANN *hover around on qui vive while* JAKE
proceeds.)

JAKE

(*As if listening to some one speaking from the mug.*)

I's a-lissenin'.

(*As if repeating a message.*)

Tell Bud I can't res' in my grave tell he quits that drinkin'.
I'm miser'ble here twix heben an' earth. Tell him I heered
his sister ax him fur his pass tonight an' it hurt my soul
when he didn't give it. Tell him to han' it to her quick an'

then run down to the sycamoo tree at the corner of de fence
in de back yard, an' fall down on his knees an' pray. My
sperrit is on de way ther now to bless him whilst he prays.
Tell him to do all I said now this very minite.

(JAKE *shakes himself as if throwing off a trance and
then looks at* BUD *who seems dazed.*)

You heered yore Ma, Bud?

(BUD *starts up as if to go to the door.*)

ANN

Ma said . . . .

BUD

(*Hurriedly reaching down into his boot top for pass,
hands it to* ANN *who has followed him.*)

Heah!

(*He rushes out of doors.*)

(*As* BUD *reaches for pass and hands it to* ANN, FRED
*snatches the bundle of clothes from the cot, leaving
the cap there in his haste. He rushes to inner room.*
JAKE *picks up cap, brushes it off on his trousers,
follows* FRED.)

ANN

(*Holding pass in hands exultantly.*)

Thank God fur this! Jake done it.

(*She hurries over to stove and gets a piece of the ginger
bread and wraps it up in a piece of cloth for* FRED's
lunch.)

JAKE

(*Emerging from other room helping* FRED *into his
coat.*)

Yeah, but ef you goin' to ketch de North Boun', you gotter
fly.

FRED

(*Putting his money into his sailor pants pocket.*)

It won't take me a minite to cut across to the junction; she ain't blowed yet.

JAKE

No, but it's time fur her.

(*Urging* FRED *toward the door.*)

ANN

(*Handing him the pass and the cake.*)

Here 'tis.

(*Slips cake into his pocket.*)

Eat that when you is hongry.

(*Pushes him toward door. As* FRED *lingers she urges him on.*)

Don't stop to say good bye. Hurry!

(*Train is heard blowing at a distance.*)

JAKE

(*At door holding it slightly ajar.*)

Fur God's sake, cummon, man, you ain't got a minite to lose.

FRED

(*With one arm around* ANN *at door.*)

Bye, Ann. I'll send for you, honey.

ANN

(*Pushing* FRED *out of door, agitatedly.*)

Bye, Fred. Hurry! Hurry!

(*Ann turns quickly and goes to window, pushes back curtain and looks out. She listens. The rumble of the train can be heard as it nears the junction. All is still a few minutes and then the sound of the train bell is heard to ring and the gradually accelerating sound of a train gaining momentum is heard. There is a long whistle.* ANN *seems satisfied.*)

Thank God!

(*She falls down beside the cot as if in prayer as the curtain falls.*)

WILLIAM AND ELLEN CRAFT

A Play in One Act

BY

Georgia Douglas Johnson

WILLIAM AND ELLEN CRAFT

CHARACTERS

William Craft.

Ellen Craft.

Aunt Mandy.

Sam.

Time: Before the Civil War.

Place: On the Upper Mississippi.

WILLIAM AND ELLEN CRAFT

A log cabin with a window and door at rear. A fireplace at right with sweet potatoes baking in the ashes. At center a table. At left sheet drawn across the room to screen the bed. A box of wood beside the fireplace. Two chairs near the table. On the back of one chair an old black coat with a needle in it. Near the window a bench on which are a bucket of water and a gourd. ELLEN *is looking out of the window at the setting sun. Seeming to be in deep thought she begins to pick up articles of clothing and ties them in a bundle. Hearing a knock at the door she throws the bundle behind the curtain and taking the coat begins to sew.*

ELLEN

Who dere?

MANDY

(*Entering.*)
It's me. Mandy. Want you spectin' me?

ELLEN

Course, but I's so nervous an' figety.

MANDY

An' skeered too, I be boun'. You better be, cause—

ELLEN

Cause what?

MANDY

Cause I got bad news for you.

ELLEN

Bad news? What you mean, bad news?

165

MANDY

Chile, ole Missus done foun' out 'bout der undergroun' railroad an' now can't none ov you all git away. Dey watchin' you alls hidin' places like hawks.

(ELLEN *drops her sewing and puts her hands to her face moaning.*)

MANDY

(*Picks up sewing and starts to darn.*)

I'll finish dis coat for you, chile. I reckon you lowed William was goin' to wear it tonight, didn' you?

ELLEN

(*Brokenly.*)

Eugh-hu. But, Aunt Mandy, do they know 'bout our last secret hidin' place in the woods where Cap'n Smith meets the slaves an' takes um to the boat?

MANDY

Yes, honey, dey knows all 'bout ev'ything. You sho can't go now 'cause dey'll ketch you.

ELLEN

But, I got to go! I got to!

MANDY

(*Exasperated.*)

No you ain't, you can't. How ken you?

ELLEN

I don't know, I don't know. But sho'ly dere must be some way ayuther.

MANDY

(*Soothingly.*)

Po' chile! I know it's hard, but you got to ben' to de rod. You got to stan' it.

(*Looks at potatoes on hearth.*)

Don't no trouble las' all de time. Evething passes sometime.
Come on, less us eat one of these taters—I'll peel you one.

ELLEN

(*Shaking her head.*)
You go on an' eat. I'd choke. Dem traders will be here at
sun up an' you knows they means to take me down de
river!

MANDY

(*Peeling and eating potato.*)
I'll finish dis coat for you. Now chile be sensible—life's
moughty sweet if it is bitter!

ELLEN

(*Agitatedly.*)
Oh, you don't know, you don't know what dey mean to make
out of me do you?

MANDY

(*Soothingly.*)
Yes I knows . . . Yo' prutty white face is yo' cuss. You's just
the spittin' image ov your daddy, ole Marse Charles.

ELLEN

I hate him! Hate him!

MANDY

Don't say dat. Don't say dat. He was good to you while he
was alivin'. Now ole Miss is takin' out her spite out on you
sendin' you down de river.

ELLEN

I hate her fur it. I'd ruther stay here an' work like a
dog in de field than go down de river.

MANDY

No honey, your hands too white fur field work. Dey makes
ladies outen sech as you.

ELLEN

(*Sarcastically.*)
Lady! Eugh!

MANDY

If you was black an' ugly you would sho' get along lots
better. Dem white debils!

ELLEN

(*Goes up to* MANDY *supplicatingly.*)
Don't you see I just got to get away tonight?

MANDY

(*Shaking her head.*)
Poor chile, you's just most plum crazy wid skeer but we's
all in the han's of de good Lord.
        (*As she speaks a sound is heard at the door.* WILLIAM
        enters hurriedly. ELLEN *flies to him and flings her-
        self into his arms crying.*)

ELLEN

Oh! William, Aunt Mandy says you can't go tonight.

WILLIAM

(*Excitedly.*)
Whut you mean?

MANDY

De white folks done found all about de underground.

WILLIAM

Who tole em?

MANDY

Dey caught Jack and Sophie las night an' whupped em till
dey tole all 'bout de secret plans an' meetin' places. Liza's
boy Bill overheered em frum de kitchen door whilse dey was
talkin' in de dinin' room. Dey said they want goin' to be no

more gol darn niggers runnin' away soon, said dey'd shoot
any nigger full o buck shot that sot foot nigh dat river
bottom.

WILLIAM

(*Putting his hand up to his face thoughtfully, then sinks
weakly into a chair and puts both hands up to his
face.* ELLEN *drags over to the fireplace and cries
hopelessly. There is a tense stillness in the cabin for
some minutes, then* WILLIAM *jumps to his feet snapping his finger.*)

I got it! I know whut I'll do!

ELLEN

(*Rushing over to him eagerly.*)

Whut, William, whut?

WILLIAM

(*Walking up and down excitedly.*)

If I kin get the things I needs we kin do it. I bet my life
on it.

MANDY

Whut tomfoolry you goin' to start, William? I done tole
you de white folks is spicious an' all de pateroles is out
tonight. You can't git away!

WILLIAM

You don't understand Aunt Mandy. I got to git Ellen away
from here tonight or I'll die a tryin'.

ELLEN

You right William. I'd rather be dead than stay here till
mornin', an' . . .

WILLIAM

(*Still nervously moving about.*)

If I kin jus git some things I need we kin steal cross de
corn fields an' ketch the north bound when she stops at de

flag station. I done it many o times wit young Marse Charles when we used to go up to Philadelphia.
(*Stops dead still.*)
But I got to git a suit of Master's clothes.

MANDY

Lord sakes. Whut you mindin' to do wid em?

WILLIAM
(*Speaking excitedly.*)
You see if I could git a suit of Master's clothes I could dress Ellen up like a white man an' I could go long an' be her slave. Jus like I done wid young Marse Charles.

MANDY

You crazy boy!

ELLEN

Oh, William, how could we do that?

WILLIAM

You see when I used to go off to school wit young Master I looked after eveything for him. That's why he learned me to read an' write an' figger. I knows how to do travelin'. I kin do it. I must do it, but I got to git de clothes.

ELLEN

But where?

WILLIAM

I kin steal em from de big house. I knows where all ole Marse clothes is hung up. I kin sneak in there . . .

ELLEN
(*Breaking in.*)
Oh William they might ketch you!

MANDY

That's mighty dangus.

WILLIAM

Can't hep it. Ellen can't stay here till mornin'. No matter whut happens I wunt let her!

ELLEN

(*Moaning.*)
Oh Lord, whut's goin to become ov me?

WILLIAM

(*Rising.*)
Stay wid her Aunt Mandy; I'm a goin to git a suit ov clothes from somewhere.

MANDY

I thinks youse plum crazy William runnin' way like white folks, you an' Ellen—if dey ketches you—um-m-mh!

WILLIAM

(*Moving toward the door.*)
Don't youall worry. I kin do it! I'm bleeged to do it. Young Marse used to say my head was too good for a nigger an' now I'm goin to try it out.

ELLEN

(*Moving toward door with* WILLIAM *solicitously.*)
Be keerful, William.

MANDY

(*Standing up hesitatingly, as if trying to make up her mind about something.*)
Wait, William, I lows you done gone plum crazy an' loss your mind doin' this here thing. But since you gwine go anyhow, I'll hep you! I got a suit!

WILLIAM

(*Turning back toward* MANDY *excitedly.*)
A suit! You is?

MANDY

Yes, I is.

WILLIAM

Oh Aunt Mandy, where ya got it?

MANDY

In my lof'. You see ole Miss din't wunt nothin' lef round here to put her in de mind of dat terrible time when young Masser died. She told me to burn up all his close 'cause you know he had dat ketchin' sickness.

WILLIAM

It sho is lucky fur us! You didn't burn nothin' 'tall?

MANDY

Nothin' 'tall. After I done washed an' laid out young Marse Charles I took evey stitch uv his close an' burned sulfur thru em in my hut . . .

WILLIAM

(*Interrupting, lowering his voice earnestly.*)
You ain't got his tall hat, is you?

MANDY

I sho is! Eben down to his walkin' stick.

WILLIAM

What a God send! Will—will you let Ellen wear em?

MANDY

Sho she kin, since you two goin' to play fool I kin do dis much to hep.

WILLIAM

(*Pulling* AUNT MANDY *up from chair.*)
Hurry Aunt Mandy! Go an' get em, an' we kin ketch dat north bound at dat crossin' in no time.

ELLEN

(*Moving over to* WILLIAM.)
I'm skeered, William, I'm sho skeered.

WILLIAM

Shucks, buck up! You don't want to be here in de mornin',
do you, when de slave traders come?

ELLEN

Oh, no, William, no. I'll go—I'll go.

WILLIAM

(*Urging* AUNT MANDY *toward the door.*)
Do hurry, Aunt Mandy!

MANDY

(*Going toward the door.*)
I'll be right back. Thase all right in my lof'.

WILLIAM

Put em in a quilt an' if anybody sees you tell em you com·
in' to do some quiltin' wid Ellen.

MANDY

(*Going out of the door.*)
Don't you worry—I'm er ole fox, I knows.

ELLEN

(*Going up to* WILLIAM *trembling.*)
You sho you kin git us through, William?

WILLIAM

Sho honey; ain't I been on the train time an' time agin
wid young Marse, an' can't I read and write?

ELLEN

But how kin I be like young Marse? I'm all a shakin' now.

WILLIAM

(*Soothing her.*)
All you got to do is to walk. You don't have to talk, you

don't have to do a thing but just walk along bigity like a white man. See here.

(Shows her how to walk.)

Try it.

ELLEN

(Tries to walk like him.)

Dis way?

WILLIAM

You doin fine! You see now you is supposed to be sick, you got a toothache, you goin' to a doctor in Philadelphia, you is nearly deaf, an' yo' nigger slave is takin' you—understand? Oh-o-o-.

ELLEN

What's wrong?

WILLIAM

Nothin' 'tall. Gimme yo' shears. I got to cut yo' hair. You see you is a man now.

ELLEN

(Despairingly.)

Oh my hair!

(She gets the scissors from the sewing basket, and brings them to him.)

WILLIAM

(Placing chair near table where the candle is lighted.)

Set here.

(He goes to shutter, makes sure it is tight, walks back to ELLEN, *who has let down her long hair.)*

I hates to cut yo' pretty hair, but . . .

ELLEN

(Resignedly.)

Anything is better than goin' down de ribber.

WILLIAM

(Takes a lock of hair to cut it when there is a sound of voices and footsteps outside of the door.)

Specks you better git behind the curtain, somebody might drop in.

ELLEN

Yes.

(*Rising.*)
That tale-tellin' Sam's got a way ov droppin' in here right free lak.

WILLIAM

That would be terrible! He'd be sho to git suspicious.

ELLEN

(*Halting as she raises the curtain.*)
If he do drap in whut we goin' to say? How we goin' to git him out?

WILLIAM

Oh, I'll say you sick—got a headache or something or other, an' gone to bed. I'll git a few horseredish leaves out of the garden an' lay one or two on de table to make it look natul like.

ELLEN

(*Entering into the spirit.*)
Yes, an' I'll put de coffee pot on some coals an' you kin say you makin' me some coffee to he'p me.

WILLIAM

You sho learn fass. You'se reel smart. I knows you'se goin' to make this trip perfect.

ELLEN

(*Beaming, moves toward the table as* WILLIAM *moves toward the door.*)
Hurry William!

WILLIAM

(*Going out of door.*)
Awright, honey, put on the coffee.

ELLEN

(Takes some water from the bucket with the gourd, puts it in the coffee pot, puts some coffee in it, sets it on some coals at the fireplace. Goes to the window, cracks it open a little, looks anxiously down the road and sighs. After a moment there is a soft scraping at the door, then MANDY *comes in with a big bundle tied up in a quilt.)*

Oh you got em!

MANDY

(Placing bundle on floor.)

Sho, where's William?

ELLEN

He's in de garden gittin' some horseridish so's if anybody draps in we can play lak I'm sick behind the curtain here.

MANDY

Dat's right! I'll put dese things behind the curtain too. You can't never tell—dere's many a slip.

WILLIAM

(Coming in with leaves. Puts them on table; saying breathless to MANDY. *)*

Got em?

MANDY

(Points.)

Sho, I put em behind the curtain.

WILLIAM

May the good Lord bless you, Aunt Mandy.

MANDY

Dat coffee smells good!

ELLEN

You drink some Aunt Mandy while William's cuttin' off

my hair over here behin' de curtain. We got to be careful now.

(ELLEN *goes behind curtain.*)

MANDY

You'se right! I clean forgot 'bout yo' hair. William sho got a good head on him.

WILLIAM

If anybody happens to drap in please git rid o' 'em, Auntie.
(*Takes scissors and follows* ELLEN *behind screen.*)

MANDY

Just leave it to me, I knows whut to do.
(*Pouring some coffee in a mug, tastes it.*)
Um-m-m, sho is good. Bof o' you better swallow a mug befo you starts tonight—it'll buck you up.

WILLIAM

(*From behind curtain.*)
You right, we sho will. Leave it where it'll keep hot.

ELLEN

(*From behind curtain.*)
Did you git some molasses for your coffee, Aunt Mandy?

MANDY

Yes, chile, I done sweetened it.

WILLIAM

(*Poking his head out from behind the curtain.*)
You sho done fine Aunt Mandy! Dese things sho fit! I'll hep Ellen git into de britches an' she kin do de ress.

MANDY

Dey ought to fit for she's just de size of her haf brother, Marse Charles.

ELLEN

(*From behind the curtain.*)
Don't talk about dat Aunt Mandy!

WILLIAM

(*Coming out and pouring himself a mug of coffee.*)
Well, dat's done.

MANDY

You got nuff money to git to Philadelphia?

WILLIAM

(*Snapping his finger.*)
Goodness! I jest recollect I got my money buried under a tomato bush in de garden. I'm goin' to dig it up.
(*Drinks down his coffee.*)

MANDY

It's high time!

WILLIAM

(*Goes to window, cracks shutter a little, peers into the darkness, then closes it.*)
We ain't got much more time to lose. Hurry Ellen!

ELLEN

(*From behind curtain.*)
I's mos' ready.

MANDY

It sho would be too bad if you'd miss dat train.

WILLIAM

We mos' ready to git out ov here now.

MANDY

I hope nothin' hinders you.

WILLIAM

Nothin' is a goin to.

ELLEN

(*Steps out from behind curtain dressed in a man's suit, tall silk hat, and a muffler, shrinkingly.*)

Oh, I feels terrible!

MANDY

(*Admiringly.*)

You looks just like Marse Charles. I would o' said you was him if I hadn't a laid him out myself.

WILLIAM

(*Standing up and looking her over critically, wrapping the scarf up around her face.*)

Like dis.

(*He then takes a large handkerchief from the pocket of the suit and pins it to her coat and puts one arm in it, explaining.*)

You see you can't write so I make out you got rheumatism; now you won't have to sign for nothin'.

MANDY

(*Admiringly.*)

You sho is smart, William.

ELLEN

(*Breathlessly.*)

Do you think we will make it, Aunt Mandy?

MANDY

I sho hopes so.

(*Sighs.*)

WILLIAM

(*To* ELLEN.)

Now take a mug of coffee, while I go out and dig up dat money out of de garden.

(*As he goes out of door, says.*)

Practice walkin' like a white man while I'm gone.

ELLEN

Awright, William.
(*Nervously.*)
You hurry.
(*Drinks coffee and walks up and down cabin, as* WIL-
LIAM *had shown her.*)

MANDY

(*Solicitously.*)
Got eveything in your valise?

ELLEN

I think I is.

MANDY

Let me see.
(*Gets valise from behind curtain, looks in it.   Says
um-m, then goes to cupboard.*)
I'll put a piece of dis here bread an' some herrin' in it
cause I hern tell you can't tell nothin' tall bout dem trains.
(*Fixes bread and herring and puts in valise while
ELLEN is stalking up and down the cabin practicing.*)
(*Listening.*)
Ain't dat somebody at de door?

ELLEN

'Taint William. Who dat?

MANDY

(*To* ELLEN.)
You git behind de curtain.
(*Then sets valise behind curtain quickly.*)   (*Louder.*)
Who dere?

VOICE

(*Outside.*)
It's me, Sam!

MANDY

(*To* ELLEN, *softly.*)
We better let him in.

ELLEN

(*Softly to* MANDY.)
Yes, but do get rid of him quick.

MANDY

(*Opening the door.*)
What you doin' runnin' up an' down the road worrin' sick
people fur tonight?

SAM

(*Coming in and looking around.*)
Who sick?

MANDY

Ellen. She got a terrable headache an' gone to bed.

SAM

Wher' William?

MANDY

Out in de garden.

SAM

Pretty time o night gardenin'.

WILLIAM

(*Entering rather upset and overhearing Sam's last re-
mark.*)
I'm a trying out a new secret on my tomatoes this year.
Everytime I gits a piece o' iron I buries it under em.
Makes em blood red an' big as your fist.

SAM

I never hearn o' that. I'm goin to watch yourn from now on.

WILLIAM

(*To* MANDY.)
How's Ellen feeling?

MANDY

I think she's 'bout to drap off to sleep.

WILLIAM

May be we had better change the poltis on her head. (*Takes up another horseradish leaf and bruises it.*)

MANDY
(*Softly.*)
You gimme I'll put it on er, then we better put out the light an' let er go to sleep.

SAM
(*Riled.*)
You all putin me out?

WILLIAM

No, we ain't, but Ellen a got to get up before day in de mornin' to do some work fur ole Miss an' she got to git some sleep tonight.

SAM
(*Slyly.*)
I been hern an' tell the traders was comin' tomorrow an' there was some talk about ole Miss a sendin' Ellen down the river.

MANDY

Don't you pay no 'tention to dem low lak niggers talkin'. 'Taint no such thing. Ole Miss ain't thunkin' about sendin' Ellen no wheres.

SAM
(*Rising slowly.*)
Well, tain't none o' my business, no how.
(*Slyly.*)
Kin I have a drink o' water fore I goes?

WILLIAM

Sho, take a gourd full.

(WILLIAM *moves toward the gourd but* SAM *wheels
suddenly and ducks toward the curtain, peeping behind it.* ELLEN *screams, then stifles it.*)

WILLIAM

You mangy dog!
(*Angrily.*)
What you mean by doin' dat?

SAM

(*Sneeringly.*)
So you is goin' to try to get away, is ya?
(*Moves toward the door.*)
Goin' to tell ole Miss goodbye?

WILLIAM

(*Excitedly.*)
What you goin' to do?

SAM

(*Snarlingly.*)
What you reckon, Mr. edicated nigger?

WILLIAM

(*Rushes to him and catches him about the throat.*)
So you is goin' to tell! Spyin' on us! I sho ya!

MANDY

(*Jumping up overturning her chair in excitement.*)
What you goin' to do, William?

WILLIAM

I'm a goin' to shut his mouth. Give me a piece er rag,
Mandy.

MANDY

(*Hunts around the cabin, finds a piece of cloth in the*

sewing basket and brings it to WILLIAM.)   (*Looking at* SAM.)
Dirty pup!

WILLIAM

(*Stuffs cloth into* SAM's *mouth, while he presses him down into a chair with his knees.*)   (*To* MANDY.)
Now git me Ellen's close line over there in the corner.

MANDY

(*Running to corner getting clothes line, bringing it to* WILLIAM *excitedly.*)
Lord, Jesus, hep us!

WILLIAM

(*Tying rope around* SAM's *arms with a loop knot.*)
(*To* MANDY.)
Peep out first, then open de door.
(*Takes* SAM *and drags him out of the door as* ELLEN *comes trembling from behind the curtain.*)

ELLEN

(*Crying.*)
What will we do now, Aunt Mandy?

MANDY

(*Shaking her head despondingly.*)
Things look mighty bad, honey, I dunno.
(*For a few minutes there is a strained silence in the cabin while the two women strain their ears listening for sounds outside.* ELLEN *nervously moves about the room, picking up things and putting them down.* AUNT MANDY *picks up* WILLIAM's *coat she has darned, shakes it.*)

MANDY

(*Head on one side listening outside.*)
Wonder what William is a doin' to Sam?

ELLEN

(*Tearfully.*)

I dunno. I don't wunt to know.

MANDY

He brung it on his self.

WILLIAM

(*Entering disheveled and brushing his hands on his trousers, speaking hoarsely.*)

Come on, Ellen, trains don't wait.

ELLEN

Oh, William! What ya done done?

MANDY

(*Holding* WILLIAM'S *coat for him to put on, as* WILLIAM *slips off his sweater.*)   (*To* ELLEN.)

Don' worry about dat now, it's too late!

WILLIAM

I'm sorry, Aunt Mandy, but I had to do what I done to kiver you cause he saw you here.

(*Just then a train whistle blew, all listen and move excitedly.*)

Come on, Ellen, we jes kin make it by takin' the short cut, walk in fron' o' me an' don't say nothin' tall to nobody. I'll do de talkin'. Keep you arm in de sling.

(*Breathlessly.*)

Goodbye, Aunt Mandy, goodbye.

MANDY

You ain't gone yet.

ELLEN

(*Whimpering, as she hesitates at door.*)

MANDY

(*To* ELLEN.)

Buck up, chile, white men don't cry!

WILLIAM

(*To* MANDY.)

I hope no harm don' come to you for this night's work, Aunt Mandy.

MANDY

(*Appreciatingly.*)

Huh! After I done suckled all ole Miss children, gone chile, I kin take ker myself.

WILLIAM

Well, goodbye, Aunt Mandy.

(*Kisses her.*)   (*To* ELLEN.)

You go first, Ellen. I'll walk behind you in de light but I'll walk wid you in de dark. Hurry!

ELLEN

(*Throws arms around* MANDY, *kisses her, then dashes out.*)

MANDY

God bless you, William.

MANDY

(*Closes door, goes to shutter, cracks it a little, and peers out. It is quiet for a few minutes. A train whistle is heard in the distance.* MANDY *drops down on her knees on the floor, while the candle sputters and goes out.*)

CURTAIN

SAFE (C. 1929)

GEORGIA DOUGLAS JOHNSON

CHARACTERS

LIZA PETTIGREW: *The Wife*
JOHN PETTIGREW: *The Husband*
MANDY GRIMES: *Liza's Mother*
DR. JENKINS: *Physician*
HANNAH WIGGINS: *Neighbor*

SETTING

PLACE: *Southern Town*
TIME: *1893*
SCENE: *Front room of Pettigrew home*

SCENE

Front room of a three room cottage. Back door leading to kitchen. Door to left leading to LIZA'S *room. A front door and a cot along the wall. A table and oil lamp, three chairs, baby garments, a basket of socks, newspapers, etc.*

SCENE OPENS: LIZA *is discovered sewing on some small white garments.* JOHN *is reading the evening paper by an oil lamp on the table.*

LIZA: (*lifting her voice*) Ma, come on outer that kitchen—jest stack up them supper dishes and come on and set down and rest, you hear?

MANDY: (*from kitchen*) All right, Liza, I'm coming out in a minute now.

LIZA: (*to* JOHN) Ma's been on her feet all day long. She don't know how to rest herself.

JOHN: (*absently*) Eughhu. She sho don't. (*continues reading*)

LIZA: (*calling again*) Come on, Ma.

MANDY: (*appearing in the kitchen doorway*) I hate to leave them dishes all dirty overnight, but if I must, I must. (*She looks about the room for something to do.*) I reckon I will jest mend John's socks while I'm setting here. (*She brings a basket with socks, needle and thread in it over near the table light with a chair.*)

LIZA: No, Ma, you lay down on your cot and stretch out a while and rest. First thing you know I'll be down and then you got to be up and around waiting on me—so rest while you kin.

MANDY: (*obediently putting up the sewing basket*) All right, honey. I'll stretch out a minute or so if you wants me to. (*She goes over to her cot against the wall and falls down heavily with a sigh upon it.*) My, this feels good to my old bones.

LIZA: Of course, it do—you're plum wore out; you done a sight of washing today.

MANDY: (*yawning*) Yes, I been going pretty steady today. What you making on now?

LIZA: Just hemming some little flannel belly bands. (*She holds up one for her mother to see.*) I got all the night gowns ready now. My time's pretty nigh near.

MANDY: Yes, it's jest about time—nine months I count it.

JOHN: (*lowering the paper*) Well, well, well. I see they done caught Sam Hosea and put him in jail.

MANDY: When they ketch him?

JOHN: Paper says this morning. I reckon his ma is plum crazy if she's heered they got him.

LIZA: I knows her. She's a little skinny brown-skinned woman. Belong to our church. She use to bring Sam along pretty regular all the time. He was a nice motherly sort of boy, not mor'n seventeen I'd say. Lemme see. 'Twant no woman mixed up in it, was it?

JOHN: No, seems like he and his boss had some sort of dispute about wages—the boss slapped him and Sam up and hit him back they says.

MANDY: Eugh eugh—that's mighty unhealthy sounding business for this part of the country. Hittin a white man, he better hadder made tracks far away from here I'm er thinking.

(*Just then there's a soft knock at the door.*)

JOHN: I wonder who that is.

LIZA: Go see!

(JOHN *goes to the door* HANNAH WIGGINS *enters*.)

JOHN: Howdy, Miss Wiggins, come in and take a cheer.

HANNAH: (*still standing and excited like*) Howdy! I jest thought I'd drop over here, being as Liza was so near her time and, and—

MANDY: (*sitting up on the cot*) Go on Hannah; what's the matter, you look all flusterated—what's up?

LIZA: Set down, Miss Hannah, there's a cheer.

HANNAH: (*sitting down on the edge of the chair uneasily*) I, I come over here to see how Liza was most special—then I wanted to see if yaw'll knowed about the trouble—

MANDY: Liza's fine. But what trouble is it you're talking 'bout? We ain't heered nothing 'tall!

JOHN: I saw in the papers they done caught Sam Hosea—we all thought he'd got out of town. I jest read 'bout it.

HANNAH: Yes, but that ain't all. (*Shakes her head.*)

LIZA: What else is it? Tell us!

HANNAH: (*looks around the room, again floundering*) You see I heered they done formed a mob downtown and it mout be there'll be hell to pay tonight!

JOHN: (*excitedly*) Who told you that?

HANNAH: Jim Brown told me 'bout it. He dropped in our house jest now and said as how things didn't look good at all downtown. So I thought I better run over and tell yaw'll.

JOHN: Ain't they gointer call out the soldiers, did he say?

HANNAH: No, he jest said the crowds was gathering and it didn't look good in town.

LIZA: (*in awed tones*) You don't reckon they'll take Sam out of the jail, do you, John?

JOHN: I don't know. (*He gets up and goes to the door.*) I think I'll step down the streets and see what they knows by Briggze's store.

MANDY: (*to* JOHN) You think you oughter go out?

LIZA: Be keerful and don't stay long.

JOHN: I'll be right back. Don't yaw'll worry. (*goes out.*)

LIZA: I been setting here thinking 'bout that poor boy Sam—him working hard to take kere of his widder mother, doing the best he kin, trying to be a man and stan up for hissef, and what do he git? A slap in the face.

HANNAH: Chile, that ain't nothing—if he gits off with a slap. These white folks is mad—mad—he done hit a white man back.

MANDY: They ain't gointer stan for it. I done seen it happen before.

LIZA: What's little nigger boys born for anyhow? I sho hopes mine will be a girl. I don't want no boy baby to be hounded down and kicked 'round. No, I don't want to ever have no boy chile!

MANDY: Hush, honey, that's a sin. God sends what he wants us to have—we can't pick and choose.

HANNAH: No, we sho can't. We got to swaller the bitter with the sweet.

(*Just then a shot is heard.*)

MANDY: (*jumping up*) What's that?

HANNAH: Sho sounded like a shot to me. I b'lieve them white folks is up to something this night.

LIZA: Listen, ain't that noise coming this a way?

HANNAH: It sho sounds like it. (*Goes over to the door, cracks it, peeps out and listens.*) They's coming—a big crowd headed this way.

MANDY: (*excitedly*) We better put out the light and pull that curtain way down.

HANNAH: Yes, that's right, you can't tell what them devils might git it in they heads to do.

(*There is an increasing sound.*)

LIZA: (*in awed tones*) They wouldn't come in here? Would they?

MANDY: (*consolingly*) No, they wouldn't, but then we better keep it dark.

(*Another shot rings out. The women jump and look at each other in fear.*)

LIZA: (*plaintively*) I wonder where John is—

MANDY: He oughter been back here before now. (*She goes to the window and peeps cautiously out from behind [the] shade.* HANNAH *follows and then* LIZA.)

HANNAH: You stay back, Liza. You oughtenter see sich things—not in your delicate state.

LIZA: But what they doing? Where they goin to?

MANDY: Yes, go back, Liza, and set down. Let us watch.

(*a confusion of many footsteps and tramping horses as the roar becomes louder*)

LIZA: (*beginning to walk up and down the room restlessly*) Ma, Ma, do you think they got him—do you think they'll hang him . . . ?

MANDY: (*patting* LIZA *on the shoulder*) I don't know. You try and kep quiet. You hadn't ought to hear all this screeching hell— God help you! (*goes back to window*)

HANNAH: She sho oughten. It's a sin and a shame! Coming right by here, too . . .

(*Then a voice rises above the men outside shouting, "Don't hang me, don't hang me! I don't want to die! Mother! Mother!"*)

LIZA: (*jumping up*) That's him! That's Sam! They got him. (*She runs to the door and looks out.* HANNAH *and* MANDY *follow her quickly and drag her back, shutting the door quickly.*)

MANDY: They'll shoot you! You can't do that! They're mad—mad!

LIZA: (*crumpling up on the chair shivering, her teeth chattering*) Oh my God, did you hear that poor boy crying for his mother? He's jest a boy—jest a boy—jest a little boy!

(*The roar outside continues*)

HANNAH: (*to* MANDY) This is mighty bad for her, mighty bad—

MANDY: (*looking at* LIZA *critically*) Yes, it sho is. (*She thinks a minute.*) I hates to ast you, but John ain't got back and we ought to git a doctor. Could you steal out the back and git him?

HANNAH: Yes, I'll go—I kin steal out the back ways.

MANDY: Better hurry, Hannah. I don't like the looks of her.

(HANNAH *goes out through back.*)

LIZA: (*continues to shiver and shake*) Oh, where is John? Where is John? What you reckon has happened? Oh, that poor boy— poor little nigger boy!

MANDY: Try not to worry so, honey. We's in the Lord's hands. (*shaking her head*) My poor, poor chile. I'll heat a kettle of water, then I'm gointer fix your bed so you can lay down when you feel like it.

(*Hoarse laughter is heard outside as the noise grows less and less.* MANDY *goes into small bedroom adjoining [the] kitchen for a moment, then comes back, looks at* LIZA, *shakes her head. Then* LIZA *begins walking up and down the floor all doubled over as if in pain. She goes to the window occasionally and looks out from behind the shade. The noise of the countless passing feet are heard and an occasional curse or laugh. She trembles slightly every time she looks and begins pacing up and down again*)

SAFE

MANDY: (*coming over from the bedroom*) Come on and lay down now, chile; the doctor'll be here to reckly. I'll git all your little things together for you. (*goes over and begins to gather up the little white garments* LIZA. *had been sewing on*)

LIZA: (*stands stooped over in the opening of her bedroom door*) Did you hear him cry for his mother? Did you?

MANDY: Yes, honey chile, I heard him, but you musn't think about that now. Fergit it. Remember your own little baby—you got him to think about You got to born him safe!

LIZA: (*looks at* MANDY *wild-eyed*) What you say?

MANDY: Born him safe! Born him safe! That's what you got to do.

LIZA: (*turning her head from side to side as she stands half stooped in the doorway. She repeats.*) Born him safe! . . . Safe . . . (*She hysterically disappears into the next room.*)

MANDY: (*sighs and continues picking up the little garments, smoothing them out nervously. Just then the door opens and* JOHN *enters.*) Oh, where you been, John? Why didn't you come back before now?

JOHN: I tried to but I got headed off—they come right by here too. It was terrible, terrible . . . Where's she?

MANDY: In the room I done sent fur the Doctor; he'll be here any minute.

JOHN: (*nervously going toward* LIZA'*s bedroom*) I'll go in and see her. Poor little LIZA. (*enters room*)

MANDY: (*goes to the window and peers out and listens as scattering footsteps sound outside on the sidewalk. Then she busies herself about the room, turns down her bed, lights the lamp and turns it down low. Just then there is a knock at the kitchen door Calling*) John! John! (JOHN *comes to the door.*) See if that ain't Hannah at the back door with the Doctor.

JOHN: (*hurrying*) All right. (*He goes through the kitchen and returns with* THE DOCTOR.)

MANDY: I'm sho glad you come, Doctor; she's right in there. Please hurry.

DR. JENKINS: (*to* MANDY) Get me some hot water.

MANDY: I got it ready for you, John, git the kettle! (JOHN *goes in kitchen.*) She's terrible upset, Doctor, terrible . . .

DR. JENKINS: I know—Hannah told me all about it; she stopped at her house a minute or two, but said tell you she'd be here to help.

JOHN: (*returning with kettle*) Here 'tis.

MANDY: Set it in the room.

(THE DOCTOR *goes into the room with his bag and* JOHN *comes out.*)

MANDY: How is she?

JOHN: Mighty upset.

MANDY: She ain't never seen no lynching not before, and it was terrible—her being so nigh her time too.

JOHN: Do you think she'll git through all right?

MANDY: I pray God she do. But she's shook to pieces.

JOHN: I oughter been here myself, but I didn't know I was gointer be cut off.

MANDY: Course you didn't. We's all in the hands of the Lawd.

JOHN: (*drops his hands helplessly on his knees*) What a terrible night.

MANDY: I wish Hannah would come on back. I'm that nervish.

JOHN: She was right brave to go for the Doctor.

MANDY: Want she?

(*Just then a baby's cry is heard from the next room and both of them jump up and look toward the closed door. They take a step forward and wait.*)

JOHN: You reckon she's all right?

MANDY: I hope so, but . . .

JOHN: But what?

MANDY: I don't know zactly; I never did see her look like she looked tonight.

JOHN: (*groaning*) I wish the Lord this night was over.

MANDY: God knows I do too—my poor, poor chile.

(*They waited for what seemed like an eternity listening to the muffled sounds in the next room. Then* THE DOCTOR *appears at the door, closing it behind him. His face looks distressed. Nervously*)

MANDY: How is she? Can I go in?

JOHN: (*agitatedly*) How is she, Doc?

DR. JENKINS: (*holding up one hand*) Wait a minute, calm yourselves. I've got something to tell you, and I don't hardly know how . . .

MANDY: (*bursting into tears*) She ain't dead, is she? Doc, my poor chile ain't dead?

JOHN: (*biting his lips*) Tell us, Doc, tell us! What is it?

DR. JENKINS: She's all right and the baby was born all right—big and fine. You heard him cry . . .

JOHN: Yes . . .

MANDY: Yes, we heard.

DR. JENKINS: And she asked me right away, "Is it a girl?"

JOHN, MANDY: (*stretching their necks out further to listen*) Yes, yes, Doc! Go on!

DR. JENKINS: And I said, "No child, it's a fine boy," and then I turned my back a minute to wash my hands in the basin. When I looked around again she had her hands about the baby's throat choking it. I tried to stop her, but its little tongue was already hanging from its mouth. It was dead! Then she began, she kept muttering over and over again: "Now he's safe—safe from the lynchers! Safe!"

(JOHN *falls down on a chair sobbing, his face in his hands, as* MANDY, *stooped with misery, drags her feet heavily toward the closed door. She opens it, softly and goes in.* THE DOCTOR *stands, a picture of helplessness as he looks at them in their grief.*)

[*CURTAIN.*]

A SUNDAY MORNING IN THE SOUTH

CHARACTERS

SUE JONES: *the grandmother, aged seventy*
TOM GRIGGS: *her grandson, aged nine-teen*
BOSSIE GRIGGS: *her grandson, aged seven*
LIZA TRIGGS: *a friend, aged sixty*
MATILDA BROWN: *a friend, aged fifty*
A WHITE GIRL
FIRST OFFICER
SECOND OFFICER
PLACE: *A town in the South.*
TIME: *1924.*

(SCENE Kitchen in SUE JONES' *two room house. A window on left, a door leading to back yard and another leading to front room. A stove against the back wall, a table near it, four chairs, an old time safe with dishes and two bottles—one clear and one dark—a wooden water bucket with shiny brass bales, and a tin dipper hanging near it on a nail.*

As the curtain rises SUE JONES *is seen putting the breakfast on the kitchen table. She wears a red bandanna handkerchief on her grey head, a big blue gingham apron tied around her waist and big wide old lady comfort shoes. She uses a stick as she has a sore leg, and moves about with a stoop and a limp as she goes back and forth from the stove to the table)*

SUE *(calling)* Tom, Tom, you and Bossie better come on out here and git your breakfast before it gits cold; I got good hot rolls this mornin!

TOM *(from next room)* All right grannie, we're coming.

SUE You better ef you know whut's good for you (*opens stove door, looks at rolls, then begins humming and singing*)

> Eugh . . . eu . . . eugh . . .
> Jes look at the morning star
> Eugh . . . eu . . . eugh . . .
> We'll all git home bye and bye . . .

(*as she finishes the song* TOM *and* BOSSIE *come hurrying into the kitchen placing their chairs at the table; there is one already at the table for* SUE. SUE *takes rolls out of stove with her apron and brings them to the table*) It's as hard to git yawll out of the bed on Sunday morning as it is to pull hen's teeth.

TOM (*eating. The Church bell next door is heard ringing*) Eugh— there's the church bell. I sho meant to git out to meeting this morning but my back still hurts me. Remember I told you last night how I sprained it lifting them heavy boxes for Mr. John?

SUE (*giving* BOSSIE *a roll and a piece of sausage*) You hadn't oughter done it; you oughter ast him to let somebody hep you— you aint no hoss!

TOM I reckin I oughter had but I didn't know how heavy they was till I started and then he was gone.

SUE You oughter had some of my snake oil linament on it last night, that's whut?

TOM I wish I hader but I was so dead tired I got outer my clothes and went straight to bed. I muster been sleep by nine er clock I reckin.

SUE Nine er clock! You is crazy! Twant no moren eight when I called you to go to the store and git me a east cake fur my light rolls and you was sleeping like a log of wood; I had to send Bossie fur it.

BOSSIE Yes, and you snored so loud I thought you would a chocked. (*holding out his plate and licking his lips with his tongue*) Grannie kin I have some more?

SUE Whut? Where is all thot I jest give you?

BOSSIE (*rubbing his stomach with his other hand and smiling broadly*) It's gone down the red lane struttin'.

SUE Well this is all you gointer git this mornin. (*helping him to more rolls and sausage*) When you git big and work like Tom you kin stuff all you wants to.

BOSSIE I aint never gointer break my back like Tom working hard—
I'm a gointer be a—a preacher that's whut and . . .

SUE (*catching sight of someone passing the window as she
approached the back door*) I bleve that's Liza Twiggs must be
on her way to church and smelled these light rolls and coffee.
(*a knock is heard at the back door*) Let her in, Bossie!

(BOSSIE *jumps up from the table, hurries to the door and opens
it*)

LIZA (*enters sniffling*) Mawning yawll.

SUE Morning Liza—on your way to church?

LIZA Yes the first bell just rung and I thought I'd drop in a minute.
(*whiffs again*) Coffee sho smells good!

SUE Tastes better'n it smells—Pull up a cheer and swaller a cupful
with one of these light rolls.

LIZA (*drawing up a chair*) Dont keer if I do. (*she is helped to coffee and rolls while* BOSSIE *looks at her disapprovingly. To* SUE)
How is your leg gitting on?

SUE Well as I kin expect. I won't never walk on it good no mo. It
eats and eats. She is lucky I'm right here next door to church
(*to* TOM) Open that winder Tom so I kin hear the singing. (TOM
opens window. To LIZA) Folks don't like to set next to me in
church no mo. Tinks its ketching—a cancer or somethin': (*then
brightly*) Whut you know good?

(*From the church next door is heard the hymn drifting through
the window:* "Amazing grace how sweet the sound / That saves a
wretch like me . . .")

LIZA (*listening*) They done started "Amazing grace." (*music continues as a background for their talk*) (*still eating*) That music
she is sweet but I got to finish eatin first, then I'll go . . .

SUE I ast you whut you know good.

LIZA Well, I don't know nothin tall good, but I did hear as how the
police is all over now trying to run down some po Nigger they
say that's tacked a white woman last night right up here near
the Pine Street market. They says as how the white folks is
shonuff mad too, and if they ketch him they gointer make short
work of him.

SUE (*still drinking coffee*) Eugh, eugh, eugh, you don't say. I don't
hold wid no rascality and I bleves in meeting out punishment to
the guilty but they fust ought to fine out who done it tho and
then let the law hanel 'em. That's what I says.

LIZA Me too. I thinks the law oughter hanel 'em too, but you know a sight of times they gits the wrong man and goes and strings him up and don't fin out who done it till it's too late!

SUE That's so. And sometimes the white uns been knowcd to blackin they faces and make you bleve some po Nigger done it.

TOM They lynch you bout anything too, not jest women. They say Zeb Brooks was strung up because he and his boss had er argiment.

LIZA Sho did. I says the law's the law and it ought er be er ark uv safty to perfect the weak and not some little old flimsy shack that a puff of wind can blow down.

TOM I been thinking a whole lot about these things and I mean to go to night school and git a little book learning so as I can do something to help—help change the laws . . . make em strong . . . I sometimes get right upset and wonder whut would I do if they ever tried to put something on me . . .

LIZA Pshaw . . . everybody knows you . . . nobody would bother you . . .

SUE No sonnie, you won't never hafter worry bout sich like that but you kin hep to save them po devels that they do git after. (*Singing comes from the church next door*:

>Shine on me, shine on me.
>Let the light from the lighthouse shine on me,
>Shine on me, shine on me,
>Let the light from the lighthouse shine on me.

TOM It takes a sight of learning to understand the law and I'm a gointer . . . (*a quick rap is heard at the door and it is almost immediately pushed open and an* OFFICER *enters as the four at table look up at him in open mouthed amazement*)

FIRST OFFICER Tom Griggs live here?

SUE (*starting up excitedly*) Yes Sir (*stammering*)

FIRST OFFICER (*looking at* TOM) You Tom Griggs?

TOM (*puzzled*) Yes sir.

FIRST OFFICER (*roughly*) Where were you last night at ten o'clock?

SUE (*answering quickly for* TOM) Right here sir, he was right here at home. Whut you want to know fer?

FIRST OFFICER (*to* SUE) You keep quiet, old woman. (*to* TOM) Say, you answer up. Can't you talk? Where were you last night at ten o'clock.

TOM (*uneasily*) Gramma told you. I was right here at home—in bed at eight o'clock.

FIRST OFFICER That sounds fishy to me—in bed at eight o'clock! And who else knows you were here?

SUE Say Mr. Officer, whut you trying to do to my granson. Shore as God Amighty is up in them heabens he was right here in bed. I seed him and his little brother Bossie there saw him, didn't you Bossie?

BOSSIE (*in a frightened whisper*) Yessum, I seed him and I heered him!

FIRST OFFICER (*to* BOSSIE) Shut up. Your word's nothing, (*looking at* SUE) Not yours either. Both of you'd lie for him. (*steps to back door and makes a sign to someone outside, then comes back into the room taking a piece of paper from his vest pocket and reads slowly, looking at* TOM *critically as he checks each item*) Age around twenty, five feet five or six, brown skin . . . (*he folds up the paper and puts it back into his vest*) Yep! fits like a glove. (SUE, LIZA *and* TOM *look from one to the other with growing amazement and terror as* SECOND OFFICER *pushes open the door and stands there supporting a young white girl on his arm*)

SECOND OFFICER (*to girl*) Is this the man?

WHITE GIRL (*hesitatingly* I—I'm not sure . . . but . . . but he looks something like him . . . (*holding back*)

FIRST OFFICER (*encouragingly*) Take a good look, Miss. He fits your description perfect. Color, size, age, everything. Pine Street Market ain't no where from here, and he surely did pass that way last night. He was there all right, all right! We got it figgered all out. (*to* GIRL, *who looks down at her feet*) You say he looks like him?

WHITE GIRL (*looking at him again quickly*) Y-e-s (*slowly and undecidedly*) I think so. I . . . I . . . (*then she covers her face with her arm and turns quickly and moves away from the door, supported by* SECOND OFFICER. FIRST OFFICER *makes a step toward* TOM *and slips handcuffs on him before any one is aware what is happening*)

SUE (*holding on to her chair and shaking her cane at the* OFFICER, *while* BOSSIE *comes up close to her and snivels in her apron*) Whut you doing? What you doing? You can't rest my granson— he ain't done nothing—you can't rest him!

FIRST OFFICER Be quiet, old woman. I'm just going to take him along to the sheriff to question him and if he's telling the truth he'll be right back home here in no time.

SUE But you can't rest him; he don't know no mo bout that po little white chile than I do—You can't take him!

TOM (*utterly bewildered*) Granma, don't take on so. I'll go long with him to the sheriff. I'll splain to him how I couldn't a done it when I was here sleep all the time—I never laid eyes on that white lady before in all my life.

SUE (*to* TOM) Course you ain't. (*to* OFFICER) Mr. Officer, that white chile ain't never seed my granson before—All Niggers looks alike to her; she so upset she don't know whut she's saying.

FIRST OFFICER (*to* SUE *as he pulls* TOM *along*) You just keep cool Grannie, he'll be right back—if he's innocent. (*to* TOM) And the quieter you comes along the better it will be for you.

TOM (*looking back at his grandma from the doorway with terror in his eyes*) I'll be right back granny—don't cry—don't cry—Jest as soon as I see—(*the* OFFICER *pulls him out of the doorway*)

LIZA (*standing with her hands clasped together, her head bowed and swaying from side to side with emotion. She prays*) Sweet Jesus, do come down and hep us this mornin. You knows our hearts and you knows this po boy ain't done nothing wrong. You said you would hep the fatherless and the motherless; do Jesus bring this po orphan back to his ole cripple grannie safe and sound, do Jesus!

BOSSIE (*crying and pulling at his grandma's apron*) Grannie, grannie, whut they gointer do to my brother? Whut they gointer do to him?

SUE (*brokenly*) The good Jesus only knows, but I'm a talking to the Lord now asting Him to . . . (*a rap is heard at the door; it is almost immediately pushed open and* MATILDA BROWN *enters hurriedly and excitedly*)

MATILDA (*breathlessly*) Miss Liza, as I was coming long I seed Tom wid the police and there was some white mens wid guns a trying to take him away from the police—said he'd done been dentified and they want gointer be cheated outen they Nigger this time. I, I flew on down here to tell you, you better do somethin'.

SUE (*shaking nervously from side to side as she leans on her cane for support*) Oh my God, whut kin I do?

LIZA (*alertly*) You got to git word to some of your good white folks, that's whut and git em to save him.

SUE Yes ... That's whut ... Lemme see ... (*she stands tense thinking a moment*) I got it ... Miss Vilet ... I got to git to Miss Vilet ... I nused her when she was a baby and she'll do it . . . Her pa's the Jedge.

LIZA That's right! I'll go. You can't go quick.

MATILDA No. Lemme go; I kin move in a hurry, lemme go!

SUE All right Tildy. Tell Miss Vilet her ole nuse Sue is callin on her and don't fail me; tell her they done took Tom and he is perfect innercent, and they gointer take him away from the police, and ax her to ax her pa the Jedge to go git Tom and save him fur God's sake. Now hurry, Tildy, fly!

BOSSIE (*to* SUE) Lemme go long; I knows how to git there quick cutting through the ole field.

LIZA Yes they knows Bossie and he kin hep tell.

SUE Yes Bossie, gone, yawll hurry, hurry! (MATILDA *and* BOSSIE *hurry out of the back door and* SUE *sinks down into a chair exhausted while* LIZA *comes over to her and pats her on the back*)

LIZA Now, now evrything's gointer be all right ... Miss Vilet 'll fix it ... she ain't gointer let her ole mammy call on her for nothing ... she'll make her pa save him.

SUE Yes, she's a good chile ... I knows she'll save him.

(SUE *moves her lips in prayer. From the church next door comes the sound of singing; the two women listen to the words with emotion*

> *Alas and did my savior bleed*
> *And did my sovereign die*
> *Would he devote his sacred head*
> *For such a worm as I.*
> *Must Jesus bear the cross alone*
> *And all the world go free,*
> *No, there's a cross for every one*
> *And there's a cross for me.*

SUE *rocks back and forth in chair, head buried in her apron.* LIZA *walks up and down the floor, throws her hands up imploringly now and then*)

LIZA Oh Lord, hep us to bear our cross! Hep us!

SUE (*drooping*) Liza. I'm feeling sorter fainty lack; git me my bottle of camphor out of the safe yonder.

LIZA (*going to safe*) Yes chile, I'll git it. You done gone through a whole lot this mornin, God knows. (*takes up a bottle and holds it up for* SUE *to see*) This it?

SUE (*shaking her head*) Eugh eugh, that's my sweet oil. It's the yuther one in the black bottle . . . see it?

LIZA (*taking out bottle and smelling it*) Yes here it is. Strong too. It'll do you good. I has them sinking spells too sometimes (*comes over to* SUE *with stopper out of bottle and holds it to her nose*) There draw a deep bref of it; feel better?

SUE I'll feel better tereckly. My old heart is gittin weak.

LIZA Set back comfortable in your cheer and listen to the singin; they all sho talkin to the Lord fur you in that church this mornin. Listen!

(*The church is singing*):

> I must tell Jesus, I cannot bear my burdens alone
> In my distress he surely will help me
> I cannot bear my burdens alone.
> I must tell Jesus, I cannot bear my burdens alone
> Jesus my Lord he surely will help me
> Jesus will help me, Jesus alone

LIZA That's all, that's all we kin do jes tell Jesus! Jesus! Jesus please bow down your ear! (*walks up and down mumbling a soft prayer as the singing continues mournfully*)

SUE I reckin Tildy's bout on her way back now. I knows Miss Vilet done got her pa by now, don't you reckin, Liza.

LIZA (*sympathetically*) Course; I spects Tom'll be coming back too any minit now. Everybody knows he ain't done no harm.

SUE (*listening to running feet at the door and sitting up straight in chair*) Who dat coming? (MATILDA *pushes open the door and comes in all excited and panting while* BOSSIE *follows her crying*) Whut's the matter? Didn't you find Miss Vilet?

MATILDA (*reluctantly*) It want no use.

SUE No use?

LIZA Whut you mean?

MATILDA I mean—I mean—

LIZA For God's sake Tildy, whut's happened?

MATILDA They—they done lynched him.

SUE (*screams*) Jesus! (*gasps and falls limp in her chair. Singing from church begins.* BOSSIE *runs to her, crying afresh.* LIZA *puts the camphor bottle to her nose again as* MATILDA *feels her heart; they work over her a few minutes, shake their heads and with drooping shoulders, wring their hands. While this action takes place the words of this song pour forth from church*:

> Lord have mercy.
> Lord have mercy,
> Lord have mercy over me.

Sung first time with words and repeated in a low hum as curtain slowly falls)

Starting Point

ONE ACT PLAY IN
3 SCENES

CHARACTERS

FATHER: *Henry Robinson*
SON: *Tom Robinson*
MOTHER: *Martha Robinson*
GIRL: *Belle*
Place: *Charleston, S.C.*
Props: *Kitchen table—stove—cabinet—5 chairs—dishes—food for meal.*

SCENE OPENS

Martha discovered laying table for dinner—takes a letter from apron pocket and with a pleased expression places it under her husband's plate.
(Henry Robinson enters, stage right)

ROBINSON: *(Walks over to his wife and kisses her lightly on the cheek)* Hello Martha—How you feeling?

MARTHA: Oh—a little tired Henry, but I've had good news today.

ROBINSON: Good news, what kind of good news?

MARTHA: It'll wait—eat your supper first—I know you're tired and hungry after being on your feet all day long at the beck and call of Tom, Dick and Harry.

ROBINSON: You're mighty right—my feet seem like they don't belong to me a tall they're that tired—Let me get my slippers— *(Goes off stage left)*

(Martha puts food on table)

ROBINSON: *(reenters—sits down at head of table and asks blessing—They begin to eat—)*

MARTHA: How's things at the bank today?

ROBINSON: Well, there's been a whole lot of howdy do down there today over Jim Boyd's son Toby—you know, from in Cat fish row—seem like he's been writing numbers for the white folks round the bank, and them fedral investigators caught him red-handed.

MARTHA: You don't say—Poor Jim—I know he's all broke up—he set such store on that boy of his—Suppose there's anything we do to help em out?

ROBINSON: I don't know, I'll ask him tomorrow. We got a lot to be thankful for our son's doing so fine up there in the doctor's school in Washington.

MARTHA: It sure is—it won't be long now before he gets his doctor's license—Euhm hum *(she smiles)*

ROBINSON: I can see him now going about from house to house.

MARTHA: Doctoring sick folks now! My but I'll be proud!

ROBINSON: Proud's no name for it. Thank God he's got a fine profession and won't have to set at no white man's door and fetching and carrying all his life like me.

MARTHA: Yes, and he'll make a lot of money and help you like you helped him.

ROBINSON: Sure he'll want to. Fine boy—but I don't need him to help me—I an get along alright—, I just want him to be a man and stand up on his own two feet, that's all—be a real man!

MARTHA: *(Gets up, lifts up Henry's plate and discloses letter underneath—)* Here's your surprise Henry read it! *(proudly)*

ROBINSON: *(Takes letter and looks at it quizzingly)*

MARTHA: Read it out loud.

ROBINSON: *(Reading)* Dear mother and dad: I'm coming for a day or two. Will be there almost as soon as this letter. Have a surprise for you. Your loving son, Tom

ROBINSON: I wonder what's bringing him home.

MARTHA: I wonder what the surprise is.

ROBINSON: School's not through yet—

MARTHA: Maybe he's got his license already—maybe that's the surprise.

ROBINSON: *(Scratching his head)* I don't believe that's it—It's something else.

MARTHA: Go long Henry you know—Tom's a smart boy—Why couldn't they give it to him already.

ROBINSON: Maybe they might, but it seems like to me that's too good to be true. *(They hear a voice from outside calling, "Dad, mother, Dad".)*

(The two look at each other startled)

MARTHA: *(Excitedly)* Oh my lands Henry—here we've been talking ourselves to death and here's the child already. Go see.

(Henry goes out stage right)

(Martha bustles about kitchen—snatching off her apron and smoothing her hair)

(Noise of greeting in yard come faintly into the kitchen.)

(Martha listens perplexedly, then draws back upon noting the dazed expression on her husband's face—as he reenters.)

ROBINSON: *(Walks toward Martha and puts his arm tenderly around her shoulder as Tom and Belle follow upon his heels.)*

TOM: Mother! *(dashes over and kisses her.)*

MARTHA: My little boy—my son—my! *(then notices the girl just behind Tom's shoulder. She stops short again as Tom leaves her, approaches the girl and leads her back to his mother.)*

TOM: My surprise, Mother, your new daughter Belle—!

MARTHA: *(Staggered—swallows as tho trying to collect herself then putting out her arms slowoly embraces the girl, then faintly)* Belle—welcome. My, but I'm glad to see you. I'm so surprised—I don't know what to say.—I, I, thought maybe you———

TOM: Don't worry little mother—*(fondles her)* I'm o.k.

MARTHA: But—Well supposin you go upstairs children a little while—you must be dead beat out, riding on the train all that way.

TOM: Oh, we're not tired mother. How about a little snack *(goes over to the stove and peers in the pots.)* What you got to eat?

MARTHA: You go long Tom and take Belle to wash up, she's dusty I know. I'll fix you'all something and call you in no time.

BELLE: Don't bother about me—I'm not hungry and you oughtn't put your mother out either Tom after all the hot dogs you ate on the train.

TOM: *(Takes the hint from Belle)* Come to think of it I'm not hungry—a bit [I bet] it's just the smell of ma's good cooking and bein home, I guess that's what I was hungering after. My stomach and my heart is both full—Now I got you too.

TOM: Come on up, Belle, and wash up. *(As Tom and Belle exit— The father looks in blank amazement toward the door they passed through, turns his gaze from the door to Martha—then wearily drags himself to the table and falls down limply into a chair—his head falling on his outstretched arms. Martha walks over quietly to him, leans over him tenderly and pats him on the shoulders.)*

END OF SCENE I

SCENE 2

(An hour later)
Same Scene—Table is cleared. Father and Mother are seated at the table. Father is playing a game of solitaire and Mother darning a pair of socks—looking up furtively now and then at herr husband who holds one card looking at it as if he had forgotten where to put it.

TOM: *(Hurries in from stage left. Coat off, collar open)* Gee its great to be home. Same old place—Same old kitchen.

MARTHA: *(Smiling)* Its good to see you too son.

TOM: It sure was sweet of you take Belle right in, but I knew you would.

ROBINSON: *(grunts)* Eughn.

MARTHA: Well son—your happiness is our happiness. Tho we did think maybe you'd get your license. We thought that was the surprise you had for us.

TOM: Well you see Mother—*(Belle's voice is heard in a popular blues song off stage. All three lift their heads with varying expressions. Father and Mother taken aback look askance at each other because of the type of song and rowdy music.)*

TOM: *(proudly)* That girl's a wow! She sure can sing. Knocked em cold in Washington! *(continues with broken speech)* Well as I was saying. It's like this. They're as tricky as can be at these schools. Always trying to put stumbling blocks in your path and making you go through a lot of red tape. I won't finish this year after all.

397

(Belle who has caught the last few [words] *of his sentence as she hesitates for a minute in the doorway stage left.)*

TOM: You see *(haltingly as he looks at Belle)* I won't get my medical degree until next year.

BELLE: What kind of cock and bull story is that that you're pulling on your folks, Tom.

(Father and Mother look from Belle to Tom wonderingly)

ROBINSON: What does she mean, Tom?

BELLE: I mean *(Tom looks at her imploringly)* Tom's not in school.

MARTHA: *(aghast)* Not in school!

BELLE: No, he's not in school.

ROBINSON: *(looking from Belle to Tom)* What do you mean not in school?

BELLE: Come on, Tom, make a clean breast of it. Tell them the truth.

TOM: *(Sheepishly)* Well—No father I had to have some money, I couldn't ask you or ma for any more—so—Well I had to get busy.

ROBINSON: Busy! Busy doing what?

TOM: *(Hesitatingly)* Well

BELLE: For God's sake be honest. Tell em. They've a right to know. *(Pauses as she waits for Tom to speak.)* He's in the number racket.

ROBINSON: My God!

MARTHA: *(whispers)* My son!

TOM: Well I had to do something.

MARTHA: You should have told us—we would have helped you.

ROBINSON: What a mess—what a mess. *(Knock is heard at door)*

TOM: *(goes to front door through entrance stage right)*

MARTHA: *(absently)* I wonder who's that knocking so sharp this time of night.

ROBINSON: *(Mechanically)* I don't know.

TOM: *(reenters with a telegram in his hand)*

MARTHA: A telegram! Who's it for?

TOM: *(Who's torn it open with a quick jerk and is now reading it with a worried expression)*

BELLE: What is it Tom?

ROBINSON: Yes what is it?

TOM: *(Flicking the telegram with one hand and then quickly jabbing it into his pocket.)* Oh it's nothing. Just a little line from a friend in Washington.

BELLE: Quit stalling Tom—Come clean——You've got bad news—Spill it.

ROBINSON: Yes what is it. I demand to know.

MARTHA: Now Henry, Don't be harsh with the boy. What is it son?

BELLE: *(Going up to him)* Here give it to me Tom. If you won't say what's in it I'll find out for myself.

TOM: *(reluctantly drags telegram from his pocket) (reads)* "you're [Your]—place raided. Town's hot. Don't come back."
(Looks of consternation pass between mother and father.)

BELLE: *(Belle stands knitting her brow—arms a-kimbo.)* Well that's that. What's the next move?

TOM: Oh it'll blow over—we've been in jams before—we can go back under cover when this has all quieted down.

BELLE: Oh, no we don't either. I told you before if this happened again either go straight now or never. *(Looks at parents)* I'm sorry, I know its tough on you but we've got to face it. Looks like he'll have to stay here.

TOM: *(Heatedly)* Now wait a minute Belle. I've been man enough to make my own decisions up to now. You shut your mouth. I'll decide what I'm going to do and I'm to stay in this dead hole—There's other fields for a smart fellow like me. I can go to New York, Chicago, Pittsburgh—

BELLE: *(shouting)* Oh no you won't over my dead body. You've been cock of the roast too long now. You've got to take low. *(pleadingly)* Please Tom, you know it's the toughest game in the world you can't beat it.

TOM: I been beating it—Nobody's going to tell me what to do.

ROBINSON: Oh yes they are—-You listen to me boy—-You've had your way long enough. You've fooled your mother and me up till now. But by God I'm going to have my say and your going to do as I say if I have to thrash you to bring you to your senses.

TOM: Who in the Hell do think you are? You're only my father, you're not God. *(Father rushes at Tom and slaps him)*

MARTHA: Henry!—Tom! *(Faints)*

399

SCENE 3

Same Scene
Next morning early
Scene opens with Belle and Tom entering kitchen

BELLE: *(continuing argument that evidently has been going on all night)* I don't understand how you can't see it Tom. It's plain as the nose on your face. You can't go back. You've got to start anew and from scratch.

TOM: Scratch! Why I got enough now to buy up everybody in this little burg!

BELLE: Got! — What you got? A car—a few dollars and a few suits of clothes, that's what you've got and that don't amount to a hill of beans!

TOM: That's what you say . . . But I got mother wit and that's worth a million dollars!

BELLE: Humph—-That's what all hustlers think and where do they wind up, behind the bars. The easy way is the hardest way and after all's said and done it don't pan out the way you want it to. You've already found that out, Tom. So don't be a sucker. After all what kind of sport are you. You always prided yourself on the fact that everyone said you were one of the squarest shooters in the game. Well what about it—here you have two of the finest folks in the world. How about giving them a break? What about what you owe them? You've taken everything and given them nothing... They bet on you and you failed them. Don't you see Tom you've got to square yourself.

TOM: Square myself for what? I didn't ask to be born.

BELLE: So you are a heel. You've only been a big bluff, a whole lot of wind. I drew the booby prize for a husband. *(She walks away from him, walks over to the stove lights a cigarette as Father comes in with Mother leaning weakly on his arm. He seats her at the table.)*

MARTHA: Good morning, son . . . Good morning, Belle.

ROBINSON: Morning, Belle

MARTHA: Did you sleep well children . . . seems like to me you were up pretty late.

BELLE: I hope we didn't keep you awake. I've got some breakfast ready for you.

MARTHA: Thank you child . . . I just want a cup of strong coffee . . .
(Belle and Martha are watching the two men furtively. Robinson exits stage right and comes right back in carrying the

400

morning paper. While Tom is fidgeting about the kitchen nervously.)

BELLE: *(To Robinson who is glancing through the paper. Timidly)* Father your breakfast is on the table.

(A tense silence is felt in the room. Martha sips her coffee in the electric atmosphere.)

ROBINSON: Thank you, Belle.

TOM: I'm . . . I'm sorry about last night Dad.

ROBINSON: That's all right son—We all make mistakes but it's never too late to start over again. Now I been thinking and your Ma and me figured that since I'm old and about played out ... you could step in and take my place. I feel almost certain my boss would be willing.

TOM: You mean?

ROBINSON: Yes son.

(Tom looks at Belle who stands with clasped hands . . . looks at Tom imploringly and nods her head approvingly.)

ROBINSON: *(Rises, gets his hat, walks a step or two, turns to Tom and says)* Ready now?

(Tom stands irresolutely looking at the three of them as if for direction then with a sudden turn exits left saying)

TOM: Just a minute Dad.

(Robinson walks over and kisses Martha who is quietly weeping then walks to Belle and tenderly kisses her. As he walks toward door, Belle moves toward Martha and stands behind her protectingly.)

(Off stage left, Tom calls)

TOM: I'm coming Dad.

Paupaulekejo

A THREE-ACT PLAY

BY JOHN TREMAINE

CAST OF CHARACTERS

PAUPAULEKEJO: *(half caste) son of Zoagoa*
ZOAGOA: *chief of the tribe of Tahaka*
CLAIRE: *daughter of missionary*
DUGLEY MCKENZIE: *missionary*
EDWARD LONSDALE: *cynic, trader*
SAHDJI: *dancer*
MISCELLANEOUS: *warriors, witch doctor, wives*

ACT 1-SCENE 1

Scene opens in a jungle clearing in interior of Africa. In the left center a fire around which are warriors squatting, the women in the rear standing. In the right center to right of fire, a little back stage, three tom-toms, a rattler, reed-lower.

Curtain rises on Sahdji dancing to jungle music. This dance is significant to Paupaulekejo. Sahdji throws her beads at Paupaulekejo's feet.

Curtain falls on this scene, slowly.

Interior of a trader's store, printed cloths of cotton and cheap silk, gaudy jewelry, glass beads. Open packing cases showing cheap toys, tobacco and cheap candies in glass jars, crates of soda crackers, demi-johns of cheap liquars, saw-dust floors, kerosene lamps, cheap print pictures on walls. Door to back right center, window to left of door with cheap print muslin curtain, couple of folding chairs. Scene opens with Lonsdale talking to missionary.

CYNIC: So this is the great day your daughter will be here. You'll be happy, eh?

MISSIONARY: Yes. Haven't seen her for five years. I suppose she'll be a big girl now.

CYNIC: How old is she?

MISSIONARY: Let me see. She—Oh, there she is now. *(Rushes out of doorway)*.

(Offstage, you can see him pass by the window running. Sounds from without, dropping of ropes, snorts, grunts, then from without is heard girl's voice.)

From *without*: Father, Father! *(The missionary's voice is heard)*. My darling! *(They pass the window, arms about each other, she impeding his steps)*.

(Enter Missionary and Claire)

MISSIONARY: How was the trip on—

CLAIRE: *(breaking in)* Oh wonderful, wonderful!

MISSIONARY: How did you leave Aunt Roberta?

CLAIRE: Distressed to death! Said the natives would kill us both!

MISSIONARY: Bah! This is my little girl, Claire McKenzie—the apple of my eye.

CYNIC: Little girl—ho! She's a great dame. Glad to see you. Good for the eyes. Hope you'll like these parts.

CLAIRE: Oh, I'll like it! Seems very interesting already.

Missionary *(patting daughter on back lovingly)*: Wait, dear, I'll speak to my men outside, then we'll go over to my hut. *(Goes outside)*.

CLAIRE: The natives have such splendid physiques.

Missionary *[Cynic]*: Yeh, the blacks have big healthy bodies. They're so bloody lazy they ought to have.

CLAIRE: They seem very kind—pleasant.

CYNIC: Wait till you see 'em drunk; they're awful then.

CLAIRE: You'd never believe it to see them now.

CYNIC: By and by—

CLAIRE *(cutting him off)*: You have lots of British goods here. So far from England. What's this? *(Picks up fetish)*.

CYNIC: Some black tomfoolery! That's the sort of thing they bring in here and trade for rum.

CLAIRE *(Noticing book with pictures in it, then laughing)* Do you sell these to the natives too?

CYNIC: Oh no, there's only one of 'em here with brains enough even to look at the pictures *(afterthought)* and he's half white.

CLAIRE: Oh, I think I must have seen him—a big handsome specimen of manhood. He was leading a troop of blacks. He was marching like a king! I wondered who he was. He wasn't—well—black like the rest!

CYNIC: Paupaulekejo!

CLAIRE: Whom did you say?

CYNIC: Paupaulekejo. He thinks he's the king around here; a sort of despot.

CLAIRE: Tell me about him.

CYNIC: Well, his father's black; his mother came out from England, at least, they say so.

CLAIRE: How singular!

CYNIC: Not strange. He was a handsome black and she—well she came out without a man.

CLAIRE: This is going to prove interesting.

CYNIC: Oh yes— *(Interrupted by missionary's return)*.

MISSIONARY: *(Entering speaking)* Well, everything is ready, darling. Let's go.

CLAIRE: *(Turning to Cynic)* It has been very pleasant to have known you and—and I'd like to know more about—

CYNIC: Oh you'll learn.

CURTAIN

SCENE II

Missionary's hut. Rude sitting room. A wooden center table with books. A rudely constructed book-shelf with rows of books. A door leading to a small room that Claire occupies. A door leading into another room back. Front door leading to the porch and window to the left of door. A settee near bookcases.

Claire and missionary discovered in sitting room having tea as curtain rises.

MISSIONARY: Well, darling, what do you think of my bringing black souls to Christ?

DAUGHTER: I think you've been a perfect St. Xavier, considering all the difficulties you encounter here.

MISSIONARY: I don't think I have been so great as all that, but at least I have been successful in planting the Spirit of the Master here among other gods. The natives seen to take to Christianity well enough, but they don't seem to think that they are under any obligation to give up their false gods.

DAUGHTER: *(Thinking somewhat)* I—I—from what I've seen of them I think they make good Christians, provided they could be persuaded to adopt a more civilized dress.

MISSIONARY: That also is one of the serious drawbacks. They seem to think that the body in [is] something to be proud of and shown at all times.

DAUGHTER: I do think they have splendid bodies, but the flesh is not everything.

MISSIONARY: That's just it! The flesh is not everything and they must learn to overcome the desires of the flesh if they would be good Christians.

DAUGHTER: I think I shall be able to offer some suggestions whereby you will be able to make further progress, provided, of course, they are acceptable and practicable to you.

MISSIONARY *(Somewhat beaming)*: I am glad to hear you say that since for so long I have labored here without the help or suggestion of anyone ggenuinely interested in the work.

DAUGHTER: First, I would suggest that we get in touch with the most influential leaders, whoever they are.

MISSIONARY: I have met and talked with most of the leaders, but—

DAUGHTER: Are they sympathetic?

MISSIONARY: Yes, at least as far as I can see.

DAUGHTER: How about inviting the most influential one to a sort of conference here?

MISSIONARY: That's a good idea. We might send for Paupaulekejo. He's the most influential native. King in fact.

DAUGHTER: Oh yes. He is the one that—that reads the picture books.

MISSIONARY: Yes—if only we can influence him—but I've tried. God knows I have but—

DAUGHTER: Now father, nothing beats a trial but a failure and I do want to help.

MISSIONARY: I'll do it. I'll send for him. *(Calling)* Sahdji!

SAHDJI: Yes, Teacher.

MISSIONARY: Sahdji, I wish you to go to Paupaulekejo. Tell him— Ask him to come here please.

SAHDJI: He no come. Me go for he though. *(Exits)*

MISSIONARY *(Rising)*: It is always best to humor the natives, to *ask* for Paupaulekejo. *(Laughs slightly).*

DAUGHTER *(Also rising)*: Now father, you go and take a smoke. I'll finish clearing off the tea dishes. *(Gently pushes him to the door).*

MISSIONARY: Yes, daughter. I will take a walk through the garden, but I will be back before Paupaulekejo arrives or Sahdji returns with his no.

DAUGHTER: I think he will come. Now out with you *(Shoos Paupaulekejo [Missionary] on).*

MISSIONARY: It won't be the first time he has sent a refusal! *(exits wagging his head).*

(Daughter makes busy over the dishes, humming the Kashmit song. Every now and then she speaks to herself). If no other way works, a picture Bible might. That's it, a picture Bible. *(Stoops before a bookcase in corner away from door, humming Kashmir song. A native enters, stands with folded arms, speaks:)* I am Paupaulekejo. *(She stands abruptly; the books in her lap fall. Sees Paupaulekejo).*

CURTAIN

ACT II—SCENE I

Three months have elapsed between Act I and Act II. Living room. Sahdji is dusting around. Offstage in distance can be heard male voice singing love song, bizarre. Sahdji listens, dusts dilatorily. Paupaulekejo enters.

SAHDJI: Paupaulekejo!

PAUPAULEKEJO: Where is your mistress?

SAHDJI: She here.

PAUPAULEKEJO: Tell her I am here.

SAHDJI: She come—bymby.

PAUPAULEKEJO: Sahdji, I am here!

(Sahdji leaves the room).

(Paupaulekejo looks around furtively, then tips over to bookcase, gets Bible, and tips out. Returns in a few moments and is curiously looking at prints on the wall when Claire enters.)

CLAIRE: Well, I see you are on time.

PAUPAULEKEJO: What this? *(Pointing to picture on wall)*.

CLAIRE: That is the Pantheon.

PAUPAULEKEJO: What that?

CLAIRE: Oh a building that—but never mind, we will get to our lesson first. *(Goes to bookcase, searches)*. Where is that Bible? *(Calls)* Sahdji!

SAHDJI *(entering)*: Yes, tasmamy?

CLAIRE: Where did you put the Bible?

SAHDJI: Me put him there. *(Goes to case)*.

CLAIRE: But it's not there.

SAHDJI: Me put him there.

CLAIRE: Oh pshaw! Help me find it, Sahdji. *(They look)*.

PAUPAULEKEJO: You tell me. All the same.

CLAIRE: Where is it? It was right here this morning.

PAUPAULEKEJO: You find him bimeby. You tell me.

CLAIRE *(absently)*: You will find it *soon*, Paupaulekejo.

PAUPAULEKEJO: Yes you will find him soon.

CLAIRE: Where on earth can it be? Sahdji, ask father! Or ask him to lend me another. *(Sahdji leaves)*. Now, where did we leave off before? *(Turns to Paupaulekejo)*.

PAUPAULEKEJO: You say your god is love?

CLAIRE: Yes, and what did you learn?

PAUPAULEKEJO: To love everybody.

CLAIRE: Every *one*.

PAUPAULEKEJO: Sahdji?

CLAIRE: Yes.

PAUPAULEKEJO: Slaves?

CLAIRE: Yes.

PAUPAULEKEJO: That White man give me rum?

CLAIRE: Yes, Paupaulekejo, every one. That is God's message.

PAUPAULEKEJO: Love you?

CLAIRE *(embarrassed)*: Yes of course. Now what?

PAUPAULEKEJO: Love much?

CLAIRE *(blushing)*: Yes, you must love every one—every one!

PAUPAULEKEJO: I no like to love every one!

CLAIRE: But you must! That's what I have been—

PAUPAULEKEJO: I love you!

CLAIRE: That is right, but—

PAUPAULEKEJO: I no love Sahdji!

CLAIRE: Oh Paupaulekejo, but you must.

PAUPAULEKEJO: You love Sahdji?

CLAIRE: Of course.

PAUPAULEKEJO: Me?

CLAIRE: Yes, every—

PAUPAULEKEJO: Love long time?

CLAIRE: Always every one.

PAUPAULEKEJO: I no want you love every one.

CLAIRE: Paupaulekejo, stop it. I want to teach you.

PAUPAULEKEJO: I know how to love.

CLAIRE: Then do it! Love every one!

PAUPAULEKEJO: Can I call your name?

CLAIRE: *May I*, Paupaulekejo.

PAUPAULEKEJO: Claire—you here—night time—tom-tom go boom, boom, boom!

CLAIRE: Yes, but—

PAUPAULEKEJO: An' air in grass blow by young bucks, sound sweet—like song?

CLAIRE: Yes, Paupaulekejo, but that is not the lesson.

PAUPAULEKEJO: Yes him is. That my men, tom-tom love for you, for me.

CLAIRE: All right now.

PAUPAULEKEJO: And I sing for wind to bring you love song like this *(sings).*

(Claire listens.)

PAUPAULEKEJO: *Him go Goaro njubomotbo sale.* I sing him for you.

CLAIRE: But you mustn't, Paupaulekejo. It's wrong.

PAUPAULEKEJO: What wrong? I love you?

CLAIRE *(faintly)*: Yes.

PAUPAULEKEJO: But you say, your God say love; I love you more everybody.

CLAIRE: But you mustn't, Paupaulekejo, not like that.

408

PAUPAULEKEJO: I only know one love. I love you that one.

CLAIRE: Please.

PAUPAULEKEJO: Love you that one all time. Claire, Claire, make sound like love song in grass; Claire sound like love song on wind. Paupaulekejo sound like love song on tom-tom. Love song on wind, you Claire, love song on tom-tom, me. Go all time together. Paupaulekejo and Claire.

CLAIRE: Please, Paupaulekejo, it isn't right.

PAUPAULEKEJO: You no love me?

CLAIRE: Yes, but—

PAUPAULEKEJO: You put your lip on my lip.

CLAIRE *(frantically)*: No!

PAUPAULEKEJO: Then Paupaulekejo no think your God.

CLAIRE: But a kiss doesn't mean love. Judas kissed Christ.

PAUPAULEKEJO: You love me then?

CLAIRE: In my country a white woman must not love a—a—black man.

PAUPAULEKEJO: In your country no think your God?

CLAIRE: Oh, God, yes! But—Oh, I can't explain.

PAUPAULEKEJO: You no love me?—Your God no love me?

CLAIRE: I do love you—I do—Oh, God, what have I said?

PAUPAULEKEJO: I do love you—Claire—*(kisses her warmly)*

CLAIRE: Stop—father might *(pushes him away)*

PAUPAULEKEJO: Paupaulekejo love you love your God—love Sahdji—love everybody—every one—*(enter father)*

PAUPAULEKEJO: Me know—my mother—she white—my father him black—she think your God—you no think Him.

CLAIRE: But I do—I—

PAUPAULEKEJO: Then you love me?

CLAIRE: I—I can't say.

PAUPAULEKEJO: Him mean yes.

CLAIRE: Paupaulekejo!

PAUPAULEKEJO: You love me? Put your lip on my lip.

CLAIRE: If father should hear you.

PAUPAULEKEJO: Him tell me your God—him think Him.

CLAIRE: I know but—

PAUPAULEKEJO: Claire love me?

CLAIRE: It cannot be—not here or anywhere on God's green earth.

PAUPAULEKEJO: Why—why?

CLAIRE: Because—Oh, Paupaulekejo—

(Enter Missionary. Looks vexed): Better stop the lesson for the night, Claire! Let Paupaulekejo go!

CLAIRE: Why father! *(turning to Paupaulekejo)* We'll take this up next Friday, Paupaulekejo.

(Missionary walks up and down agitatedly. Paupaulekejo gathers his book and paper, looks perplexed, salutes and leaves hastily. Sahdji is seen darting out of the door in the wake of Paupaulekejo. Missionary glowering as curtain descends.)

ACT III

Scene III same as Scene II, one day later.

CLAIRE *(whispering to Sahdji)*: Sahdji, run and find Paupaulekejo. Tell him to come right away. *(Sahdji, with peculiar expression, hurries out).*

Claire, getting things together in a grip perturbedly, stands in doorway.

Enter Paupaulekejo quietly and Sahdji enters behind him.

CLAIRE: Run without, Sahdji! *(Sahdji leaves reluctantly).*

PAUPAULEKEJO: You send for Paupaulekejo?

CLAIRE: Yes, I had to see you to—er—say good-bye.

PAUPAULEKEJO: Good-bye—what you mean?

CLAIRE: I'm going away. I take the next ship. It leaves shortly. I've enjoyed teaching you.

PAUPAULEKEJO: You what? You go leave Paupaulekejo? You say good-bye all time—Never see Paupaulekejo again, no?

CLAIRE: Yes, Paupualekejo. Father says I must go. He is angry with me. I must go.

PAUPUALEKEJO: Why you want to leave Paupaulekejo?

CLAIRE: I don't want to but I must.

PAUPAULEKEJO: No, you stay.

CLAIRE: My father forbids and I—I—Oh you can't understand!

PAUPAULEKEJO: I do. You love me and I love you. What more?

410

CLAIRE: Everything. We are different. I can't live as you live. We're different, different!

PAUPAULEKEJO: You don't want go. Stay. Paupaulekejo marry you. Me buy you everything—big house, pretty dress—me get him.

CLAIRE: No, I cannot live your life. It's terrible.

PAUPAULEKEJO: What wrong?

CLAIRE: I'm bewitched! Bewitched!

PAUPAULEKEJO: No. No you not. You love. You happy with me, yes.

CLAIRE: Yes, happy! Too happy! But you must go. Father will be returning. He said he would kill you.

PAUPAULEKEJO: Kill me? I ready. My braves outside; they wait, I know and ready, trick with trick.

CLAIRE: But you mustn't shed blood.

PAUPAULEKEJO: Ha! Shed blood! I make the rivers red with blood for you. For you, Paupualekejo drown the world in blood!

CLAIRE: Hush! You must leave now! I'm sorry we met.

PAUPAULEKEJO: Sorry? You sorry?

CLAIRE: I mean since we must—must part.

PAUPAULEKEJO: Part? Must? Claire, once more your lip on my lip once last time, then Paupaulekejo go. Come!

CLAIRE: Last time. Good-bye. *(They embrace).*

PAUPAULEKEJO: We go same God. Your God, my God. We same there; we love there. Your heart, Claire, my heart. We go together!

Swiftly he plunges knife into Claire's heart and then into his own. They fall on couch.

Sound of returning voices. Sahdji enters hastily, rushes across room, looks around quickly, dashes to couch and throws her hands up in horror. Screams and moans, pulls Paupaulekejo away from Claire and falls with her arms about him.

Missionary and Cynic enter and then both stop in horror. Missionary slowly advances and kneels at the side of his dead daughter.

CURTAIN

411

SHORT STORIES

THE SMILE

All of her life, Florence Rowe had wanted romance. Romance of the smart, sophisticated, modern sort one reads about now. And all of her life she had lived & taught school in the little New England village that was her home. She had grown to be thirty five years old, an old maid school teacher, before the impossible happened. Her aunt Florence had died and left her a little money. It was then that Florence became courageous. Had resigned from the school, packed her things & set out to see the world. The smart world of France & the Riviera.

Then almost before she could enter the Riviera she had had the accident. The car she had hired had been struck and she had been injured. The wealthy family in the other car did everything for her of course. And when Florence had realized that her torn face would be scarred for life, they had sent her to Dr Blanks Sanitarium, it was called, in Austria. Dr Blank the plastic surgeon who had taken her torn and broken face and remodled & molded it. Then there had been weeks of pain and despair. Weeks of despair after the pain had left and she moved around the beautiful grounds with her face in a mask. Meeting people, women who had come to be rejuvenated. Who took the procedure as every day recurrence. Brittle sophisticated women. And Florence discovered conversation. The smart brilliant conversation she had so desired. And entered into it. Her wit slightly cynical and biting, her voice from behind its plaster mask, low & beautiful and throaty.

In her spare moments she had written. Little bitingly witty stories of the women who came there to be rebeautified. And the stories of Flordé—for she used that name now—became well known and popular. Then came the day the mask was removed. And Flordé looked at her new face. It was beautiful. In some strange way so sophisticated. The torn muscles in her face had knit so that

415

her lips always would be curved in a slight hint of a smile. A faint sceptical, cynical smile. And the new Florence—or Flordé as she was now came out into the world.

In Paris, London and New York literary circles she was much sought after. And her wit became even more softly caustic and intangible. For suddenly she had conquered the world—as women always did in smart novels, and like them, believed that the admiration of the men who pursued her, was superficial. Was for her face, her face that wasn't hers.

Then she had met Gene. Gene who was the most brilliant and cynical of the younger writers. They had met at a party and had imediately been drawn to each other. They were excellent foils for each other. And had seen more & more of each other. Then Flordé had realized that she loved Gene. And believed that Gene loved her. The fact that she was ten years older than he ceased to matter. She knew they loved and that was enough.

Then one day Gene had come to her and flung himself in tears at her feet, his head in her lap. His mother had died. And his cynicism stood in no good stead now. His friends had not been sympathetic, for his past cynical attitudes to human things had be[come] too well known. There was no one to whom he could turn. From whom he could expect sympathy. So he turned to her. He loved her.

And she, with the knowledge of a woman in love, was silent as he wept his heart out to her. And soothed his hair with her fingers silently.

And finally he had quieted and said he had known he could depend on her for understanding, he loved her. And as he repeated his love, looked up and stopped in the middle of a phrase. Then with a gesture of loathing & and heart break, jumped to his feet, blaspheming, calling her, heartless, unnatural—a damn cynic. And flung himself out of the room slamming the door behind him. Leaving her with heart break—empty & un-understanding, looking at the door he had closed behind him—.

Then she got to her feet and walked slowly toward her room and as she did, caught a glimpse of herself in a mirror—smiling, aloof, cool.

TRAMP LOVE

PAUL TREMAINE

I rode the street car to the end of the line just a little way inside the city limits the north side of Columbus. Then I walked a hundred yards or so and sat down on the grass underneath a tree. It was nice there out of the sun; the ground seemed so cool after hot pavements of the city. Automobiles skimmed almost silently over the highway. A freight engine moved lazily up and down bumping cars around in the yard, across the road, and down in the gully. I could see the engineer in the window mopping his face with a red bandana. The almost colorless smoke went right up straight from the hot stack; little heat waves jiggled before my eyes.

Stretching out on my stomach, I rolled a cigarette. I had turned my back on the highway and the railroad track. A golf course began here, a little way from the road. Men and women moved around in pairs all over the course. The grass was brown and dry, and dust came up in little whirls from their steps. As I watched I envied them just a little. Their nice white clothes, their parked automobiles, their homes and dinners awaiting them. Cool drinks, cool salads. Mothers, fathers, babies, everything that a homeless tramp often longs for, for a moment.

I rolled over on my back and gazed up at the clear, hot sky. Winged seeds drifted by up there in the air. They seemed alive as they moved. I knew they were moving swiftly, for as I looked through the leaves of the tree they passed out of sight like a flash. The air was so dead and still that not a leaf on the tree stirred. I fell to wondering about the air currents that must be moving up above where the seeds floated. I was almost asleep.

Another street car had come out and stopped with a jangling noise at the end of the line. I sat up to watch it. The conductor was already out, changing the trolley around for the return to the city, when a girl stepped down from the car carrying a small black bag. She began walking up the highway. Her hair was very blond. The sun shone from it as she turned her head once to look back at the car. She wore white slacks and seemed quite neat and trim as she tripped swiftly along the highway toward where I was sitting.

I pushed my battered old felt hat back on my head and let the brown paper cigarette dangle unlighted from my lower lip. A car or two passed her before she neared me. I knew by the way she looked up that she was a hitch-hiker. The cars were crowded and didn't stop. When she came opposite where I sat, she looked easily at me. She hesitated only an instant, then the little black bag sailed through the air to light on the ground beside me. She took off her white knitted beret, and with it dangling in her hand, she walked through the shallow ditch toward me.

"Hello," she called out. "It looks cool in the shade there."

She came nearer, fluffing her hair with one hand. It was wispy and curly like white gold.

I lay back on my side and one elbow and watched her as she kicked the bag over with one foot, sat down on it, kicked her slippers off, wiggled her toes and observed them seriously for a moment.

She looked at me. "Have you a cigarette?"

"I have the makin's."

She held out her hand. "Gimme, please."

I picked up the can and papers and handed them to her. She was expert. Her fingers twisted a dandy smoke as rapidly as I could. I scratched a match on my shoe and held it out to her. When she had a light I relighted my own dead butt. She inhaled deeply and then looked around her. She observed everything all around on both sides of us in silence, smoking.

I, too, was silent; just looked at her. She was only a kid. Not more than twenty. Hardly that. Clean and neat, just like she had stepped out of a band-box, so to speak. Her slacks were ordinary white duck. They were men's slacks, worked over. Above them she wore a waist of thin, white silk. I could see the pale green lace brassiere over the tiny breasts. Her throat was delicate and the skin a little red but very smooth. No paint on her face or lips. Just a light coat of powder.

My elbow and shoulder began to ache from lying like that. I dropped down on my back and blew smoke towards the sky.

A motor or two hummed by on the road. The engine over in the yards blew a shrill blast. A bell clanged.

She began to talk. Her voice was soft. It came easily, and not too deep. She had a peculiar, almost Southern accent, or maybe more Western than Southern.

"It's nice to be sitting here in the shade. It's summer—quiet and still. No one cares about us. Automobiles go zipping past. Nothing to bother about. Nothing to worry about. We can sit here as long as we like or leave when we want to. I don't have nothing to—we don't have nothing," she finished suddenly. "Do we?"

I turned my head to look at her. "No, nothing," I agreed. "We just lay down when we're tired and rest. The world is ours. Always there is someone who will give us a ride when we want to go. Some may scowl at us and shake their heads, but always there is one. Yeah, girlie, it's sure nice in the summer. Sure is."

I sat up and began to roll another cigarette.

A couple of men, hitch-hikers, came past on the road. They stopped to wave thumbs, half-heartedly, at a passing car which didn't stop. They looked at us. We looked at them. One of them eyed my tobacco greedily.

"Smoke, fellas," I called.

They scrambled through the grass and eagerly accepted my tobacco and papers. They were dirty and tired out. Long, deeply lined faces. Belts with long flapping tongues pulled tightly around thin waists. The older of the two returned my papers and tobacco with a "Thanks, buddy." His eyes lowered as if in shame. I noticed that neither man met the girl's glance.

Her face was a study of pity and sympathy. The men turned swiftly, shambled back to the road, and walked down it out of sight.

We were silent, our thoughts much alike or poles apart. The girl then took a file from her pocket and began to work on her nails. I broke twigs into tiny lengths.

"You're not like the rest of the fellows. I mean like any of the fellows I've met on the road. I mean—I mean—oh, you're different," she finished lamely. Her hand waved uncertainly in a circle. She studied my face, my clothes, my eyes.

"Have you been out a long time, then," I asked.

Her blue eyes dimmed and again she bent to her manicuring. "Three years. I've been going from place to place three years."

She stopped her manicuring and stretched out beside me on the grass. She nibbled a grass stem as she told me her story.

She was from Nebraska. Her parents were farmers and very poor. That is, there was a big family and they didn't have much money. She had finished high school and gone to the city. No work. She hated to return home and be a burden to them, so she left first one city and then another. Sometimes she worked, sometimes she just traveled, hitch-hiking on the highways. She had been in every state, and done all sorts of work, waitress, child's nurse, and everything else. She wanted to work, liked to work, but there were so many girls looking for jobs, and so many reasons for jobs suddenly ending. Most times the reasons were men.

And the men who picked her up on highways. Sure, she had to be nice to them. She had to pay for many a ride. Not with money, but in the only way a poor girl could pay. Especially a nice-looking young girl. She was not bitter about it. It was the only practical way. She had tried to be clean, had tried to find work first, and at first it had seemed tough to find that all the men were alike in one respect. But she held no ill feeling toward the majority of them. It was that or starve or walk. Some of them had been kind, had given her money. She never asked for it. She went to hotels with them or stayed in the car with them. Sometimes they had been rough truck drivers. They had big roomy bunks in those freight trucks. At first it was pretty hard to take, but one learns it doesn't matter. A bath in the morning, and one forgets the bad taste.

She picked up the tobacco and built another smoke. I lighted it for her. After the first puff she talked again.

"But one thing I refuse to do, and that is work at waiting table or something, and then sleep with the boss to hold the job. I'm willing to do one or the other to get by, but both! Nuheugh, not this little gal! I've been waiting table here in Columbus, getting five dollars a week, paying two for a room and three to spend. Not much, but it was enough. The boss has been trying to make me every since I've been here, three weeks now. Last night he told me plain. I'd either come to his room or get out. I got out. He's the kind of man I hate. The others? Well, I'm just fair game for them."

Her voice went dreamy. "I just keep going and going. Doing the best I can, keeping as close to ways I was taught as I can, and still exist. Lots of soap and water and clean clothes, hoping and dreamin' that a day will come when I can get a break, a good guy, a fairy prince." She broke off, "Oh hell! I'm crazy, I guess."

I lay with my chin on my hands, gazing out across the golf course. In my heart I pitied her, liked her spirit, admired her. She was a square little thing—frank and practical as hell. I had met many girls on the road, but none like her. She had a brain to think with. She lived as best she could.

"Tell me," she questioned. "Why are you so different from the others I've met?"

"I don't know," I answered, "unless it's because I've always been a tramp. Always. I don't care about anything. I'm pretty much like you, I guess, mentally speaking. Of couse, I'm a man; that's our only difference. Do you understand?"

"I think I do," she answered. "I see it now. We're alike. I should have known that without asking. But tell me, isn't there anything you long for? Something you're really crazy to have?"

I thought for awhile. "No. There's nothing. And most of the things I do get or have, I care nothing about."

She turned on her side and studied me again. "How about girls? Don't you ever crave that kind of companionship? Most men do."

"There are times when I think about them. There've been times when the idea seemed rather nice, but to really care or crave or long for them or for one, I don't think I ever did."

She put a hand on my arm. "If I stayed here with you all night, I mean. Would it make you happy? Would you like to have me?"

I jerked my head to look into her frank eyes. She was just being kind, wanting to share what she had of happiness with one she thought in need of it.

"I would be happy while you were here," I answered softly, "but tomorrow after you had gone, I would be more unhappy than ever."

She nodded slowly, slapping me once or twice on the back. "Fella," she said, "if things were different I reckon I could learn to love you like I dream of loving someone. You're the kind. But we haven't anything. We don't want anything except security or nothing. Do we?"

I shook my head.

She got to her feet saying, "I better be going. I want to get to another town tonight."

I got up, too, and stretched and sat down again. She combed her hair down smooth and picked up her bag to go. Then she set it down again and reached inside her white blouse. Her brassiere had a pocket in it. She brought out a few folded bills.

"You got any money?" she asked. "I know a guy can't raise money on the road so easy as a girl."

"You're a good little egg, girlie," I replied. "Sure I've got dough. I was in a crap game last night." I showed her a roll of bills.

She tucked hers back into the little pocket and picked up the bag again. She stood looking at me almost tenderly.

"Well, if you ever see me again, sing out, won't you?"

I nodded. She turned and walked out to the road.

A car came. A seaman. I knew from his appearance, for one learns on the road. One glance and a driver is labeled.

He slowed and stopped. She put her bag in the back and got in front beside him. He looked down at her, smiling, then shifted gears. The car started. She turned and looked back. She didn't wave.

I smoked for hours, then I dropped off to sleep. When I awoke it was dark. The skies were clouded. A stiff breeze had come up. Off toward the south a rain storm was blowing up. A train was just whistling out of the yards. I had time to make it, and started to walk over to the yards. A few drops of rain splattered on my hat. I ran then, and just swung up into a car as the skies exploded with tons of water. The whistle sounded eerie and weak as it came drifting back along the train.

GESTURE

PAUL TREMAINE

Clouds of dust spun skyward in swirls of fury, behind the speeding automobile, going north on the desert highway. It hovered an instant and then settled slowly over the terrain as it had been doing for countless ages. The highway wound in and out among the rocky bluffs and deep gullies, to end somewhere out of sight in the distant mountains. The auto soon disappeared beyond that last tiny line that marked the end of the road, to the seeing eye. Once more it was quiet and still along the Hassayampa river road in the Arizona desert.

A hundred feet or so from the highway, in a clump of bushes, that afforded shade from the hot sun, a young man lay flat on his back gazing up into the dusty skies. The noise of the roaring motor had awakened him. He listened intently for a moment to determine the direction taken by the automobile, then yawning and stretching luxuriously, sat up grinning and said aloud, "Well old man, better be getting out on that highway and thumbing yourself a ride or else . . . ?" He studied the sun and the skies a little while and decided it must be about four o'clock.

Searching thru his pockets for a cigarette, he found the butt of one he had smoked the night before. Carefully he smoothed it out with his fingers, put it between his lips and searched again for a match. At last he had a light. There were not more than two or three drags left in the short butt, but he inhaled deeply and let the smoke out thru his nostrils slowly with a sigh of deep satisfaction. His eyes roved slowly around his immediate tiny horizon, and a grin of appreciation stole slowly over his boyish countenance as he drank in the strange beauty of the desert.

A bee droned noisily above him. A grey bit of bird chirped tonelessly somewhere in a mosquito clump. A tiny lizard crawled out on a small dead limb and blinked at him in unwavering study. The cigarette burned his fingers and he quickly flipped it away. The suddenness of his movement frightened the lizard and it scuttled away with a great noise for so small an animal. The man threw back his head and laughed loud and heartily. He was amused.

Suddenly he stopped laughing. He spied an old desert cow and calf standing near in some bushes eyeing him curiously. Soberly the old cow's jaw moved in continous chewing on her cud, her eyes unblinking as she stared at the man. The calf stood close to its mother with lifted head, as if trying to satisfy its own small-brained curiosity. The man studied them in silent amusement, then laughed loudly, frightening the cow, who suddenly broke into a fast lope, with the calf running close behind her. She looked back once or twice, but the sound of the man's continued laughter seemed to make her run faster. They disappeared beyond a fringe of bushes and desert growth along the river. Once more the man was alone, and now even the tiny noises were stilled.

His face sobered. Anxiously he listened again with his ears to the earth, then quickly got to his feet, looked down at the dusty blue serge, and flicked the dust carelessly with his hands before stepping out to the highway to hail the car he had heard. Desert dust brushes off easily. He did not look like a fellow who had been out in the desert most all night nor like one who had slept on the ground most of the hot hours of the day. His shoulders squared as he walked.

The night before he had ridden out from Phoenix with a fellow who had turned off somewhere back down the road. So he had walked on, stopping now and then to sit on a rock and smoke. Daylight had come and with it no rides with friendly motorists. When it had become too hot he had found the shade of the bushes and slept as comfortably as if he had been in a hotel.

The motor he had heard coming turned out to be a stage. It bore down upon him rapidly. He stepped out of the road to watch it go past. Passengers turned to stare at the lonely fellow in the middle of the desert. Some of them waved and he waved back, muttering, "Why in the world do people always wave and grin at a fellow walking when they are riding." He laughed deep in his throat as he watched the stage move out of sight on the winding road. Then he turned and looked back south a long time. No other car was coming. He faced north and began walking. His steps were slow and careless. He might have been any man strolling in a city park.

As he walked he began to recite a few lines to himself and to the silence of the desert at large.

> "Strange about thuh the desert—how it
> sorta gits a man
> Thuh rusty, dusty desert wheh no
> rivahs eveh ran
> Thuh eart' so hot below yuh, thuh
> hot blue skies above,
> A funny sort of country for a man
> to learn to love."

He didn't know about those lines; whether he had read them somewhere long before, or whether he had made them up in his own mind as he thought and walked. A roaring motor coming from behind him stopped his reciting. He looked back. A large shiny car was coming, and a horse looked at him from a trailer hauled behind. He stood [to] one side, ready to hail the car for a ride. It neared, and he waved his hand politely. The car didn't slow down. The cowboy driver looked a bit guilty as he passed by but the lone woman passenger in the rear seat ignored the man in the road. Only the horse looked over his shoulder curiously as they passed. In a cloud of dust, they were gone. The man in the road cursed as they disappeared. "Goddam such lowdown stingy scared to death people. Great, big empty car and wouldn't give me a ride."

His anger passed and he grinned. "What to hell," he chided himself. "It is their car, ain't it? They don't have to give a bum a ride if they don't want to. A good hombre will come along any time anyway!"

Far ahead up the road he saw the car top a rise, the trailer with the the horse bobbing after them. Then they passed out of sight. He shrugged his shoulders carelessly and dismissed them from his mind. Once again his thoughts returned to the poem he had been reciting.

> "Yuh have t'learn t'love thuh des-
> ert for at first yuh hate it all—
> Thuh cactus and the sage brush and
> the sands where lizards crawl—"

He stopped reciting, searched for a smoke again, and not finding one, walked on, up one rise and down thru a gully, and then up another long rise, climbing easily and unhurriedly. He halted and stared as he topped the rise. A little way below him the shiny car with the trailer had stopped. The cowboy driver was out and kneeling beside a rear wheel. The man grinned and walked carelessly toward the car, stopping first at the horse and looking him over admiringly. The two people were unaware that he had neared them, and not until he had spoken did either of them look up.

"Cowboy," he said, "I reckon you could shoe a hoss much handier than you can fix that tire?"

The cowboy looked up at him, grinning. "Sure could, stranger. Never did fix one of these nohow. We ain't got no more spares. Been having lots of tire trouble."

The woman stared coldly at the newcomer, her eyes pale and unfriendly. For a second the man looked into her eyes just as coldly. Then he said to the cowboy, "All right, Buddy, you sit on that rock, and I'll fix it for you."

He took his coat off and flung it over the side of the car, then knelt and expertly removed the tire from the rim. He yanked the tube out, and walking over to a rock, began to patch the hole with the repair kit he had picked up from the running board.

The cowboy rolled a cigarette and smoked, eyeing the stranger with a knowing expression in his eyes. The woman smoked and watched also. In a very few minutes the man had the tire back on the rim. "There yuh are, cowboy, pump it up. I'll take the makin's while you're doing it. I'm plumb out of smokes."

The cowboy handed the sack of tobacco and papers over to him and went to work on the pumping business. Soon the tools were in the car, and they were ready to travel once more.

The tramp took his coat from the car door, saying, "That sure is a fine looking hoss to be bringing out in this country. Bet my shoes he's a long way from where he was born." He turned to the horse and said, "Old fellow, you sure are going to miss that bluegrass out here."

The woman was studying him closely. Now she asked, "What are you doing way out here alone in the middle of the desert?"

The fellow grinned. The cowboy turned and looked soberly. "I was walking, mam. Slept out here most of the day." He looked toward dark mountains. "Walking to Prescott."

The woman asked, "Don't you want to ride with us? We are going to Prescott."

The fellow smiled oddly, and shook his head, "No mam, I don't want to ride. I'll walk."

Her voice was tense with surprise. "It's getting dark already. You'll be out here all night!"

"I know it, mam. I like it in the desert at night."

"Why don't you want a ride now?" she demanded. "You hailed us for one back there."

"Oh did I? Well, I must have changed my mind."

He looked into her eyes with a cold smile.

"Can I pay you for fixing my tire?" she asked indifferently as she picked up her purse.

He shook his head. "You don't owe me nothing, mam. You understand, courtesy of the road. We're in the west now."

Curtly she ordered the grinning cowboy to drive on. Her face settled into haughty indifference as she stared straight ahead toward the distant mountains. The cowboy started the motor and shifted slowly, looking around and winking slyly at the vagabond as the car moved away. His left hand dropped over the side of the car and a sack of tobacco and papers slipped through his fingers to the road.

Like a graven image the man stood and watched the car and horse pass out of sight again. Then once more he began to walk and recite,

> "Yuh come t'find it beautiful 'n'
> glorious and grand

427

Gesture

> With its colors splashed regardless
> by some giant's careless hand."

He shivered and walked faster, drawing his coat closer around him. The sun had gone down behind the western hills. The coolness of the desert night was rolling down from the darkening hills. Her walked faster as he recited,

> "Yuh come to love thuh the desert where
> the air is crystal like and clear
> Where the stars come down at night
> time sorta friendly like and near."

He shivered again and pulled his collar higher, shoving his hands deeper into his pockets and walking faster.

Far ahead in the mountains he could hear the echoing of a roaring motor as it labored up some steep grade. He stared at the darkness approaching from the mountain side, then swore an oath and raised a heel of his shoe hard into the seat of his trousers.

"Damn, damn fool," he muttered.

FREE

GEORGIA DOUGLAS JOHNSON

The funeral was over. The wife and the mistress sat facing each other in the old fashioned parlor of their common home, waiting for the will to be read. A September drizzle had set in and lent to the somber air of the house an added gloom. Stray bits of faded leaves and flowers from the many lovely floral wreathes were here and there upon the green plush carpet that covered the rectangular surface of the quiet room. Nashville had not seen such a long procession of carriages as had curled through her narrow streets at this noon hour in many a year. Dr. Ryan had been very popular. These two strangely linked women had just returned from the cemetery where all that remained of the tie that bound them, the late Paul Ryan—had been laid to rest. What would happen now that his portly, beaming, and genial personality had left them— poles apart together?

As Martha Ryan, hidden in the thick crepe of her black veil sat in church, her mind was darting here and there, picking at the tangled threads of her life. What would she do now? Always he had made decisions for her, now he lay there so still and cold in front of the altar as the preacher's voice threw sweet flattering words across his upturned face. Even when she had tried once to put her foot down on his bringing this young woman Rose Delaney to live right in the house with them, twenty-five years ago . . . twenty-five long years! Had called her his new nurse, her lips curled in derision. For her, this baby-eyed woman, he had decided against her, his own wife. But the whole town knew the truth . . . you can't

---

From Marci Knopf, ed., *The Sleeper Wakes* (New Brunswick, NJ: Rutgers University Press, 1992).

throw dust in people's eyes . . . nurse . . . nurse forsooth! And what could she do about it? Nothing, she was old and the girl was young!

Out of one corner of her eye she could see Rose's head bowed beside her. She was weeping, and well she might, for now, her protector was gone, and she herself was boss. At last, boss in her own house, and out she'd go! Her friends had taunted her long enough, she'd show them how she'd handle the situation. Martha tightened her lips in determination. Tears, tears, let her cry, cry her eyes out. He'd stood between them and taken her part! Protected her against his own wife. Men were queer. Yet he had been good to her. She'd had nothing, nothing of which to complain but this, this one thing. Strange how numb and far-away like she had felt at the funeral, not like it was her own dead she was burying, but maybe the feeling would come later and then. . . . So now, here she was back home at last, waiting, waiting to hear his last commands!

The clock on the mantle struck two. Martha shivered. Lawyer Green had promised to follow them from the funeral. He should be here now. Said he just had to stop by his office and get the will. The will! What did it say? Would it leave her anything? Yes, she guessed it would. Something anyhow, so's she could go away—somewhere! Martha sighed, free, free from her at last!

Rose Delaney sitting across from Mrs. Ryan, her black hat a little awry, had noted the sign and seen the shiver. She was keenly aware of her deep agitation. Something called to her from this woman's silence . . . she had always administered to her, served her . . . she needed her even now. Interestingly, she arose, casting a solicitous glance toward the brooding woman as she announced timidly that she was going to make a cup of hot tea. "You're chilly," she added, "it was awfully damp under foot at the cemetery."

A faint sound came from Mrs. Ryan's throat, whether of approval or not Rose couldn't make out, but she passed on out to the little kitchen where the soft tinkle of china was soon heard.

To make a cup of tea was an easy pleasure for Rose. She liked to serve, but somehow, today her hands seemed strangely awkward and she stumbled as she moved about the little kitchen. She was saying "Goodbye, Goodbye," to every little pot and pan that hung so shiny on the wall. She had loved to make them shine, for the woman with sad, sad questioning eyes liked them so. She had done her best. The day was over and now she must go—go away from this refuge that she had learned to love, this home, hers no longer.

As she placed the little silver tray before the tense woman with the steaming odor of the fragrant tea stealing upward she thought she detected a faint softening of her face, a small relaxation of the set jaw. She wasn't sure.

Sitting there with her hat still slantwise on her bowed head, Rose looked like a lonely traveler who sits in the station without a time table waiting for the next train with no fixed destination— just going!

A ring at the front door. Rose jumped. "It must be Lawyer Green," she murmured. She started for the door, then stopped suddenly and looked toward Mrs. Ryan; she was conscious of the new situation, its tenseness—was she expected to go—There was no movement, no sign from the still woman bent over her tea. Rose walked toward the door. As she moved away, Mrs. Ryan gradually raised her head and fixed her gaze upon Rose's retreating form. She had not been unmindful of Rose's hesitation about the door—aha! She had realized at once the change that had come about—she wasn't sure of herself anymore, not that she had been forward before, in fact, she had always deferred to her, served her well, had been kind and considerate, nursing her, but as her eyes followed the form moving bent and slow, another thought—another thought awoke like a thunder-clap in her mind! A new thought, so strangely new that she felt stunned . . . this woman who moved so slowly before her was not a young woman—she was old! old!!! Rose too was old. The years had passed and even Rose had lost her youth.

Mrs. Ryan was sitting in a kind of daze when Rose led Lawyer Green into the room. She paid no heed to his apologetic words, just sat gazing into space. Her mind had rushed back over the years to that day so long ago when Rose had first come into her home—a lovely young brown-eyed girl. Breaking away from her thoughts she fastened her eyes upon Rose as upon a stranger. This woman was new to her, new in her oldness. There was something sweet and comforting in the thought.

The tall solemn faced lawyer dropped awkwardly into a chair. He had a difficult duty to perform.

"I ask you two ladies to hear the will at once because—because . . ." He cleared his throat in embarrassment, then finished, "I thought it best for you both to have an understanding."

Placing his horn-rimmed glasses firmly on his nose, he looked at both women apprehensively and began reading: "I, Paul Ryan, being of sound mind—." He read on and on. There were several small bequests to former patients and to the hospital, and then— "The house and all my remaining property I bequeath and devise to my wife Martha Ryan, and my adopted daughter, Rose Delaney, equally share and share alike—"

The eyes of the two women met, hung together for a moment, and then Rose's glance fell.

The lawyer finished and again cleared his throat. "I'm sorry."

"I'm sorry," Rose whispered faintly. "I'll go away of course, Mrs. Ryan."

"Either of you can sell your share of the house to the other," the lawyer added. "You'd be willing to sell wouldn't you, Miss Delaney?"

"Oh certainly yes—anything Mrs. Ryan suggests will be all right with me. I'll cause no trouble at all. Now if you will excuse me I'll get a few things together and be leaving." She looked bewilderedly about her and stumbled from the room.

Lawyer Green looked at the set face of the widowed woman, arose and tried to offer some further advice. "Everything will be all right, I'm sure, Mrs. Ryan. Just consult me when you've come to a decision. The will is a little peculiar, but—ah—ah—the situation is a bit unusual."

She continued to hold the door ajar, her eyes following the lawyer's retreating form as it grew dimmer and dimmer and then vanished down the street.

How quiet it was, both outside and in. Not a sound. Death-like in the street. She closed the door—still, how still outside. Her footfall was hushed in the red velvet carpet. Her world had come to an end—All things had come to an end.

Descending the stairs slowly came a bowed figure. She seemed to be feeling her way blindly, one hand slipping along the balustrade, the other holding a brown valise.

Martha stood near the door—waiting. She wondered why she waited. She didn't know. . . . Was it to say "Good-bye"? Did you stop to say "Good-bye" when you were asking, even demanding that some one should leave your house?

Rose knew that she was waiting for her to go—had waited for twenty-five years, waited for this moment for nearly a life-time!

Nearer and nearer crept the drooping form—she came alongside, set down the valise and slowly lifted her swimming eyes to Martha's face. Haltingly, how haltingly, she formed the words—her throat tightening like cords about them, they seemed squeezed from it.

"Well, well, I'll . . . be . . . going. . . ." Martha's lips pressed more firmly together, her eyes following Rose's every move as she bent down to pick up the valise. A kind of stupor seemed to hold her speechless, she just watched and watched. Why didn't she say, "It's time you were going!" But no, she just stood still and watched wordless. Motionless.

How still the house was. Still and empty. It would be more still and empty . . . there would be no one to do little things for her . . . nurse her . . . comfort her . . . decide for her . .. no one to lean upon. . . . With a start she awoke to the moment. . . . Rose was going, her hand was turning the knob. . . . Martha watched with growing panic. . . . Rose paused a moment on the threshold, she looked back! and then Mrs. Ryan flung open her arms and cried brokenly, "Rose!"

SELECTIONS OF MAGAZINE AND ANTHOLOGIZED VERSE

Omnipresence

Whether I travel by land or by sea,
There is a face that is ever with me;
By night or by day we are never apart,
For *ever* his image looms large in my heart!

Hope

Frail children of sorrow, dethroned by a hue,
The shadows are flecked by the rose sifting through,
The world has its motion, all things pass away;
No night is omnipotent, there must be day!

The oak tarries long in the depths of the seed
But swift is the season of nettle and weed,
Abide yet awhile in the mellowing shade
And rise with the hour for which you were made.

The cycle of seasons, the tidals of man,
Revolve in the orb of an infinite plan;
We move to the rhythm of ages long done,
And each has his hour—to dwell in the sun!

Woman

UNSELFISH, silent potently
Behind each man of history
A woman stands, upon whose strength
He leans to cast his shadow's length.

She is his stairway to the sky,
His bow of hope, his inward eye,
His rhythm, yea his very breath
That plays betwixt his lips and death.

Aye, some brave woman without crown
Behind each male-throne huddles down,
A sentinel to guard his sleep,
A bosom where he kneels to weep.

To woman then! whose urge to live
Is summed within the right to give,
To merge her own identify
Into another's entity!

To Gallant France

THE Lord Himself died on the cross
He was not spared, and we
Must follow in his tortured steps
The road to Calvary.

Then why should France feel desolate
Believe her fight was vain
For who can tell what glory lies
Beyond her voiceless pain?

Surely since God's own son had need
To die upon the tree
France, too, though nailed upon the cross
Shall rise in victory!

Return

I'm sending out a thousand ships upon the world-wide
    sea,
Each one a tendril of my heart, a living part of me.
They seek an unfamiliar port, a strange uncharted
    clime,
But they will all come sailing back again, to me, some-
    time!

I Sing of Love

I sing of love who have no love
Just weary wintry days,
I sing of halcyon happiness
Along my arid ways.

I sing of love, and make the songs
From out my ailing heart,
I sing them to myself to hold
My closing world apart.

I sing of love who have no love
For something I must keep
Of beauty, and of loveliness,
To lull my heart to sleep.

A Song of Courage

Brave as a lion I must be
To face this jeering world
With my black face and rugged hair,
When every lip is curled
In bold derision as I pass
A shadow on the looking glass.

Braver than lions must I be
To give to child of mine
A heritage of certain scorn,
A place amid the swine
And bind him over to the sod—
A tethered exile sorrow shod.

Braver than all the brave must be
The race of men I bear,
Forged in the furnaces of hell
And wrought to iron there.
The future years have need of them
I sense it tho my sight is dim.

The Man to Be

I ride a-tilt because
Life charges through my veins—
Mixed forces guide the reins
And I must on.

Astride the universe
I go, nor pause nor rest,
With sharp swords at my breast
To lean upon.

These fierce contending bloods
Churn in the depths of me;
Merged in a mighty sea
They urge me on.

O white men, black and red
Look through God's lens and see
This fused intensity—
The man to be,
Your son!

SELECTIONS FROM UNPUBLISHED WORKS

Celibacy

Where is the love that might have been
Flung to the four far ends of earth
In my body stamping round
In my body like a hound
Leashed and restless
Biding time.

You

I do not want a jeweled crown
To place upon my head
I'd rather have your loving kiss
Upon my lips instead.

I do not care for cheering throngs
To shout my name about
I only want within your arms
To shut the whole world out.

I'd mount the cross of thorns for you
And hold the feat sublime
If, as I go you whisper low
"I loved you all the time."

Upon Passing an Old Graveyard

Grey slabs old, awry or fallen
Across their sunken graves:
The walks, a labyrinthe of tangles
Where now no foot-step braves.

Once long ago of Life's strange chalice
They too have had their share,
But now alas all those who loved them once
Are sleeping too, somewhere.

To Keep My Heart from Breaking

To keep my heart from breaking
I tied it with a string
Of little silken memories
Woven of everything

That placed a smile upon my lips
And set my heart a-glow
And painted rainbows in my sky
In days of long ago.

To keep my heart from breaking
Grows harder day by day
I'm searching through the past to find
The bits I threw away.

I look into the ghastly years
With frantic fear and doubt
Alas, Alas, what shall I do
When all my string gives out.

446

Song of a Spinster

Ah me, life is so short
And I
Stand tethered here:
No memories or hopes
To sky me,
Naught but gray and dull routine—
If I should scream. . . .

But who would care?
While life's quick-silver hours fly
Ah me, life is so short
While I. . . .

Recessional

My life flares up like a dying torch
That leaps once again but to say,
Good-bye to the glow of the rosy morn
With its vanishing banners gay.

My life flares up—by its fitful light
I gaze once again around
To say farewell to the fond sweet hopes
That I leave in the upturned ground.

Gloamtide

The shades of the gloaming around me are stealing,
The lure of the dusk through the silences call,
While blossoming incense comes mutely appealing,
And choiring wood-voices, vespering, fall.
Immersed in the deep of my dim sylvan-bower,
Upborne on the breast of its emerald tide,
I drift with the gleam of the vanishing hour
Afar—where my uttermost longings abide.

Dispossessed

Day by day
The pristine glory of my frame
Declines,
Life, a lurid flame, devours me.

Helplessly
I view the wreck
Within its wake
Tomorrow . . . hide me
I would weep.

No more the triumvirate
Youth, wit and beauty win
No more the noon's Capricious Jest:

Faint lights and few
My portion–
And twilight kindliness!

ABOUT THE EDITORS

Henry Louis Gates, Jr., is the W. E. B. Du Bois Professor of the Humanities, Chair of the Afro-American Studies Department, and Director of the W. E. B. Du Bois Institute for Afro-American Research at Harvard University. One of the leading scholars of African-American literature and culture, he is the author of *Figures in Black: Words, Signs, and the Racial Self* (1987), *The Signifying Monkey: A Theory of Afro-American Literary Criticism* (1988), *Loose Canons: Notes on the Culture Wars* (1992), and the memoir *Colored People* (1994).

Jennifer Burton is in the Ph.D. program in English Language and Literature at Harvard University. She is the volume editor of *The Prize Plays and Other One-Acts* in this series. She is a contributor to *The Oxford Companion to African-American Literature* and to *Great Lives from History: American Women*. With her mother and sister, she coauthored two one-act plays, *Rita's Haircut* and *Litany of the Clothes*. Her fiction and personal essays have appeared in *Sun Dog, There and Back*, and *Buffalo*, the Sunday magazine of the *Buffalo News*.

Claudia Tate is Professor of English at the George Washington University. She is the author of *Domestic Allegories of Political Desire:The Black Heroine's Text* (1992) and the forthcoming study *Desire and Protocols of Race: Black Novels and Psychoanalysis*.